# CULTURE SHOCK!

*China*

## Kevin Sinclair
## with Iris Wong Po-yee

**Graphic Arts Center Publishing Company**
Portland, Oregon

## In the same series

| | | | |
|---|---|---|---|
| Argentina | Egypt | Laos | Sri Lanka |
| Australia | Finland | Malaysia | Sweden |
| Austria | France | Mauritius | Switzerland |
| Belgium | Germany | Mexico | Syria |
| Bolivia | Greece | Morocco | Taiwan |
| Borneo | Hong Kong | Myanmar | Thailand |
| Britain | Hungary | Nepal | Turkey |
| California | India | Netherlands | UAE |
| Canada | Indonesia | Norway | Ukraine |
| Chile | Iran | Pakistan | USA |
| China | Ireland | Philippines | USA—The South |
| Cuba | Israel | Scotland | Venezuela |
| Czech Republic | Italy | Singapore | Vietnam |
| Denmark | Japan | South Africa | |
| Ecuador | Korea | Spain | |

| | | |
|---|---|---|
| Barcelona At Your Door | New York At Your Door | A Student's Guide |
| Chicago At Your Door | Paris At Your Door | A Traveller's Medical Guide |
| Havana At Your Door | Rome At Your Door | A Wife's Guide |
| Jakarta At Your Door | San Francisco At Your Door | Living and Working Abroad |
| Kuala Lumpur, Malaysia At Your Door | A Globe-Trotter's Guide | Working Holidays Abroad |
| London At Your Door | A Parent's Guide | |

Illustrations by TRIGG
Photographs by Kevin Sinclair and Chris Davis

© 1990 Kevin Sinclair
Revised 1996, 1999, 2001
Reprinted 1997, 1998, 1999, 2000, 2001

This book is published by special
arrangement with Times Media Private Limited
Times Centre, 1 New Industrial Road, Singapore 536196
International Standard Book Number 1-55868-615-0
Library of Congress Catalog Number 90-085618
Graphic Arts Center Publishing Company
P.O. Box 10306 • Portland, Oregon 97296-0306 • (503) 226-2402

Printed in Singapore

*To Kit, my wife and companion on journeys along the
China Coast.*

*And to Iris Wong Po-yee, who has been with me to ports,
paddyfields, coal mines, steel works, kindergartens, factories,
vegetable farms, plantations and shipyards in every province
between Guangdong and the Mongol border.*

*And to Prudence Lui Lai-kuen, Nelson Ng Kwok-chueng, Cindy
Cheng Mei-fun, Raini Hamdi and scores of other friends and
workmates with whom I have toiled, laughed, drunk
and eaten in China.*

# CONTENTS

# PREFACE

I first glimpsed China from a camouflaged British army lookout station atop a jagged crest on the Hongkong border. Across the narrow Shenzhen River, the Cultural Revolution was ripping China apart. Below me, on the far side of the border fence, blue-suited figures marched below the scarlet banners of the Red Guards.

What was going on in the forbidden land over the muddy river? As a young newspaperman, I wanted to know. But I never really worked out what the Cultural Revolution was all about; neither did anyone else. What I did know was that China had me in her grip.

My unlikely fascination with China came about when I was a farm boy growing up in distant New Zealand. One day, I borrowed Edgar Snow's *Red Star Over China*, the compelling story that first told the world in 1936 about Mao Zedong, the Red Army, and the Long March. I started to read as much as I could about China.

A decade later, I arrived at the magnificent Hongkong harbour on a rusty old liner. I could smell the frying bean curd on the breeze, hear the raucous shout of Cantonese vendors in the crowded street, see the junks with dusty tan sails stretching as they lumbered through Fragrant Harbour. I had never been here before, but I was home.

In those days, it was exciting to be a reporter in Hongkong. Across the border, China settled down as Mao sank to his end. Then, the twice-purged great survivor Deng Xiaoping climbed once more out of disgrace. Finally, I was allowed to cross the border bridge at Lowu.

What made China work? What made this ancient, gracious, great civilisation operate in such a bewildering manner? I've lost count of how many times I have been to China. Certainly, well over 100 and to many far corners of the country.

Over the years, I have learned a little of how to get around China. I hope that some of what I picked up would aid you on your personal Long March into China.

# INTRODUCTION

In 1983, after many years of rejections I was finally given a visa to visit China. I had lived in Hongkong for 16 years and from that unlikely political cockpit had watched, partly enthralled, frequently horrified, as China went through the self-inflicted agonies of the Great Proletarian Cultural Revolution.

In 1976, the thrice-purged Deng Xiaoping emerged once again from political disgrace to pick up the shattered pieces. Like a magical Humpty Dumpty, the diminutive dynamo patched China together again. When he introduced new economic freedoms in 1978, he relaxed the reigns of Maoist dogma that had kept China in poverty. Five years later, the China I entered was still a drab, grey and dimly lit land. But hope was starting to emerge. The country, even those huge, sprawling industrial cities, was strangely quiet; people seemed to move in shuffling armies, dressed in identical faded blue, black or grey high-necked jackets. There was little colour, apart from the emerald of the rice fields of the south and the crimson banners of the national flag. The brave new economic freedoms announced five years earlier by Paramount Leader Deng had still to bite. Personal freedoms were largely unknown.

That was another era, almost another universe. Today, the streets of Chinese cities are vibrant, bustling, bursting with life and vigour. It is a transformed land. The changes of the past 20 years have seen China turn from a wary and sullen society full of fear of its own rulers and resentment of the West into a nation brimming with confidence, full of hope.

There remain problems, of course, huge challenges. But China today is a land of hope and optimism. Much of that hope is centred on the remarkable figure of the prime minister, Zhu Rongji. He is steering China on a course that will, by early in the new millennium, make it the largest economic power on earth.

What he is attempting seems an impossible task, akin to the ancient legend of the Chinese peasant who tried to move a mountain. Zhu has abolished the vast, unwieldy, corrupt and hugely inefficient and over-staffed state enterprises which were once the bulwark of production and the pride of the nation. Not only did these enormous government-owned conglomerates turn out rivers of steel and landslides of basic goods, but they also provided comfortable berths for millions. They were uneconomic industrial dinosaurs.

These combined answered the socialist dream of a job for all for life. But they doomed China to be an uncompetitive giant, an industrial colossus producing basic machinery and goods that were badly designed and shoddy.

With amazing courage, Zhu Rongqi broke up these bureaucratic manufacturing empires. He consigned them to the wastepaper basket of history. He broke the iron rice bowl that had fed complacent masses, throwing hundreds of millions out of work to find new jobs in the wave of profit-motivated private companies that sprang up in the industrial vacuum.

As it strides confidently into the 21st century, China is a land of opportunity. The people are better educated than they have been for 5,000 years of written history. Illiteracy has been abolished. Education is universal and compulsory and across the land is carried out in the national tongue – Putonghua, which is the version of standard Chinese known as Mandarin. One result of this classroom revolution is that for the first time since China was unified 2,200 years ago, every Chinese can speak to every other Chinese. No longer is the nation wrenched into divisions by the barriers of dialect and language, for so long a divisive hurdle to progress.

Today's Chinese are healthier and wealthier than ever before. They are also more free. This is not the freedom of the West, which often comes with irresponsibility, but the more basic freedoms that most Chinese never knew until this century. This is freedom from starvation and, largely, freedom from oppression.

# Chapter One

# CHINA TODAY

*Once the dragon gate is crossed,*
*One's status rises ten times.*

Observe Shanghai. This is the 21st century. Unlikely skyscrapers in glass and steel thrust high above the muddy waters of the Huang He (Yellow River), down which flows a third of China's annual export trade. See those mighty towers; from the 88th floor bar in the Grand Hyatt the enormous city spreads like a living map. That spike is the new Marriott, there's the Ritz-Carlton, the Sofitel, the Hilton; 5-star hotels proliferate and swank restaurants beckon the New Age millionaires of this thrusting industrial and business turbine.

This is Red China, about which the world quivered for two generations? This throbbing metropolis with its fashionable women, traffic jams, internet cafés, coffee shops, brand-name lingerie and a mobile phone for every ear; is this the dreaded Mainland China that Western propagandists demonised? Yes, it's still China and it is still ruled firmly by the Chinese Communist Party. But this is the New, New, New China, the Mark IV China, the post-revolutionary China that is surging into the top ranks of economic superpowers. It's China, yes, but with a vast difference.

Broadly speaking, what Shanghai does today, the nation does tomorrow, or a year hence, or a decade later. Shanghai leads, and as the 21st century was born, the vast city was striding down a new road, leading the country into an era of confident expansion and prosperity. It was, proclaimed many, the start of a new golden era, as the Tang Dynasty had been 13 centuries before.

Chinese cities today are vibrant, bustling, bursting with life and vigour. Bicycles still chaotically outnumber cars. But in towns from Haikou on tropical Hainan Island to the old Russian-built city of Harbin in the far reaches of the frigid north, cars honk frenetically, buses are packed, trucks carry the new lifeblood of industry and vans unload consumer goods that would have been a dangerous dream two decades ago. Traffic jams are a major problem, one which big cities like Shanghai and Guangzhou are trying to solve with ambitious underground railways.

Elevated inner-city expressways sweep through Shanghai, 200 miles of them built only in recent years. Bridges are thrown across the Huang He, tunnels bored underneath the river. Four subway lines were opened in a decade; 21 more were being constructed or planned.

You can see into the future in Shanghai. Pay 20 yuan to visit the urban planning museum, next to the stately city hall, and you view an enormous model of the city as it will be in 10 years time. The model covers and area the size of a basketball court and every individual building, existing or planned, is there in miniature.

What's the secret to Shanghai's success? Well, in large part, it's because the city has been run for a half century by can-do, hands-on engineers. Every mayor, back to the 1950s, was an engineer first, a communist party official second. It's thanks to these no-nonsense men, whose ideology is founded on slide rules and science rather than little red books, that Shanghai seems to work so well. The President, Jiang Zemin, was an engineer. So was the man who followed him, the Premier Zhu Rongji.

Throughout eastern and southern China, shops are crammed. The tidal wave of electronics and appliances that flood from China's factories to the world's markets are also eagerly sought in local stores. The name of every famous Italian designer glows in brilliant neon; most of these garments are made under license in Chinese factories. The drab unisex Mao suits have disappeared. Young Chinese in the cities dress in high international fashion; indeed, they appear considerably neater than their counterparts in the West.

It is a transformed land. The changes of the past 20 years have seen China turn from a wary and sullen society full of fear of its own rulers and resentment of the West into a nation brimming with confidence, full of hope.

There remain problems, of course, huge challenges. The incredible prosperity of the highly industrialised coastal cities with their merchant kings and glittering hotels contrasts with the backward poverty that still stalks large swathes of the arid, cold Northnand Northnest. Progress is uneven, inescapably so as it was the ancient trading ports of Xiamen and Guangzhou, with their strong links to the vast riches of the Overseas Chinese, which started the new economic dynasty. But, overall, China today is a land of hope and optimism.

Much of that hope is centred on the remarkable figure of the prime minister, Zhu Rongji. He is a man of enormous stature, a soft-spoken, steel-willed economist. He is steering China on a course that will, by early in the new millennium, make it the largest economic power on earth. Zhu is propelled by determination moderated by pragmatism. He is a master of the possible. What he and his government are now attempting is yet another historic challenge. "Go west, young man," was the call made by Americans to open up their plains and mountains in the 1860s; that's being echoed in China today with appeals for business to look at challenges in a vast swathe of interior China.

Places like Ningxia, the autonomous Muslim province in the far Northwest, have enormous assets in agriculture and minerals. But exploiting those advantages, getting their produce to markets, is the problem. This theme of opening up the west, helping the backward, under-developed regions to catch up with the prosperous coastal regions, is the next great theme to the China story.

## WHICH NEW CHINA?

In 1949, Mao Zedong and his ragged peasant armies conquered the Nationalists, ending decisively a bloody civil war that had begun 22 years earlier. The Guomindang armies had been lavishly equipped by America. The communists, however, had weapons stronger than modern artillery and air power; they were armed with the will to win. Generalissimo Chiang Kaishek and the remnants of his vast military retreated over the Straits to the island province of Taiwan. Their descendants remain there today, both parts of China warily striving to find some common ground which will allow eventual unification.

On 1 October 1949, Mao Zedong stood at the Gate of Heavenly Peace and proclaimed the birth of the People's Republic. It was the New China. In 1978, Deng Xiaoping outlined the sweeping economic reforms that would usher in a fresh era; that was the New New China.

Today, President Jiang Zemin and Prime Minister Zhu are struggling to scrap the vast state-owned enterprises that drain the lifeblood and enterprise of the nation, to battle widespread corruption, rejuvenate industries, invigorate education and introduce a small – but unprecedented! – element of democracy. They are creating the New, New, New China. It is unlike any society the nation has seen since the first China stirred 5,000 years ago on the banks of the Yellow River.

It is a vast challenge, as big as the country, as sweeping as the Manchurian plains. In the decade after Deng's 1978 reforms, China changed immensely. In the decade since the disastrous student-led disturbances in Tiananmen Square and the government's tardy and heavy-handed response, that thrust of change has been even swifter.

The last of the Long March generation, battle-hardened idealists who fought with blind courage for their holy cause, have died. They were mighty warriors; their grip on economic and social policies was far less certain than on the rifles and swords they wielded on the road to power. The rigorous dictates of socialist purity are long dead. Today, pragmatism and profits are the motivations that lead China. They are heading on a high road not only to prosperity but also to a better and fairer society.

The Chinese people today are healthier, wealthier and more free than at any time in their long history. Free? Yes, although not perhaps in the sense accepted in the West.

By and large, people in China are free to say what they want, to read newspapers which are increasingly vocal with complaints about the way their country is run and free to believe what they want. There are restrictions, however. Individuals, organisations and newspapers can roundly abuse and criticise local government officials and provincial administrations, pointing out their failings and calling for better performance. They can poke fingers at the Central Government and disagree about policies and methods of the ministries of state. But what is sacrosanct, what may not be questioned, is the right of the Chinese Communist Party to rule China. The way the party and government run the country can be criticised. The role of the party as fount of all power is above challenge.

All this is not to say that China is a free country in the accepted Western sense of a social democracy with guaranteed rights. It's not. Journalists who offend those in power are arrested and sometimes jailed for long periods, like the unfortunate charged with disclosing state secrets; anywhere else in the world he would be promoted for getting a scoop. And all too often, it is rule by whim rather than rule of law that decides issues. People are taking power into their own hands – as Chairman Mao preached 70 years ago – to the frequent embarrassment of provincial and national governments. Cases of peasants staging angry riots and demonstrations because of incompetent or corrupt local cadres are common. The Central Government takes notice of such outbreaks.

But in the bosom of this New, New, New China, the past lives on. In wide swathes of the countryside, where 85% of the vast population still live, quiet villages slumber still in placid tranquillity. The visitor can see arched bridges, weeping willows, ducks on village ponds and aged matriarchs standing at the worn wooden doors of stone houses, peering quizzically as modishly dressed teenagers with mobile phones stroll by.

It's a land and society in transition. Still, it always was. The notion of the changeless face of China was never totally accurate. If the country didn't change significantly for centuries, it was because the vast bulk of the people were chained down by poverty, ignorance and oppression. Chinese are as eager as any other people to take advantage of improvements in technology that will improve their way of life.

## INTO THE NEW MILLENNIUM

A decade ago, a visit to China required determination. Getting a visa, changing money, buying internal rail or air tickets was challenging, demanding and required patience. Today, going to Beijing or Shanghai is akin to landing in Manchester or Melbourne. It's normal. It's like travelling anywhere in the dawn of the new millennium. That very normality marks a vast change. The truth is, as China has soared in every sphere at such a blinding pace, spurred on by brave new economic policies, it becomes inevitably linked with other parts of the global village. Modern airport arrival halls and towering hotel spires are universally similar. Yet the Middle Kingdom remains different, sometimes delightfully so, sometimes frustratingly and infuriatingly apart from the rest of the world.

The nation is developing at an unhealthy and uneven rate. The Pearl River Delta gallops ahead to become what some visionaries see as the world's most immense and potentially most wealthy conurbations, a vast metropolis embracing the cities of Hong Kong, Macau, Guangzhou, Shenzhen, Zhuhai, Dongguan, Zhongshan, Foshan, Jiangmen, Dayawan and Huizhou. There are more than 400 cites and towns in the region. The important cites are Guangzhou (the capital of Guangdong Province), Shenzhen Special Economic Zone, Zhuhai

Special Economic Zone, and Foshan, which is a well-known historical city. It has now a population of 45 million and spending power that rivals that of the whole of the United Kingdom. For mile after mile after mile, new factories and high-rise housing rises from what used to be vegetable plots and paddy fields. Elsewhere in the key province of Guangdong – the Shantou region with its distinctive Teochew people and the Wuyi (Five Counties) area (which comprises Taishan, Xinhui, Kaiping, Enping and Heshan City) of the Pearl River Delta area – are as large and as populous as European nations like Holland or Belgium. They are all within just one of the nation's 30 provinces.

Hongkong is set on becoming the capital of this explosive region, a metropolis seen by some enthusiastic observers (like Britain's Lord Rees-Mogg) as the greatest city in the history of the world. Meanwhile, in the remote backwardness of places like Anhui and Gansu, superstition and poverty still haunt isolated rural villages.

The new leadership, notably that of the brilliant economics boss Zhu Rongji, is trying to keep China on course. It's tough and tricky, rather like a lone oarsman attempting to steer an overloaded bamboo raft through the wild turbulence of the Yangtze River's Three Gorges. One part of the vessel – the advanced coastal belt hurtling towards the superstar economic status of the 21st century – bobs lightly atop the torrent. The more backward interior provinces are a heavyweight ballast threatening to drag the craft under the rushing waters.

Everything about China is vast. The opportunities are great. So are the problems. The potential is enormous. So are the economic hurdles. Every time China comes to another crisis – and there are crises aplenty as the enormous population tries to drag itself into the 21st century and its destiny as an economic superpower – some outsiders point to its inevitable problems as proof that the country and its leadership are bound to fail. This is wishful thinking on their part. China is determined to succeed – not just the government, but the people – and realise that on the way to success, there will be many setbacks. Transforming the world's largest society is no easy overnight task.

China since 1978 has made strides that would have once been unimaginable. These have not only seen more Chinese become well-to-do than at any time in history, but have also given more Chinese genuine, if limited, freedom. Admittedly, this is in a unique authoritarian Confucian framework and under the rigid, though increasingly flexible, rule of the Chinese Communist Party. It may not be the full political freedoms of the Western democracy, but it gives a degree of personal liberty and choice, coupled with security and safety, that has been rare for most Chinese for the last 30 centuries. The country is now united – except for the island province of Taiwan – and there is no likelihood of outside intrusion. The dangers that threatened a weak nation so alarmingly a century ago – Japanese greed, Russian imperialism, grasping and arrogant demands by British, French, Americans and Germans – have been washed away by the strong currents of history.

For all his many faults and blindnesses, Mao Zedong led the Chinese people to self-sufficiency and pride. China has stood up. It will never again allow itself to be humbled.

## SHADOW OF TIANANMEN SQUARE

China's history since the spring of 1989 has been dominated by the military action that led to the end of the uprising in Tiananmen Square. It's fashionable for the Western press and politicians to blithely label this as "oppression of democracy-loving students striving for freedom". Reality is very different to this widely-perceived romantic fiction. A large part of the anger and irritation of the Chinese leadership is directly due to a refusal by the outside world to appreciate the very real likelihood that the so-called "pro-democracy" movement could have ripped China asunder.

Imagine, if you can, London held under siege for six weeks, with a half-million people crammed into Trafalgar Square. Contemplate Paris brought to a near-total halt with gendarmes being lynched in the industrial suburbs and their weapons stolen by riotous mobs. Consider Washington in chaotic shambles with hundreds of thousands of protestors demanding the President of the United States and the

*Vegetable vendors cart their produce past the watchful eyes of Mao Zedong in Tiananmen Square.*

chairman of the Republican Party and the Leader of the Senate explain their policies in person. And imagine these worthies going into the streets to personally plead with arrogant youthful student leaders to return to the classroom, only to be derided and lectured on national television. What would other strong governments have done to save their nations from total collapse? With the regime in peril, with unrest spreading into the provinces, the very darkest nightmare of any Chinese leadership aroused – disintegration of the nation.

Today, China's leadership points back to 1989 and the tanks rolling into the Square with a degree of justification. Look, they say, pointing to a decade of ethnic terror in what used to be communist Yugoslavia. Look at the economic misery of the former Soviet Union. Look how the Soviet Union has been split into so many disintergrating splinters and – look again! – at the civil wars which have broken out in some of the Central Asian republics that border China. And then look at the 1,270,000,000 Chinese people: do you prefer your well-stocked shops and your brimming rice bowls and our rigid leadership, or would you risk your future and that of your child on the spinning wheel of reform? The vast majority of Chinese on the free enterprise farms, in the factories and the schools are not prepared to gamble an increasingly prosperous and secure future on a desperate gamble to change the system.

Indeed, the system is changing itself. The Chinese Communist Party remains in power, but the old warriors of the Long March generation have all but faded away. The age of the can-do technocrat has dawned. This is not democracy – something China has never enjoyed or experienced – and it is not personal freedom in the Western sense. But China is not Europe or North America. And even in the field of democracy (in a very limited and restricted way, admittedly) China is changing. It's estimated that 280 million people voted in the latest nation-wide village elections.

What do the Chinese people want? Basically, the same as anyone else. They want a home, a decent job, security for their family, the prospect of a better future. The present regime has provided the opportunity for this to more Chinese than any other government has in the long history of the Chinese people. It has also eradicated some of the most hated symbols of rigid rule, like the inefficient communes and the strict work assignment system that virtually forced young graduates into careers they did not want to follow.

Democracy? It's like walking into a bar in the Western world and asking who wants a Rolls-Royce. Most people would put up their hands. Then you tell them it's going to cost 90% of their wages to pay for the car and 85% of their spare time to look after it. Thanks, I'll stick to my Ford. Same with democracy. Do you want it? Chances are, many Chinese would vote yes. Then explain the consequences. Would the rich south want to subsidise the backward west? No. Would a democratic government be able to enforce the strict one-child policy? No; this would lead to an almost instant surge in the birthrate, swamping China with scores of millions of children the nation cannot afford. And what sort of democracy? Should it be based on an American federal mould? If so, wouldn't this rip apart a multiracial country with 56 recognised ethnic groups, including ancient and proud nations like the Mongols, Manchus and Turkic Uighurs? Would it mean self-determination for regions like Tibet, an area which foreigners seem to think is not part of China? Almost every Han Chinese would oppose the shrinkage of the nation.

The complexities are awesome. But this does not stop interfering foreigners who live in total blissful ignorance of the realities of governing a diverse, vast and complicated land from laying down simplistic judgements. Give the people democracy, cry liberal yuppies in California, and all will be well. Not true, say many thoughtful close observers of Chinese affairs, pointing to the nightmare across the border in Central Asia and poverty in the Russian Far East.

The truth is, the Chinese Communist Party, for its many faults, has given the country stability. There is corruption, yes, and rule by decree against which people cannot appeal. By and large, however, the Chinese people are today wealthier, healthier, better fed and housed and educated, than at any time in history. This is not opinion. These are facts.

## *NATION IN TRANSITION*

The transition has spanned a generation. The revolutionary flame is being passed from the now-tottering old soldiers who marched with Mao to men and women who learned to use computers while they studied for their MBAs in Stanford or Edinburgh. It's a whole new world.

The very face of the landscape is changing. Roll north on the train taking tourists and businessmen across the Shenzhen River on the border of Hongkong. For mile after mile, new factories rise, gleaming estates of apartments spring up. The placid water buffalo in the paddy field, that classical symbol of rural China, is seldom seen. In this part of China, the paddy field itself is disappearing as the concrete and steel tide of industrialising turns the country into the world's premier manufacturing power. New industries rise from the paddy fields and the vegetable plots. The policies of free enterprise and wealth –

anathema to the brave peasant soldiers of Mao's Red Army who sought to bring equality to the countryside – have radically changed the face of the nation. And the pace of that change continues, like a huge waterwheel gaining momentum from the spring rains. All projections predict the Chinese economy being the largest on earth in the first decade of the 21st century.

## A GREAT LEAP – BACKWARDS

But is this latest turn of the Chinese wheel of fortune going to be permanent? Or will it be just another passing phase, like the Great Leap Forward and the Great Proletarian Cultural Revolution? These were two of the greatest man-made disasters in history. Each took millions of peasant lives. Like tidal waves, earthquakes and droughts, these calamities swept over the Chinese peasants in the first two decades after the communist victory.

Will the second revolution of Deng Xiaoping be more lasting? I believe so. A gigantic momentum has built up since the first hesitant and doubtful moves to unshackle the economy, back in what seems the distant past of 1978. Many were suspicious. In the 1950s, the seemingly benign Mao Zedong urged those with differing views about how the New China should be ruled to speak out and stand up. Those sufficiently naive to believe in his proclamation of constructive dissent enthusiastically took part in the One Hundred Flowers movement, in which he urged that one hundred schools of thoughts contend. The flowers that sprouted were soon plucked, the intellectuals and philosophers disappearing into the labour camps. The thought correction centres received another generation of inmates in 1979 when the large character posters bloomed on Democracy Wall in Beijing. Those who suggested China follow a different road were imprisoned.

But Deng's road is an economic super highway, not a broad path to political freedom. The party, the army and the bureaucratic administration is determined to continue to exercise all real power; the people, however, are free to make money. As long as they live within the confines of rules laid down by the party leaders – and never

23

challenge the right to rule won by the People's Army for the Chinese Communist Party – the Chinese can do what they want. But let them confront the party's right to rule, and all deals are off. The leaders of China today, in the same manner as the great emperor Qin Shihuang who united the nation 22 centuries ago, will tolerate not the slightest challenge.

## *BIRTH OF THE REPUBLIC*

Since 1911, China has seen fundamental change, not once, but several times. In that year, after decades of unrest, the Chinese people arose and overthrew the Manchus of the Qing Dynasty who had sat on the Dragon Throne since 1644. Instead of a brave new world of egalitarian rule leading towards prosperity and freedom from foreign oppression, the long-awaited revolution ushered in the convulsions of the warlord era. The country was weakened, split and fractured as squabbling local dictators imposed corrupt and selfish rule on many parts of the country.

Dr Sun Yat-sen, inspiration for modern China, died before he could see his dream of a unified nation come true. The inheritor of his vision, Generalissimo Chiang Kai-shek, grasped briefly at the chance to weld the country into one modern nation. In 1928, he led the Great Northern Expedition to unseat the warlords. He conquered all that stood before him and, briefly, China had hope. It didn't last long.

The Kuomintang (National Party) of Chiang Kai-shek split with another group of ardent reformists, the communists. A civil war started that was to drag on for two bloody decades. Simultaneously, a much more brutal threat afflicted China. In 1932, the Japanese had driven into the rich industrial plains of Manchuria, seizing the three strategic provinces. Five years later, they struck into the heart of China. For eight more years, the country was torn apart by vicious foreign invasion and brutal occupation and by civil war. When Japan surrendered in 1945, the Nationalists had largely lost its mandate from the people; and corruption, nepotism, inflation and greed had eaten away at its foundations.

In the final stages of the civil war, the communist armies hammered down the length of China from their northern strongholds, joining with local militias and underground bands in the rural areas and with workers and students who welcomed them in the cities. By 1 October 1949, Chairman Mao Zedong and his victorious marshals could stand at the Gate of Heavenly Peace in Beijing and proclaim to the world the birth of the People's Republic of China. Trumpets blared the new anthem *The March of the Volunteers*, hailing the heroes of the Long March. The few survivors of that astonishing military trek had seized power. Their heirs today are determined to cling to it.

The early promise of the new regime was soon to lose much of its lustre. The communists accomplished much good. The land was redistributed basically on the lines of the slogan that had helped carry the Red Army to victory: 'The land to the sower'. But then this promise was largely negated; the landlords had been purged (often executed) and dispossessed. Instead, there was collectivisation. At first, the communes worked. Over the years they became inefficient. The legendary productivity of the Chinese peasant drooped. Politically and economically, the government blundered time and time again. A 'hundred flowers' of intellectual freedom were urged to bloom; when the flowers put their heads up in the thaw, they were swiftly plucked. A 'great leap forward' was proclaimed with peasants urged to forge foundries, feed furnaces in their rural plots. It was disastrous. Crops suffered and at least three million people starved to death in the unwise man-made famine.

## GREAT HELMSMAN LOSES GRIP

And then, growing feeble and desperate to preserve the purity of his revolution, in 1966, Mao, the Great Helmsman, steered his people into the most extraordinary peril. He called on the youth of China to arise, to wipe out the Four Olds: Old Ideas, Old Culture, Old Customs and Old Habits. They were to be excised, the nation cleansed in renewed revolutionary fire. Even 30 years after the peak of its fury, nobody could estimate how many people died in the relentless frenzy of the Great Proletarian Cultural Revolution. Certainly, it plunged

China's progress back a thousand steps. It deprived a generation of schooling. It left its marks on millions of hearts. Scarcely a family in China was untouched somehow, sometime, in that black decade.

When it ended with the death of Mao and the arrest of his wife and other ultra-leftist leaders, the Cultural Revolution left China a shaken, poor nation. The country was like a sick patient recovering from a long and debilitating illness. A new wave of leaders took power in the Forbidden City. Like Mao, they were old revolutionaries who had tramped on the Long March, who had fought Japanese and Kuomintang. They had won their laurels, wore them proudly. But their vision of the new China was not one of eternal revolution. Rather, they shared the dream of building a modern, industrialised society which could take its place in the world community.

The first outlines of how this could be achieved were disclosed by Deng Xiaoping in 1978. At the crucial foundation of these economic plans was the sturdy basis of Chinese riches for the preceding 5,000 years; the farmers were to be set free from their cooperative chains to work for themselves. This simple policy had immediate and obvious results. Farmers worked best in family groups, the traditional basis of Chinese civilisation. Now that they could plant what they wished, sell for the best price on open markets, they went to work with a will. Within five years, agricultural production had doubled in value. The peasants prospered mightily. Electricity came to the countryside. Farmers had television sets, rice cookers, watches, radios, bicycles. 'To be rich is glorious,' Deng Xiaoping preached. Few political slogans have been seized so eagerly, followed so enthusiastically.

In the cities, the obvious wealth of the peasants was envied. It was difficult to translate extra payments for hard work, initiative and productivity from farm to factory. Gradually, systems for profit sharing, for piecework pay and hefty bonuses for results raised the pay for industrial workers. In turn, this led to more problems. In the past, since 1949, it had been an honour to serve in the armed forces and the government. Now, young people were not so eager to don uniform or to work in administrative jobs. During the time when all China was poor, it had been beneficial to be a bureaucrat. At least you had face, prestige, standing and the powers of office. But who wanted to sit down in an office earning RMB70 a month when a factory worker was earning three times as much, a free enterprise hawker on the streets could earn five times as much and a humble farmer planting pumpkins on the outskirts of a suburban city could earn the fantastic wage, for China, of RMB8,000 a year? Where now was the attraction of being a soldier or a junior public servant following the communists' decree of 'Serve The People'?

One major headache, a problem of prosperity, was how to balance the national pay scales. It is a problem still unsolved, although pay rates for military and public servants have been significantly boosted to try to keep them to a reasonable level. It's a tricky acrobatic feat, akin to doing a high-wire walk across Niagara with a thousand eggs in one basket and a bulldozer on your shoulder. Senior government doctors in the great medical institutions, for instance, earn considerably less money than a street hawker selling pirate Cantopop tapes of Hongkong singers. An effective way to tackle inflation at the time of continuing growth is also a troubling worry to a government that had seen the preceding regime tumble largely because skyrocketing inflation in 1948 wiped out the urban middle class.

Alas, political developments lagged many *li* behind the swift pace of economic reform. In that other communist giant, the Soviet Union, energetic new leadership loosened the reins and allowed a long subjugated people to have their say. Russians had little on which to spend their worthless roubles, but they could complain about what they could not buy. In China, the shops were stocked with an astonishing range of consumer goods that would make Soviet citizens stare with envious disbelief. But the Chinese people remained firmly muzzled. Political dissent resulted in loss of jobs, persistence meant arrest, party discipline and a stretch in a dreaded political re-education camp.

Then, in April 1989, the former Communist Party secretary-general Hu Yaobang died. Students perceived Hu as a reformer who had tried to give China's brand of socialism a human face. They flocked to Tiananmen Square, spiritual heartland of the nation, to pay their respects. The gathering, as such meetings tend to do in China, acted as a magnet. Soon the vast square was thronged with shouting, wildly enthusiastic young people. From mourning Hu, it developed into a re-creation of the May 4th protests of 1929 when students demonstrated against the corruption, inefficiency and dictatorship of a former regime. A much vaunted ceremonial reception for Soviet leader Mikhail Gorbachev was thrown into political shadow.

## HIDING IN FORBIDDEN CITY

In their homes alongside the Forbidden City, the party leaders fumed. They had lost enormous amounts of face. But to try to placate the students, leaders such as Zhao Ziyang and Li Peng went to the square to beg and persuade demonstrators to call off their protests and to meet to discuss grievances at a later date. All such moves failed. Attempts to break up the demonstrations with police action failed. Law enforcement men were beaten up. Then the military was called in.

The People's Liberation Army had been for four decades the most respected arm of government, seen as being above politics, as incorruptible, as the army of the people, for the people. At first, as tens of thousands of Beijingers took to the streets, the army lived up to its proud reputation. Tanks ground to a halt in front of stand-fast demonstrators. Soldiers grinned at students calling for political changes to the communist system. Then roughnecks and hoodlums began attacking soldiers. More than 1,000 automatic rifles were seized from troops who were under strict orders that they were under no circumstances to fire on the crowds.

Once again, appeals were made to the student demonstrators. Once again, troops attempting to reach the historic square were stopped in their tank tracks by huge crowds. In isolated incidents, unruly youths attacked unarmed soldiers sent to break up the demonstrations. Some soldiers were lynched, others kicked to death.

Eight long weeks after the first demonstrators flocked into the square, party patience had run out. The best efforts of the conciliators had failed. The tough old soldiers who had led the Red Army to victory two generations earlier came out of retirement and in party caucus voted for the steel fist to be withdrawn from the silken glove.

Then the tanks were ordered to roll again. This time, demonstrators who stood in the way were crushed. Into Tiananmen rumbled the People's Army. Out of the square fled the people. Overnight, China had changed yet again, making yet another of the dramatic diversions in her political course that have so often marked her long and turbulent history.

The immediate upshot of the short, torrid 'Summer of the Students' was a hard and sweeping re-imposition of tough central party control. This has been somewhat relaxed, largely because economic improvements mean more money in the public wallet to spend on affordable consumer goods; it's true to say, financially, the Chinese people have never had it so good. But do not let this apparent laxity misguide you. Modern China remains, without apology, a strict, authoritarian regime. It may be glorious to grow rich, but it is incredibly foolish to misinterpret wealth as political freedom. The Chinese Communist Party, government and army will never in the slightest relax their grip on power.

## WHAT'S IT ALL MEAN?

So how do these tumultuous events affect visitors to China? They don't. Although the instant reaction of visitors at the time of Tiananmen was to stay away in droves, even as the purge of intellectuals continued, travellers headed back to Beijing. In the south, production in the booming export-oriented factories has hardly skipped a beat.

Western visitors to China should be careful how they raise such topics as the Chinese quest for democracy, the student uprising and the manner in which the Beijing spring was doused by the Chinese government. This is not for any fear that a communist secret policeman may be peering over your shoulder. He isn't. There are no bogeymen spying on your every word. (The fear of an omniscient Big Brother who keeps an efficient watchful eye on everyone in the land is not true. Chinese police and security forces are as inefficient, overmanned and incompetent as most branches of that stifling bureaucracy.)

There will be no repercussions against any tourist no matter what ill-advised and controversial questions he may ask or what anti-government expressions he may make. But the average Chinese is very wary of discussing such matters. With good reason. Even if he listens to a foreigner creating a diatribe against the leaders of the party and nation, he can place himself in peril of undergoing criticism and re-education. Just by being present when such criticism is voiced can place a Chinese in jeopardy.

And put yourself in his shoes. How would you like it if a visitor came to your country for the first time and began to aggressively criticise your political leaders. You might object to that view being expressed by a foreigner ignorant of your nation and its history.

So take care in what you say. Nobody is expecting you to parrot the self-praise of the Chinese government in 'putting down the counter-revolutionary uprising' which is how the shootings in Beijing is officially described. However, realise that any outright criticism of the government and the party will be intensely embarrassing to Chinese tour guides and others you might meet on your travels. You will put them in a situation where they will feel great unease and distress. Even if they secretly agree with you, as is likely, they will be unable to say so.

Ask questions, by all means, in your attempt to get an explanation of the events that baffled and stunned the world. But don't expect a tour guide to come out with a denunciation of the Chinese government and a well-considered statement in support of the Bill of Rights and one-man, one-vote democracy.

Anyway, it's their country and if they want to run it as a one-party dictatorship, what's it got to do with you? How would you like it if someone from a completely different culture – say a socialist military regime – landed on your front door and began questioning the very fabric of your society? You might well ask yourself: 'Who does this person think he is and what right has he got to be in my country as a guest demanding that I explain why I am not like him?'

## *THE CHINESE ONION*

China is like an onion. Observe it. Then peel off the outer skin. It looks the same. Peel off layer after layer. It still looks identical. But beneath each layer, as the observer penetrates deeper towards the inner core, there are subtle differences.

Most people will get only two or three layers deep. In doing so, they will see the patterns of the land and the people familiar to television viewers, the bamboo and the paddy fields, the immense bustling cities and the grandeur of the landscape, the pagodas poking through the mist and the Great Wall snaking over the eroded hills of Hebei.

Deep within the onion is the inner self of China. This is a lot more difficult to grasp.

It is easy, on a casual basis, to meet people in China. When you strive to speak basic Chinese, they will praise your efforts and your ability with the language. As your grasp of Chinese increases and – as a resident in the country, after a couple of years of study – you become more proficient, speaking with easy fluency about matters such as politics and philosophy, this praise for your linguistic ability becomes tinged with caution. This is particularly so among officials and intellectuals. Is the foreign devil getting too close to the kernel of how China works and how the Chinese people think?

# Chapter Two

# THE PEOPLE

*Sweat falling like rain, shoulders rubbing shoulders
and toes touching heels.*
—Poem from the Spring and Autumn period
describing a multitude.

China has too many people. And they are not all in the right place. By
2001, the population was estimated to be 1,270,000,000, give or take
a couple of million. The government had a head count, but a lot of
people felt disinclined to answer, largely because they were in some

ways in breach of the law. Take Shanghai. It's got 13 million people, legally. But any city official will tell you the population is 16 million. Those extra three million are in the city illegally, without proper work or residency status or papers. So they are now keen to disclose details to government census-takers.

China has had a strict one-child policy since 1972; that is credited with avoiding more than 300 million births. It's a matter of constant amazement to me that so many people seem able to break this law. Every time I read about a dissident or agitator (who all seem to get American residency any time they want it) they have several children. And Mainlanders coming to live in Hong Kong often have more offspring than legally permitted.

Officially, the population is growing at 15 million a year. This stupendous fertility led to the One Child policy, a regulation that has attracted much abuse from overseas critics. China's rulers dismiss complaints as unwanted interference in domestic affairs. Beijing contends that controlling the spiraling birth rate is absolutely vital to protect the welfare of the nation. It is a national priority for survival. In 1996, an emerging pattern came as a welcome surprise to family counsellors; the population growth rate slowed somewhat. This is exactly what happened in the Western world when better health facilities, rising incomes and higher education caused couples to limit the number of offspring. The population is expected to peak at 1.6 billion people around the middle of this century.

## OLD HUNDRED NAMES

The prosperity of China, now and through the ages, has rested always on the tough bent backs of the peasants. Ultimately, it was through their strong muscles, their patient skills, their endurance and strength, that the elegant civilisation of the cities was built. So it remains today. Despite impressive advances over recent decades in industry, manufacturing and such elite fields as high-tech computers, it is the farmers on whom the basic economic might of the nation depends.

*The eternal face of China, an old farmer plods home from the fields.*

There are a lot of them. Although China now has to cope with some of the biggest cities in the world, more than 80% of the population live in the countryside. Most live in villages where their ancestors toiled through the generations, bound in lifelong contracts to the soil. It is this vast majority of the people that is known as 'Old Hundred Names'. The term symbolises the mass of the Chinese peasantry working in idealised circumstances in a Confucian countryside of willow trees and dragon-backed bridges where everyone knows his place and happily keeps to it. Such a picture may be appealing; it is also largely imaginary.

Most peasants have had to stay down on the farm simply because there has been no alternative. This is changing as education becomes compulsory and universal; the degree of upward mobility may be slight but it is certainly more extensive than at any other time in China's long history.

Old Hundred Names? There are more like 5,662 written Han Chinese surnames rather than 100. Many sound the same although they are written with different characters.

## WHAT'S IN A NAME?

The five most common surnames, according to Chinese scholars, are Chang, Wang, Li, Chao and Liu. There are many millions of each. To be precise, social anthropologists tote up about 100 million Changs (or Chan in Cantonese) in modern China, about one in 12 of the population. They trace the character back to prehistoric times; it was common in the Jin territory four centuries before the Christian era. The character means 'to draw a bow'. So Mr Chang, in English, would be Mr Archer or Mr Bowman.

Similarly, many millions of one branch of the Wang clan can point to their character and claim to be descendants of emperors. Part of the character bears the symbol of imperial ruler. Rather like the Mr Kings of the Western world. Lin, another common surname, has the character of three trees grouped together; if his ancestors had been English (perish the thought!) he would be Mr Forest or Wood.

Visitors can always ask Chinese to explain their names. Point to the topmost character on a business card (the family name) and ask what it means. They will be delighted to explain and consider you polite for having asked. Then they will ask the derivation of your family name. That's okay if you are called Ford or Smith or Butcher and if you can explain how the name developed. You might have a slight problem if you should have a surname like Kaszchenowski.

## WHO'S MR LI?

I was sitting in the Dragon Boat Bar of the Hongkong Hilton Hotel one day when a message boy marched between the tables with a small blackboard atop a mahogany pole. As he rang his bell to gain attention, people looked at the board to see who was wanted on the telephone. 'Mr Wong,' read the notice. A dozen men got up to take the call. All were Mr Wong.

Such similarities are certain to cause confusion to the Western visitor unfamiliar with the system of Chinese names. You may be introduced to a group of six people, five of whom are named Li. If you ask, innocently, if they are related, the question is likely to raise a polite smile. Their names may be written in different characters so that although the surnames are pronounced the same, the written names are completely different.

It's the same when you go to a factory or an office and meet Mr Cai, the director, and Madame Cai, the sales manager. Don't assume they are married. The characters for their names may be different and, what's more, Madame Cai may be using her own birthname, a common practice in China long before women's liberation made it acceptable in the West.

## NAMES

The comparatively small number of Chinese common family names leads to an imaginative use of given names. Take ours.

Iris Wong writes: *"The family name Wong (Wang or Huang in pinyin) means descendants of the emperor. The character Po means 'treasured'. Yee means a young child. So my given name, Po-yee, means I am, literally, a Treasured Child.*

*Like most other Hongkong Chinese of my age, I also have an English given name. I was named Iris the first day I went to an English-speaking Catholic school where the teacher called us one by one to her desk and asked if we had a foreign name. What letter of the alphabet did I like most? I nominated 'I'. She gave me a list of suggested names. I have been Iris ever since."*

Sin Lok-gar writes: *"There are several ways to get a Chinese name. If you are called Smith, there is a set translation, Si Mat-sze. If you have a name which means something in Chinese, like bridge, that can be easily translated into a Chinese surname. In this instance, the character Qiao, which means 'bridge'."*

In my case, there is a set translation for the name Sinclair. But an old friend of mine helped baptise me in the Chinese manner by putting sounds which fit my name in Cantonese (the language of Hongkong) into characters. Thus I became Sin Lok-gar. In Cantonese, this translates, roughly, as 'to wash in happiness and affluence'. Not a bad name.

Then an old and knowledgeable professor I knew at Zhongshan University in Guangzhou gave me a translation that puts my name into more formal characters. In hanyu pinyin, this is Xin Ker-lai and the characters mean 'to strive with against difficulties and to come with a good personality'. Also pretty good.

But the Cantonese love playing with words and giving nicknames that reflect a person's traits and habits. So despite my two extremely auspicious formal names, to all my friends in Hongkong I am universally known by my nickname that mirrors my fondness for spicy food. They call me Sin Gar-lai, the curry man.

## THE MINORITIES

There are in China at least 90 million people who are classified as being non-Han. They are citizens of the People's Republic with all the rights of anyone else. Indeed, when it comes to such matters as family planning, it can be argued that the minority nationalities often have considerably more rights than others. They are not held so strictly to the one-child rule.

Most of the people who make up the 56 recognised minority tribes and races live in the outer ring of China. This is an enormous arc that sweeps from the plains of Manchuria, through the broad steppes of Mongolia and the Ordes, over the deserts of Xinjiang and down through the ice plateau of Tibet and Qinghai into the shrouded rain mountains of Yunnan and Guangxi.

Many live in the rich heartlands of China along with Han neighbours, but most occupy the outer areas, beyond the Great Wall in the nrth, in the deserts of the Weswnd in the jungles and mountains of the south.

Among these minority races there is diversity of astonishing variety. There are racial Koreans and Mongols, Turks, Kazaks,

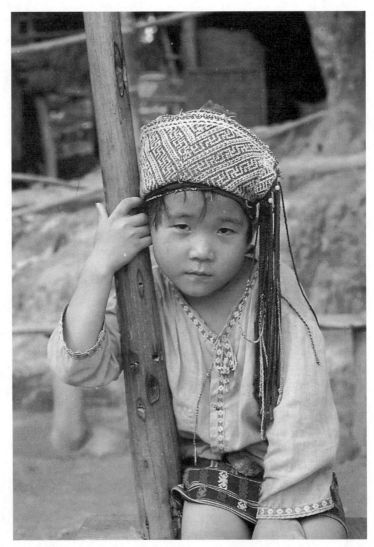

*A shy Miao girl in her traditional dress.*

Russians, Tartars and Thais. Counted among the minorities are the 7.5 million Hui, mostly racial Han but whose generations-long devotion to Islam has made them a special group who have their own autonomous province of Ningxia. Biggest of the nationalities are the Zhuang, 14 million of them who largely rule themselves in the beautiful southern province of Guangxi. In Yunnan, there is an incredible racial hodgepodge in the mountains with more than 23 racial minorities living in harmony amid the hilly valleys.

In the mountainous province of Guizhou, a natural fortress largely impenetrable until this century, there are five million Miao; their racial cousins in Laos and Vietnam have been largely exterminated by modern foes but in China they live on. Sharing Guizhou with them are many other tribes including the two million Bouyei, laughing ethnic Thais who remained behind when most of their nationality emigrated many centuries ago, in flight from the fury of another minority, the Mongols. The Bouyei still speak Thai.

Other large groups include Dong, Hani, Yao and five million Yi in the southwestern mountains. There are five million Manchus in the northwest, largely assimilated within the overwhelming Han sea, and 2.5 million Mongols. Around their lonely monasteries on the roof of the world, four million Tibetans live much as they have for centuries. All these groups cling to their own languages, customs and religions. Many follow a traditional way of life, like the nomadic Ewenki who hunt the Manchurian forests, or the million Kirghiz herders of Xinjiang.

Under the Chinese constitution, all are guaranteed a degree of self rule. The five stars on the red flag of modern China symbolise the fact that China is not one race, but a collection of peoples. Most casual visitors who go to China on one of the normal tours will be unlikely to meet any of these charming folk. But if you should stray into the tribal areas and spot people who dress differently from the average Chinese, the chances are they are one of the many minorities.

## *NORTH VERSUS SOUTH*

Even among the vast family of the Han, there is much diversity. Travelling from Beijing to Guangzhou, one can see the peoples change. The further south you go, the lighter, more delicate, finer-featured, tend to be the people. Of course, this is painting the racial picture with very broad brush strokes and talking in huge generalities. Basically, however, it's true.

Any anthropologist will tell you the Han people developed on the great curve of the Huang He somewhere around the present-day borders of Henan and Shanxi. As the population grew, there was pressure to increase the area occupied by the tribe, the dukedoms, the kingdoms and the empire. To the north there were the wild lands inhabited by the savage nomads. To the west lay uncertain deserts and to the east the sea. So the Han tended to drift south to occupy empty lands and then into areas inhabited by a colourful montage of many other tribes and races.

Going through Henan and neighbouring provinces today, the photographer's eye is drawn magnetically to those seamed, hardy peasant faces, wonderfully photogenic. These are the racial core of the Han and 2,000 years ago, most 'Chinese' would have looked like this. But as the eternal pressure of an ever-increasing population forced the boundaries of settlement inexorably towards the south, the Han met, fought, conquered, married and bred with many other races. All were absorbed into the growing Chinese family. Thus the Cantonese, for example, are now a distinctive type of people descended from the Northerners. They are Han, of course, but few can argue that they are a different variety of Han from the people who inhabit ancient ancestral homelands like Hebei or Shaanxi.

Compare China with Europe. The 'Europeans' occupied that continent in waves, most of which originated in Asia. (The Finns and Hungarians are both descended from the Huns. The Turks came from present-day Xinjiang. The Tartars who ruled Russia and Poland for centuries are Mongols.) Going from Scandinavia to Sicily, the peo-

41

ples change. It is similar in China. Just as not all Scandinavians are the picture postcard tall, blonde, blue-eyed Aryan, neither are Northern Chinese the bulky, stolid type pictured as Han. Similarly, in the south, there are many large, stocky Cantonese. There is enough truth in the general stereotype, however, to make the generalities worthwhile.

## THE DIVIDING LINE

North and south are normally separated by the line of the Yangtze. For most purposes, this is accurate enough. Settlement of the vast, rich Yangtze Valley marked an era of huge expansion for the Han. Then they moved on into the vibrant racial stew pot of the south and southwest where myriad tribes of different races were encountered. Some remained aloof and today are still distinctive minority races (the Miao of Guizhou and the Yao of Yunnan) while others blended with and married into the Han, disappearing as separate racial entities. In similar fashion, races have been absorbed in Europe by conquering nations. Where now are the Picts of Scotland?

## THE HUA QIAO

Some of the most important people in China, economically, are not there at all. These are the Overseas Chinese, the sojourners, the vastly wealthy communities which have sprung up far from the ancestral shores. There are, according to varying estimates, between 30 million and 54 million of them, depending on how you count.

Although the Hua Qiao do not live in China, they are an integral and vital part of the national economy. It is they who have provided much of the financial fuel which has powered the country towards industrialisation. Back in their ancestral villages, the more successful of these long-gone sons are venerated like living gods. In the vicinity of Chaozhou in eastern Guangdong, the name Li Kashing, the mighty mega-tycoon of Hongkong, is spoken of with awe. Little wonder; a university that any country would be proud of has been built with his

largess. Hospitals, clinics, old folks' homes, schools, temples, libraries and parks bear his name.

The Shantou region, from where Li and so many other successful
Chinese hail, has a population of 10 million. Official counts put the
Overseas Chinese population who can trace their roots to this tiny area
at a similar total. They are centred in Thailand, Hongkong and
America.

The town of Toishan in the Pearl River Delta has 800,000 souls.
In California, there are also 800,000 Toishan folk, many of them
fourth generation Americans. They include the eminent American
Chinese artist Dong Kingman who in 1987 made a sentimental
journey home after more than six decades.

Thailand has at least eight million ethnic Chinese. The six million
Hongkongers are 98% Chinese. The Philippines has three million,
Indonesia has an unknown number, depending on whether you count
Chinese by their birthplace or their ancient racial heritage. The people
of bustling Singapore are 75% Chinese and in Malaysia, 35% of the
folk are of Chinese descent. In Calgary, on the wide Canadian
prairies, there are 42,000 Chinese. Lima in Peru has three Cantonese-
language radio stations and there are Chinese daily newspapers in
Sydney and Melbourne. In Tahiti, 10% of the people are Chinese. And
there are growing Chinatowns throughout the world from Amsterdam
to Seattle.

No matter how long they have been away, a few years or 1,000
years like the Chinese of southern Borneo, they still feel their ties to
the ancestral villages. Money pours back home. Sojourners from the
Wuyi (five counties) area (Taishan, Xinhui, Kaiping, Enping and
Heshan City) of the Pearl River Delta have flooded that rich plain with
donations, bequests and investments to make it the richest area of all
China. The Shanghai textile barons of Hongkong have put some of
their profits back home into new factories on the Huang He River. In
return for this largess, areas with sizeable communal links overseas

maintain large and efficient offices to cater to the Hua Qiao when they make visits home. 'Overseas Chinese' hotels featuring local culinary delights are reserved for them.

And in places like Wuyi, every town houses a genealogical detective office to trace back the roots of families which may have left four generations earlier to go to Kam Shan (Golden Mountain – California) to dig for gold or build railways.

If a gangly young American comes to town with only the vaguest knowledge of where his great-great-grandfather hailed from, local experts can track down his native hamlet and introduce him to his distant relatives who remained behind.

# Chapter Three

# CHINA LANDSCAPE

*All the rivers flow into the sea
And yet the sea is not full.*

China is more than a country. It is a continent, a civilisation, a 5,000-year-long trek through history. To refer to China as a country is like referring to Europe as a single nation; but China is much larger, has three times as many people and in many ways is arguably more complex as a society.

Confronting outsiders, Chinese tend to form a united front. Within the homeland, they divide swiftly into provincial and local groupings.

Just as a travelling American abroad will identify himself as being from Portland, Oregon, or Houston, Texas, so will a Chinese proclaim himself from Zhejiang province or Jiangsu. If he is meeting a compatriot from the same province, he will identify himself more locally. If he hails from Guangdong and meets a fellow Cantonese, he will identify himself by county or region. Then village. Then clan. Local pride is intense; Chinese blood is a lot thicker than the muddy waters of the Yellow River.

The vast size and population of China makes generalities difficult, if not meaningless. Guangdong province, for instance, has 78 million people who speak their own distinctive dialect (with many diverse internal strains within the provincial boundaries). It is as big as Kansas and has 27 times as many people. Sichuan province, out in its France-sized mountain-guarded basin at the headwaters of the Yangtze, contains more people than the combined populations of Canada, Australia, New Zealand, Malaysia, Austria, Guatemala, Holland, Portugal and Greece. Xinjiang, which has a mere 12 million people, is larger than all Western Europe. The bulk of the people are Muslim Uigurs who speak old Turkic dialects, basically understandable even today to a resident of Istanbul.

How can one compare living conditions and culture in humid, tropical Hainan Island with those in the frigid tundra forests of northern Heilongjiang? From the Wusuli River in Manchuria to the rice paddies of Hainan is as great a distance as from London to the banks of the River Niger or from New York to Peru.

The climatic differences alone make for gulfs in the lifestyles; while tourists are splashing beneath the coconut palms on the beaches around Sanya in January, it can be 25 degrees below zero in Mongolia where the Siberian winds moan over the northern steppes.

## THE LAND

China sprawls across 9.6 million square kilometres. It runs 5,500 kilometres from the tropical sand dunes of Nansha Islands, four degrees north of the equator in the South China Sea, to the frigid banks of the Black Dragon River. When the sun rises over Shanghai, dawn is still four hours away in Kashgar, 5,200 kilometres to the west.

Along her 20,000 kilometres of land boundaries, the People's Liberation Army, biggest in the world with four million soldiers, stands watch over 16 neighbouring countries and territories. Some neighbours are friendly; others are not. They are Korea, Hongkong, Vietnam, Laos, Burma, India, Bhutan, Sikkim, Nepal, Pakistan, Afghanistan, Russia, Kyrgyzstan, Tajikistan, Kazakhstan and Outer Mongolia. Across the seas, Japan, the Philippines, Brunei, Malaysia and Indonesia have all had historic trade links with China going back well over 1,000 years.

Indeed, from the viewpoint of a mandarin at the imperial court in Kaifeng during the Tang Dynasty, China was justifiably the Middle Kingdom.

## FACE OF THE LAND

The common image of China in the West is a land of endless rice paddies with patient peasants plodding along behind equally placid water buffaloes. In large part, this likeness remains accurate. Such sights can be seen anywhere in the Yangtze valley and the fertile ricelands of the south. But hurry to get a glimpse of this; it's changing fast. Modernisation – new industries and sprawling urbanisation – has changed the face of China more radically in two decades than in the previous 20 centuries.

Two-thirds of China's 9.6 million square kilometres are hills, mountains and plateaux. The highest peak is Qomolangma (Mount Everest) at 8,848 metres, one of 100 cloud-piercers more than 7,000 metres in height.

Geographers describe China as a land of three giant steps. The lowest is the arc that faces the seas, the fertile crescent in which the bulk of the people live. Further inland, a giant step goes upwards to

the inland ranges from Yunnan and Guizhou to the Loess highlands and the Mongolian steppes. The top step is the high, icy Tibet-Qinghai plateau and the enormous mountains that gird the roof of the world.

## THE COAST

From the mouth of the Yalu River on the Korean border down to where the Beilun River separates China from Vietnam, there are 18,000 kilometres of coastline. Offshore, the two major islands of Hainan and Taiwan are the largest of many thousands of islands.

Decent deepwater harbours are surprisingly few. The best on the entire coast is the island-girded waters of Fragrant Harbour, Hongkong. Others are Dalian, Qindao and Tianjin, which serve Beijing and the northern provinces, the enormous anchorages that line the Huang He River at Shanghai, and the beautiful little snug ports of Wenzhou, Xiamen and Shantou on the jagged southeastern coastal fringe. Up the Pearl River is Guangzhou, the historic old gateway to China, and further down the coast is the oil city port of Zhanjiang.

## THE RIVERS

For thousands of years, peasants have called the Huang He (Yellow River) by a name that is sadly appropriate. 'China's Sorrow' is how they refer to the silt-choked waters of the river which nurtured the earliest Chinese civilisation. On its 5,464 kilometre journey down from the ice plateau of Qinghai province, the Huang He picks up an incredible load of silt. This is carried with the flood as it rushes down from the mountains and through the loess lands to the broad North China Plain. There, the river slows down as it meanders towards the Gulf of Bohai. When the waters slow, the silt drops to the river bed. Over millions of years the steady deposits of silt have built up the riverbed. Now, it flows high above the level of the surrounding plains. At incredible cost in toil, sweat and expenditure, China's rulers for 5,000 years have tried to raise banks to control the river. Until now, none has succeeded. Periodically, melting ice in the highlands and heavy rains in the middle reaches of the river have caused the waters to rise and overflow the banks. The results have historically been heavy death tolls in flooding and even more immense costs in lives and suffering because of starvation in the resulting famines. When the communists took control of China in 1949, one of the first things they instituted was a high-powered Yellow River Conservation Commission. Teams of engineers, hydrologists, land control experts and afforestation workers have since confined the Huang He within iron and concrete channels eight kilometres wide. For the first time in history, the Yellow River seems genuinely to be under the control of man. It is one of the proudest achievements of Beijing. Despite record rainfalls and cold spells which have frozen the waters solid for more than 100 kilometres – forming dangerous dams of natural ice – the river in recent years has not seriously threatened the scores of millions who live along its lower floodplains.

Even more majestic and certainly more impressive is the Yangtze or Changjiang as it is commonly called in Chinese. The name means 'Long River' and at 6,300 kilometres from the gaping 85-kilometre-wide mouth to the headwaters in Tibet and Qinghai, it is certainly apt. It forms a broad, muddy highway from the metropolis of Shanghai that cuts directly into the heart of China. Ships up to 10,000 tons can easily sail 300 kilometres straight upriver to Nanjing.

The Pearl River that flows through the south is one of the friendliest waterways on earth. Ferries, sampans, vessels from every port in the world and fishing fleets of thousands of sailing junks make its busy estuary a delight. It ambles through some of the most scenic areas of China; a tributary, the Li, wends its way through the sugarloaf mountains of Guilin, one of the most famed sights in China. It is also a bustling commercial waterway with many important manufacturing towns clustered along its 2,197-kilometre length. Densely populated and the richest area in China, the delta area can be explored by tourists on chugging local ferries or hovercraft that speed at 50 knots from

*North China winters can be frigid. Overseas Chinese from tropical climes dress in furs and padded clothes to cope with the chill. But, like this Hongkonger, they say the warmth of visiting the ancestral homeland keeps the cold at bay.*

Hongkong to such river ports as Guangzhou, Macau, Jiangmen or 480 kilometres upstream to Wuzhou in Guangxi province.

Cartographers have mapped more than 50,000 rivers and their combined flow of 2,600,000,000,000 million cubic metres gives China hydroelectric power reserves of 680 million kilowatts, the largest in the world.

## HOT AND COLD

It's impossible to summarise the Chinese climate simply because it is so variable over such a huge area. Basically, the north is very cold in winter; the south can also be surprising chilly.

It is one of the oddities of life in China that in winter, you are likely to be steaming, uncomfortably hot in the rigid north while you are shivering, chilled to the bone in the comparatively balmy south. Here's why ... It is an act of faith to all Chinese that north of the Yangtze, houses must be kept tightly closed through the winter months. Inside, coal fires burn below clay *kangs* and the temperatures soar. It is the same in tourist hotels where the heat is turned up as high as it can go. Outside, ice bedecks the barren branches of the plane trees and snow lies deep. Inside, it's like a sauna.

Meanwhile, it is a belief held equally firmly that south China never freezes. Just try believing this theory when the winter gales come coursing down from Siberia; in unheated southern concrete buildings, the temperature drops to icebox levels and three layers of clothes can't keep out the penetrating cold.

Bone-chilling cold in the northern winter, steambath-humid in the south in summer, delightfully pleasant everywhere in autumn, uncertain universally in the spring, the climate of China is as variable as the landscape. In summer, apart from the highlands, China is hot. There are degrees of discomfort, from the dry, arid heat of the west to the sapping, dripping humidity of the verdant moist southlands.

Chinese old wives' tales say there are four furnace cities in China: Nanchang in Jiangxi, Chongqing in Sichuan, Wuhan in Hubei and

*Typical of modern housing throughout the nation, these drab apartment blocks offer modern homes – albeit crowded – to industrial workers.*

Changsha in Hunan. Any visitor to the sauna-like south in the summer can probably nominate a few more.

## THE CITIES

The skylines of China's cities change every month. Once low and drab – and covered in a thick layer of smoke from smouldering kitchen coal fires – they are now studded with glass and steel skyscrapers that would be impressive in Manhattan. The tallest buildings are usually swank hotels, often built with investment from Overseas Chinese and managed by familiar international chains. The new financial and business centre of Pudong, across the muddy Huang He River from Old Shanghai, is dominated by a telecommunications tower taller than the Eiffel Tower in Paris and an 88-storey office spire with the top 35 floors occupied by a Grand Hyatt. In Guangzhou, the tallest building is a marble-lobbied 60-storey hotel.

Chinese cities may have been the foundries of civilisation. But in the modern era, many of them are simply vast slums with potholed, undrained streets and dusty, unpaved footpaths between endless dreary blocks of five-storey apartment buildings and factories. Dismal as is the vast suburban sprawl that surrounds most Chinese cities, the visitor must understand that these are signs of progress. With the exception of Shanghai and a handful of other cities, mostly ports, the major towns of China before 1949 were comparatively small. It was the drive towards industrialisation that saw them boom.

Formerly, city folk lived mostly in squat, single-storey brick homes with a small courtyard enclosed by a wall and the main windows facing south to catch the winter sun. In most cities, these have gone or have an imminent appointment with the bulldozers. They are replaced with five-storey buildings depressingly similar from Shenyang to Haikou. Unlovely though they be, these blocks efficiently house huge numbers of people. Families may be squeezed into tiny two- or three-room apartments in conditions which would be intolerable elsewhere by Western standards. By Chinese measures, people are deemed fortunate indeed to have such quarters.

But even here, rapid changes are taking place. In cities from Urumqi to Haikou, old city centres are being relentlessly gutted. The Russian-built heart of Harbin has almost gone, sadly, taking with it a vivid chapter of history. The same glass-shrouded commercial and hotel skyscrapers rise in Guangzhou as in Houston, stamping a global brand on Chinese city financial areas. Vast landscaped and well planned areas like Pudong in Shanghai or Tianhe in Guangzhou offer commercial environs familiar to anyone from a modern Western city.

In general, the compact old central areas of the cities – especially the waterfronts and riverbanks in ports and districts around the railway stations – tend to be the most interesting for visitors. Outside the town centres, industrial and housing blocks march off in a panorama of glum similarity.

One reason that most Chinese cityscapes are the same depressing five- or six-storey buildings with few modern high-rises poking above the squat landscape is the shortage of elevators. It's difficult to live much higher than the sixth floor if one has to use the stairs.

## *The Big City*

Although 80% of China's population lives in the countryside, this still leaves more than 200 million occupying cities. Shanghai is said to be the biggest city in the world with 13 million people. That is the official number, but town planning experts jostling to handle this mass of people admit there are at least an additional three million floating population, who cram into the city seeking work. It's a similar story in all the big cities, especially in the advanced prosperous south. The metropolitan centres act as a magnet for country youth seeking an adventure in the bright lights.

In 1984, the Central Government reorganised the political structure of the nation. While the provinces remained the same (Hainan Island was split from Guangdong to become the 30th province in 1988), the internal arrangements were changed. This meant that big chunks of provinces were put into logical regions that could be developed as sensible economic districts.

Take Shantou, in eastern Guangdong. This is the home of the Chaozhou people, a distinctive subgroup of the great Cantonese family. They speak their own language, have their own cuisine, are strongly bonded together. So the Chaozhou area was amalgamated into one region. For some reasons known only to faceless planners in Beijing, these regions were called 'cities'. Thus Shantou 'city' comprises two cities, eight counties, 10,000 square kilometres and 10 million people. The real old port town, a city in the normally accepted sense of the word, has less than two million people.

So when you hear Chinese officials talking of Beijing having eight million people, or Shanghai having a population of 13 million, they are including very extensive areas of the hinterland. It's as though Britain claimed London had 20 million people, toting up the populations of Kent, Middlesex, Surrey and the other home counties. Or if America counted the population of New Jersey, most of Connecticut and a huge swathe of New York State and proclaimed New York city held 25 million souls. Shanghai city, by my guess, has about six million people in the city proper.

In recent years, China has laid great stress on making her old cities more liveable in the era of industrialisation. Foreign experts from many disciplines have taken part in seminars aimed at teaching Chinese planners how to design functional, efficient and attractive towns. Attempts at beautification have been made in a number of cities. In Guangzhou, for instance, the go-ahead administration has planted millions of flowering shrubs and other plants. In the capital, landscaping the dull ochre soil of the northern plains has been tried in attempts to make the city more attractive.

For many Western visitors, however, the first and remaining impression of the majority of Chinese cities is of a drab, dreary landscape of endless blocks of dingy, featureless apartments marching off into the polluted haze and divided by bare plots of barren earth. Try to walk about Taiyuan, capital of Shanxi province; the dirt and filth in the air from burning low-grade coal leaves you weeping and choking.

## Beijing

The national capital is one of the great cities of the world. By Chinese standards, it is comparatively modern; it was first used as the imperial capital by Kublai Khan in the 13th century.

Its history goes back a long way before the great Mongol ruler established the seat of the Yuan Dynasty in the city on the dusty North China Plain. According to legend, a city stood near the present Tiananmen Square in 1200 B.C. It was the capital of the Kingdom of Yen before it was razed by Emperor Qin Shihuang-di in his campaign to unify China. The invading Khitan Tartars grabbed the city in A.D.

986 and declared it their capital. Successive armies of conquerors and Chinese regimes swept back and forth over the area for centuries during which the city lived under many banners, and had many names.

The Mongols called it Khanbalik (City of the Khan) and from here ruled their vast domains in China. The Chinese Ming Dynasty moved the seat of imperial rule to Nanjing (which means Southern Capital) for a brief period before moving back to Beijing (Northern Capital) so they could keep a watchful eye on the uneasy nomad borderlands.

When the Qing regime was imposed in 1644, the new rulers were happy to keep Beijing as the imperial capital because it was so close to their ancestral homeland in Manchuria. During their brief tenure in power, the Kuomintang ruled from Nanjing and in that period, Beijing was occupied by the Japanese. With the communist victory in 1949, Mao moved the seat of government back to the old imperial capital.

## Shanghai

The huge port city on the Huang He has character. It's a town of solidly built workers who proudly boast their rowdy heritage in what once gloried in its role as the wickedest city on earth. It is a pup of a city; until greedy Westerners seized the place as a treaty port after the first Opium War in 1841, it was a tiny walled town on a mudbank on a forgotten tributary of the Yangtze.

So Shanghailanders trace their roots to other places. They come mostly from the surrounding provinces of Zhejiang and Jiangsu but some look back to ancestral villages in virtually every province in the land. A walk along the Bund takes you on a stroll through an architectural museum; almost all the buildings went up there before the Japanese invasion in 1937 and the occupation of the International Settlement in 1941.

## Guangzhou

Exuberant, noisy, cheerful, smiling, quick to make a dollar, the

Cantonese are a jovial bunch. Their long tradition of links with the outside world makes foreigners familiar to them. Almost everyone you meet has a cousin in California, a brother running a restaurant in Manchester or a friend studying computers in Australia.

Vastly proud of its reputation as the culinary capital of China, the locals delight in eating, drinking and making merry. They are also the consummate traders of China, tracing their role as the major gateway to the world back to the Tang Dynasty when Arab dhows dropped anchor in the Pearl River.

## *Xian*

Famed for the buried terracotta warriors that guarded the tomb of the Great Unifier, Qin Shihuang, Xian was the capital of a dozen dynasties. A vast museum of the ages, the city has been occupied for many thousands of years, long before the first dynasty. On the outskirts of town, not far from where the Wei River joins the Huang He on the very spot where many anthropologists believe the first Chinese agronomists farmed, there is the well-preserved remains of a 6,000-year-old village.

One of the most popular axis of the tourist schedule, Xian has boomed with tourism in the past decade. The past here is profitable and new hotels – Swedish, German, Hongkong and Swiss are joint venture partners – offer high quality accommodation as a base for exploring dynastic China and its treasures.

## *Kaifeng-Zhengzhou-Luoyang*

This triumvirate of cities in Henan along the Yellow River were all at various times capitals of dukedoms, kingdoms and of all imperial China. Visitors who go to one of these cities are urged strongly not to depart without seeing all three of them. There are frequent inexpensive bus trips between the cities and each has a charm and character of its own. Each also preserves with great enthusiasm the relics of the past that make this area of the Huang He Valley stake its claim to being the cradle of Chinese civilisation.

Kaifeng was a major staging post on the Silk Route and the family Shih who still live in the town are the last remnants of the practising Judaic Chinese community.

Near Luoyang, at Longmen, are the grottoes carved over a period of seven dynasties where 100,000 figures of Buddha once occupied caves hacked out of the solid rock cliffs. Vandals over the centuries have destroyed most of the figures but thousands, some partly shattered, remain as reminders of a persistent faith.

Not far from Zhengzhou, modern commercial and political capital of Henan, carved stone monuments stand sentinel on lonely hillsides, looking out over rolling loess hills where they guard the graves of Song Dynasty rulers. This area is rich in artefacts, museums, legend and history.

## *Chongqing*

What a dump. The site is scenic enough, set on a spur surrounded on three sides by the Yangtze and a major tributary. But the high steps that allow river craft to rise up the steep flanks as the water level rises and falls with the season are normally covered with filth. The climate is dreadful, usually overcast and smoggy and the town is one big slum. Despite that, it has a certain charm and the historical links are fascinating. It was to this remote town that Chiang Kai-shek and the Nationalists retreated in 1937 in front of the advancing Japanese and it was here that Free China had its capital during the wartime years.

## *Tianjin*

Drab and miserable, the huge northern port has little to recommend it to visitors unless you have a penchant for looking at factories and chimneys belching choking clouds of smoke.

As major entrepot for the Northern Plains, as a huge industrial base and a hub for transport, Tianjin is a vital economic force in China. As a place of interest, it has virtually nothing to offer except boredom and phenomenal pollution.

## *Wuhan*

The capital of Hubei province in the central Yangtze has a population of about 3.5 million. It is a conurbation formed by the three old cities of Hankou, Wuchang and Hanyang, set on the banks where the Han River joins the mighty Yangtze. Wuhan has considerable charm. Although far inland, its history as a major treaty port has given its lively people a cosmopolitan outlook.

## *Qingdao*

What a delight! A lovely city which still largely bears the proud Teutonic architectural stamp put on the harbour promenades by Germany when the city was capital of the Kaiser's colony in China before the Second World War. Old castles that look as though they belong at home alongside the Rhine and sturdy stone cathedrals which appear to have been built to withstand a siege dominate the skyline. Shandong folk are renowned for their hearty appetites, good humour and capacity for hard work.

## *Nanning*

Very few foreigners ever make it to the southernmost provincial capital in the land. This is a great pity. The sleepy little city on the upper reaches of the Pearl River in Guangxi is a marvellous gem. Girded by clumps of enormous bamboo, the city echoes in the spring to the sound of local Zhuang tribesmen (there are 14 million of them!) singing in their local dialect to attract lovers. Gracious parks, hotels set amid gardens and broad tree-lined avenues speak of the French heritage which seeped up from Vietnam less than 100 kilometres to the south.

## *Xiamen*

Another favourite city of mine, this wonderful port city in southern Fujian is the homeland of many millions of Overseas Chinese. It is outward-looking and has been for well over 1,000 years during which the intrepid traders of Amoy (its old name) put out to sea in their junks to the distant savage lands of the South Seas. Today, in museums as far distant as Borneo and India, the jars and ornaments they carried as trade goods can be seen.

It is a city of smiles. Wander the narrow, bustling streets and drop into free enterprise restaurants, stop to admire clay teapots or simply go into a restaurant and you will meet friendly folk eager to help.

## *Hangzhou*

Imperial seat of power during the Southern Song Dynasty (when barbarian invaders held sway in the traditional northern capitals), Hangzhou makes the most of its past. For centuries, it was regarded as a cultural citadel where painting, literature, landscape gardening, architecture and drama flourished. Today, local folk like to think much of this rich legacy remains.

The focal point of the town is the scenic West Lake. For at least 800 years, poets have waxed lyrical about this willow-fringed expanse of shallow water, an artificial expanse lined by swept roof pavilions, studded with temple-dotted islands. It's pleasant enough, but hardly one of the great sights of China despite endless enthusing by Hangzhou citizens to whom West Lake is the centre of the universe.

As the terminus of the Silk Road and southern port of the Grand Canal, Hangzhou was once a vital economic hub. It is still an important city for both manufacturing and tourism. It's a typical bizarre twist of Chinese business that Hangzhou for some reason is a global capital for the leather industry, with more than 1,200 factories making jackets, shoes and designer clothes. But there's no cattle; the hides are imported from Africa, Australia and Argentina. Work this out!

## Changsha

The stamp of Chairman Mao is still very much evident in the provincial capital where he spent much of his early life, worked as a teacher and where, so legend has it, he wrote his first thesis *On Revolution* while sitting in an orange grove on the Xiang River.

Changsha is an interesting place if only for the remembrance of Mao and other revolutionary heroes. The late president of China, Liu Shaochi, was also born nearby. In glorious brotherly harmony, Liu was purged by Mao in 1966 and sent down to the countryside to learn from the peasants. He died of cancer of the nose after Comrade Jiang Qing, Mao's wife, forbade doctors to give him treatment. Lovely lady, I don't think.

Changsha is a major printing and publishing city, putting out school textbooks and medical tomes in scores of languages.

## Nanjing

Capital of China during the Kuomintang era, Nanjing is set on the banks of the Yangtze where the Zijin Shan (Purple and Gold Mountains) meet the river. The venerated father of modern China, Dr Sun Yat-sen, lies in his stately mausoleum atop a magnificent open staircase that climbs Purple Mountain.

The city was the subject of the horrific Rape of Nanjing in 1937 when Japanese soldiers murdered an estimated 300,000 people in one of the most vicious war crimes in history. More people than this, however, were slain when the Taiping rebels took the city in the 1860s and probably just as many were butchered when the Ever Victorious Army of General Charles Gordon reclaimed the city for the Manchu rulers.

Today, Nanjing is a pleasant city of trees and boulevards. One notable feature is the gigantic double-layered bridge crossing the Yangtze, a symbol of Chinese pride and progress.

## *PLACE NAMES*

It comes as a disappointment to visitors to find those exotic, romantic names of provinces and towns are, when translated, often boring and as mundane as those back home.

There are, to be sure, places called The Temple of Eternal Enlightenment and The Pond of the Pure White Egret.

But most names are nothing as exciting.

Take some of the provinces. Shandong means Mountain East. Henan means South of the River. Guangdong means Broad East while, logically, the next province up the Xi (West) River is Guangxi which means Broad West. Sichuan means Four Rivers, because that's where four rivers join to form the broad Yangtze, the real name of which is – boring! – Changjiang or Long River.

Yunnan means Beneath the Clouds because of the misty weather.

The three Manchurian provinces are known collectively as Dong Bei, the Northeast. Thankfully, the most northern one of all has an exotic name, Heilongjiang, which means Black Dragon River.

Ask your tour guide or hotel staff for the name of the city and province and what the characters mean in English. They will be happy to tell you. Then ask them for the other, unofficial names of local places. These are almost invariably more interesting.

Guangzhou, for example, means Broad City. Terrific. Much more romantic is the legend of how the place was founded by five fairies who rode into town on five goats. The fairies flew off but the goats remained in the form of an imposing statue in the city's Yue Xie Park. The legend is the basis for Old Canton being known to locals as The City of the Five Rams. Most other towns and cities have similar stories and local folk will delight in explaining them to you.

# Chapter Four

# BELIEFS

*When men are sincere, the gods are moved and they answer.*

*Accept your destiny, as you do your duty,*
*Be satisfied with your position*
*And obey the voice of heaven.*

The Chinese leadership, along with a large proportion of the Chinese people, harbour deep and well-justified suspicions about missionaries and those they see as religious extremists. Zealots have brought enormous misery and suffering to China; the deranged Hakka who thought he was the younger brother of Jesus Christ launched the Tai Ping rebellion which in the 1860s devastated south and central China at the cost of tens of millions of lives. The Boxer Rebellion largely targeted Christian missionaries, some of whom were converting starving peasants with bribes of rice. The so-called siege of the legations in the capital, romanticised into phoney heroism by Hollywood as *55 Days in Peking* was in fact a shameful episode in which Chinese were the victims, not the aggressors. It was European arrogance and effrontery that was a major cause of this conflict and the insistence on forcing foreign religious teaching on China.

Even today, foreign missionaries seem to think they have some holy calling which makes them exempt from Chinese law, a notion which the authorities in Beijing and other cities find as bemusing as it is insulting. Having said this, China tolerates and even welcomes Western religious workers who carry on with dignity and respect for Chinese institutions and laws. There is a Macau-based group consisting of friends of mine which has for years done good work, quietly, in Chinese rural areas. It's the intruders who deliberately provoke their followers into public displays of unrest who find themselves in trouble in China. These self-created martyrs who go to China with the declared intent of confronting the authorities get no sympathy from me.

Should you be religious, you will find ample opportunities to follow your faith in China. There are churches and religious groups in all major cities. If you feel the urge to go to church, mosque, synagogue or temple, the easiest thing to do is ask your hotel concierge. If you are a resident, ask your consulate.

If you are wise, you will stick to the registered, recognised institutions. The Chinese authorities look with grave disfavour on so-called underground churches, which are of the holy roller type. They are also at constant loggerheads with Rome. China recognises the Patriotic Church which has its own hierarchy. The Vatican insists that Chinese Catholics should follow the Pope. Basically, China is saying "render unto Caesar that which is Caesar's" – in other words, you stick to religion and let us run the country.

## *SECT SPRINGS SURPRISE*

Similarly, China has taken an unbending attitude towards non-Christian sects such as the Falungong. These are seen not as religious groups following truly-held beliefs, but as charlatans and conjurers misleading gullible and foolish people. What's worse, sects like this which spread like mushroom spores, unseen and uncounted, are not controlled by the state, which may be the real root cause of Beijing's implacable opposition.

The Falungong, for instance, emerged on a chilly spring morning in 1999. It stunned the Chinese leadership. Silently, with no warning, 15,000 people lined up in quiet protest outside Zhongnanhai, the sealed suburb in the Forbidden City where the nation's top leadership lives in a privileged enclave. There was no trouble. The crowd stood mute.

Officials from the Beijing Public Security Bureau, the capital's police, were taken aback. There had been no hint that members of the Falungong movement planned any such show of force. Despite their stolid good behaviour, the mass protest was a potent signal that Chinese in a communist state were able and willing to stand up for their beliefs. It was also a worrying sign to the leadership that the entire police and security apparatus had no hint that such a massive demonstration had been organised, particularly when the leadership was bracing for possible trouble on the 10th anniversary of the Tiananmen Square clampdown.

Who were they, these mostly well-dressed, mature men and women who lined the streets in the very heart of the nation? To the astonishment of many foreigners, they were practitioners of the martial art and physical fitness discipline, qigong. They assembled outside Communist Party headquarters to protest heavy-handed action a few days earlier in the port city of Tianjin when police broke up a demonstration by qigong adherents.

What was going on? The unexpected demonstration at the Forbidden City highlighted one of numerous movements that have seized the imagination of the masses. It focused attention on the growing number of religions, cults, groups, associations—call them what you will—that have sprouted unofficially in the past two decades.

The April 1999 demonstration ended peaceably, dispersed by polite police and cold rain. But it served a graphic warning to the national leadership. Falungong claimed a phenomenal 60 million followers. For an unlicensed and unsupervised organisation of such size—larger even than the 40 million membership of the Communist Party—to exist in a strictly controlled state was a worry. So was the membership, which included many academics, businessmen, executives and students, as well as housewives and workers. And so was the leadership; Falungong's 47-year-old qigong master Li Hongzhi lives in New York where he nurses resentment because Beijing banned his book on the practice of qigong.

Was qigong what it professed to be—a deep breathing, physical exercise and body-building discipline—or was it a political movement or a religious cult? Or was it a bit of each? Nobody knew, not even the religious and political licensing authorities who are supposed to keep a close eye on such movements. Outside China, it was likened to the Boxers who had led the nation to chaos and tumult as the Qing Dynasty collapsed, or even to the deranged neo-Christian zealots of the Taiping rebellion of the mid-19th century, whose ravages left much of China in a charred ruin.

Whatever, the baffling demonstration illustrated vividly the flowering of unofficial faiths. This is nothing new. Communists always viewed religions with dim suspicion—if you had to believe in anything, why not believe in the Party? During the Cultural Revolution, all religions were squelched, often with sickening viciousness. As the nation eased in the late 1970s, religions of every variety made a revival.

## GRABBING THE HEADLINES

Cultists or Christians, foreign followers of all persuasions cling to the notion that they should be free to go to China, break Chinese laws and be totally immune from any punishment. This is an idea fostered by Beijing. Instead of prosecuting people who break Chinese laws under Chinese law, the authorities are too eager to get potentially embarrassing troublemakers out of their hair. When you have a bunch of people turn up in Tiananmen and start unfurling yellow banners extolling the Falungong (which is banned in China) there's a fair chance that one of them has foreign links.

For reasons I have never understood, this instantly causes reporters to start scribbling that "Chinese police have detained a U.S. resident." Well, so what? Just because a Chinese has gone to live abroad doesn't make them immune to the laws. But when such a rumpus begins, the accused are generally released and deported. Those unfortunates who do not live in Australia or some other country go to jail. My advice to both tourists and expatriate residents in China is simple; don't get involved in illegal religious activities.

Like most political activists, Falungong devotees know how to milk a situation for maximum effect. That's why they always turn up on public holidays, when they can find the largest audience. And they know what Western reporters to call to ensure that when the police grab them, there are front page pictures in the world press. Meanwhile, the Falungong founder is happily ensconsed in comfortable circumstances in New York, where he can peddle his nonsensical ideas, many of which are fixated on movements of the bowel.

## RELIGIOUS REVIVAL

If you should be poking around an old temple somewhere in the hinterland and spot a lanky, gray-haired Englishman chatting in fast and colloquial Mandarin with monks or nuns, pay attention. Chances are you have spotted Keith Stevens, the world's leading expert on Chinese gods. The amiable former military intelligence officer has written books and lectured widely on the huge plethora of deities, demons, mythical figures, imposing legendary heroes and local village figures of worship. So ask him how the temple business is doing in modern China; "Booming!" he enthuses.

He's right. Religion, once banned as anti-socialist and non-communist and whose followers were persecuted relentlessly by Red Guards during the Cultural Revolution, has gone through a remarkable revival. Throughout the country, from the mass belief of Tibetans in their ornately-reincarnated lamas to underground and unregistered and unregulated Christian sects in Henan, religion of all sorts is flowering.

It sprang to life in the fertile minds of the Chinese peasants as the fury of the Cultural Revolution faded; wiping out religious belief was a cornerstone of the fanatical campaign to eliminate the Four Olds. It's ironic that probably not one of the millions of Red Guards realised their extremism in parroting the Thoughts of Mao and persecuting those suspected of being less than total believers was in itself a perverted form of religious mania.

Religion is becoming big business in China. In 1983, I was with a party of foreign diplomats and journalists being escorted around Zhejiang province. I wandered away from the group and chatted to typically friendly villagers. There was one big building in the village, a modern structure built like a large barn. Inside, we found more than 100 women and girls working at a furious pace. They were making gods.

"What you're looking at here," my wise old companion commented, "is the biggest growth industry in China.

"Religion is on the way back."

Since then, beliefs of all kinds have sprouted in the fruitful superstitious attitude in cities and countryside.

## A RELIGIOUS COCKTAIL

When it comes to choosing a religion, the Chinese have a multitude of choices. There are all those available to the Western world and a variety of home-grown selections as well. Officially, China is a secular state. The constitution (revised numerous times since 1949) guarantees freedom of religion. Just be careful how you exercise these "rights".

A Chinese can quite happily mix up a cocktail of religions. He can believe in Buddha, follow the preachings of the philosopher Confucius, hold precious The Way of Taoism and also without qualms attend Christian services. Is this hypocrisy, as some Westerners contend, or more charitably a broad outlook which takes the best aspects of all possible faiths? Or is it a multi-choice bet that covers all eventualities that guarantees backing a winner in the religious wagers? Take your pick.

If the visitor asks a modern Chinese bluntly, "What is your religion?" the answer is likely to be a confused silence. The most common answer is probably "None". At home, however, there will be ancestral portraits on the wall, hinting at a Confucian-like regard for the ancestors, and incense may burn in front of a family altar which also contains the likenesses of traditional deities.

Over the centuries, China has warmly accepted religious infusions from abroad. The basic faith of the people, however, has remained with the two codes of ethical conduct developed in China itself, Taoism and the teachings of Confucius, wedded to the imported religion of Buddhism which came over the Himalayas from India and greatly affected China during the Tang Dynasty. Interwoven, inter-mixed and mingled richly, the three beliefs have borrowed so extensively from each other it is now difficult to know where one religion ends and another faith begins. In practice, Taoism-Confucianism-Buddhism in China is one vast body of faith. There are no contradictions in finding Taoists praying in Buddhist temples and vice versa. The great underlying faith of all Chinese beliefs, and one that transcends all religions, is the most ancient of all, ancestor worship.

## THE PARTY

In practice, the state religion is orthodox communism, Marxist-Leninism with the addition of China's own Maoist legacy. This version of perceived truth has now been leavened with The Word As Spoken By Deng Xiaoping which has made the economic teachings of the Great Helmsman more realistic.

The Party has 47 million members, give or take a million. The figure is always changing as unpopular figures are dumped, the corrupt are weeded out—and frequently shot—or a new batch of upwardly-mobile Chutties (Communist Urban Technocrats) join the ranks of the Party faithful. Belief in the infallibility of the sainted Karl

Marx, the preachings of the apostle Vladimir Ilyich Lenin or the practices of Comrade Deng are not really necessary for membership. Young Chinese join the Party for the same reasons an accountant in Manchester joins the Jaycees or a Chicago draper joins Rotary—it's a way to make contacts and get ahead in life, although this necessity is fading rapidly.

Still, the Party has a kernel of True Believers who see the teachings of Marx as the broad highway towards a better and more equitable future for all. They grow fewer every year, tottering old figures from the revolutionary past. They are like dinosaurs, relics of a bygone era. Their day is done.

## THE GREAT TEACHER

It is impossible to overemphasise the importance of Confucius to Chinese civilisation. The imprint of the sage has been stamped firmly on the way of life of the nation for 24 centuries. The habits and customs of Chinese daily life today still sway to the teachings of the philosopher who laid down the precepts of filial piety, obedience and duty.

Kung Fuzi was born in Qufu in Shandong province in 551 B.C. His father died when he was young, his mother when the boy was a teenager and he grew up working 'at many despised callings'. As a teacher and a bureaucrat in local dukedoms, Master Kung developed an outlook on life which he taught to a number of disciples. He tossed out old ideas on the supernatural, so popular in peasant worship at the time, and introduced precepts of ethics and man's role in society. The stratified kinship relations and loyalties he outlined were adopted by government and scholars who, even if they did not follow his teachings, largely paid public lip service to them.

Master Kung's code forms the basis of modern Chinese moral outlook and in particular underlies that strong foundation of Chinese society through the ages, the extended family.

## THE WAY

Just as 'Chinese' a faith as the philosophy of Confucius is the great body of ethical belief known as Taoism or The Way. Taoism is based largely on the teachings of the sage Lao Tzu who was born about six centuries before the Christian era. The Way stresses the mystical side of humanity. In return for faith in its precepts, it promises followers immortality. 'Believe, therefore you are.' is the message.

With adherents in Overseas Chinese communities and in the United States and Australia led by the Reverend Timothy Yau of the Ching Chung Temple in Hongkong, it is possible there are now more active followers of the body of beliefs that make up Taoism abroad than there are in China. One reason for this is that Taoist priests were subject to special brutality by the rampaging Guards.

Taoism is built on a practical application of alchemy and medical science and an insistence on vegetarian food, a healthy lifestyle and a general code of conduct that stresses generosity of spirit and comradeship, which has helped promote modern interest in the faith.

## BUDDHISM

The Gautama Buddha lived in Northern India about the same time Confucius taught in Shandong. It took five centuries, however, for the Mahayana sect of Buddhism to transverse the Roof of the World and to be widely accepted in China. Over the centuries, the religion had undergone substantial changes and to all intents was a 'new' religion in China, distinct from the version of Buddhism practised in India. The image of the Buddha is enthroned in giant cliff paintings in many parts of the nation. He stares down with benign faith over the headwaters of the Yangtze, the Yellow River and the Pearl. His golden image can be found in temples in every province and his bland, all-seeing countenance is worshipped by young and old, male and female, Chinese resident and truth-seeker from abroad. Clouds of incense rise in shrines rebuilt in every corner of the country.

The contemplative 'Chan' form of Buddhism stressed meditation and withdrawal from the earthly life. From China, it passed over the Eastern Seas to barbarous Japan where it civilised the unruly islanders and became known as Zen. Split into myriad sects, following an array of local abbots and teachers, the religion took numerous forms. One that developed in the Shaolin monastery on a mountain in Shanxi saw those quiet monks developing a form of self-defence aimed at protecting the unarmed wandering holy men from bandits. Thus was born kung fu fighting. Another form of the faith is still practised in religious fervour by Tibetans who hold that their self-exiled ruler, the Dalai Lama, is a living god and a reincarnation of Buddha.

## *CHRISTIANITY*

Marco Polo never tried to convert his Mongol hosts to his Catholic faith. Other Europeans were not so retiring. In the Ming Dynasty, Portuguese priests, many of them fanatical Jesuits, made enormous efforts to convert the Son of Heaven and senior officials. They strove largely in vain; the court wanted elegant European timepieces, which were a curiosity of the time, but had little desire for a religion which preached all men were equal.

It wasn't until the 19th century that Christians began to success-fully penetrate China. Just as trade was forced on a reluctant regime and nation by the gunship treaties that ended the Opium War, so did the cross get carried into China by missionaries who swept in on the coat-tails of the merchants.

From America, Britain, Germany, Italy, France and Scandinavia, keen young men and women swarmed into the country. First they set up their churches in the coastal ports, then began to seep ever further inland. There was great competition for souls between dour Scots Calvinists and energetic Boston Baptists. The competing claims for holiness by various Protestant sects and Catholics led to a race for souls that saw confused Chinese converts selling out to the highest bidder. Desperate to get their children educated and to fill their bowls in time of famine, so-called 'Rice Christians' were attracted to the altars more by payments of food and aid in this life than promises of eternity in the hereafter. The missionaries did not only preach; they probably attracted more people to their faiths through the many thousands of schools, hospitals and universities they established and ran in China. All were taken over by the state after 1949 and missionaries were thrown out of the country. A few are now permitted back but by and large the government remains distrustful of them and suspicious of their motives.

Those Chinese who did forsake ancient ways to follow Christianity often paid dearly for it. They were despised targets in the Boxer Uprising when many were slaughtered and were again favoured victims in the Cultural Revolution. Despite cynical Western claims that Christianity never really got anywhere in China, churches across the land are today attracting record numbers of adherents, including a surprising percentage of young people.

## *ISLAM*

Up in the north and, certainly, in Xinjiang, people will proudly assert their belief in the One True Faith. In Ningxia, officially an autonomous region for Muslims, mosques dominate the skyline. The call to prayer echoes loudly in many surrounding provinces. There are Islamic communities in every large city.

Islam came early to China, travelling over the Silk Road routes from its birthplace in Arabia. In addition to the many millions of northern minorities who profess the faith, there are an estimated eight million Han Chinese converts. Known as Hui, they are now themselves classified as a national minority and given the right to govern themselves in Ningxia according to the laws of Islam.

## *DEITIES*

The Chinese heavens must be bursting at the seams with assorted gods, deities, mystical figures, demons, Venerable Celestial Beings, saintly apostles and legendary folk heroes. Scholars contend that there has never been a complete count of this multitude of holy figures. If there was, it could well compete in sheer numbers with the massive 1982 census of China itself which toted up the billion people of the nation.

Figures of worship abound in China. Traditionally, visitors would

*Putting new faces on ancient gods, these designers at the famed Shiwan pottery kiln at Foshan in Guangdong have brought artistic flair to ancient disciplines. The Old Dragon kiln has been lit for nine centuries and still specialises in making images of the senior 18 deities who followed Buddha.*

see them when they first approached a home. Ferocious scowling door gods stand in proud menace on either side of the entrance to guard those within. Inside, there would be a shrine where ancestors (themselves nearing the stature of respected saintliness) share honours in front of the smouldering incense sticks with local deities and such all-powerful figures as Guan Di, the God of War.

It was the ancestors, in the traditional belief in which Taoism merged with Buddhism, through which the common folk approached the more senior deities of faith and folklore. The departed male patriarchs occupied the top rung on the hierarchical totem pole (as they had done in life) but women frequently sought the aid of an ancestress, particularly in prayers for a son.

Many scholars have pointed out that the traditional Chinese view of heaven coincided with the earthly empires of the dynasties. When the emperor went to the Temple of Heaven in Beijing twice yearly to pray for crops and tranquillity, his messages were directed to Yudi, the Supreme Being. Yudi dealt only with the earthly emperor. His wife, Xi Wang Mu, the earth mother of antiquity, dealt with women's affairs and there was an entire celestial cabinet and bureaucracy staffed by multitudes of lesser gods, deputy deities, assistant August Personages and mandarins of heaven to deal with the prayers of other mortals and their affairs.

In this sprawling bureaucracy of immortals (which has an uncanny resemblance to the creaky overmanned public service of today) demigods and deities elbowed each other for responsibility. There were divine figures charged with looking after the kitchen, others with responsibility for the bedroom (a Lord and Lady of the Bedchamber, naturally) and the divine of the latrine.

Many of these gods can be traced back to humans whose valour, honesty, courage or feats of incredible strength or cunning made them famous in their lifetime, elevated them to legendary stature after death and then promoted them to the status of god or goddess. Such a one was Zai Chen. He lived around 1100 B.C., a hermit who lived in the mountains, could cast miraculous spells while he rode around on a tiger. He fought for Duke Wu, founder of the Zhou Dynasty, to help overthrow the Shang. After his death (he was supposedly slain by a rival sorcerer) Zai Chen became a god. Today, his gilded figure is a familiar one; as God of Wealth he is one of the most revered and respected of the deities and the object of countless incense sticks and prayers. Likewise venerated are the three Gods of Happiness, jolly old souls who concentrate on spreading satisfaction.

Not surprisingly, the warlike Manchus were extremely partial to Guan Di, God of War. This fearsome, burly and bearded figure must have seemed tailor-made for them. They built more than 1,600 shrines in his honour in every corner of the land and he is today not only still venerated as the deity in charge of war but also bears responsibility for detectives. Thus, even in sophisticated Chinese societies, he is honoured still. In Hongkong, when detectives are faced with a difficult crime poser, they burn offerings to the Guan Di shrine in every station, offer him fat roast pork and sweet wine and kowtow in deep respect. When the crime is solved, as often happens, they return to give thanks.

## MISSIONARIES

The Western idea of missionaries in China, largely sponsored by media-created romances, is of a brave white man or woman penetrating into an ignorant, disease-ridden and dangerous environment to spread one or another of the branches of the Christian faith and to bring sweetness, justice and light to uncouth and ill-educated savages. Needless to say, this notion is not one commonly shared by the Chinese.

The communist view of missionaries is a perception of unwanted crafty, snide foreign intruders who forced their way into the country under the unwelcome protection of gunboats to subvert traditional Chinese values, to undermine the way of life and to slyly implant perverted alien ideas. There is some truth on both sides.

Although a few exceptions have been made and an increasing number of religious figures have been permitted to enter and work in China in recent years, there are still deep suspicions harboured about missionaries. The great bulk of them were hounded out of their parishes and forced out of China in 1950 and there is no way a new generation is going to be allowed back.

The rulers in Beijing have grave – and largely justified – suspicions about foreign missionaries. They cannot control them, therefore mistrust them. The wildly irresponsible, downright stupid, attitude of some self-serving Western dogma-fuelled maniacs makes those who know the realities of modern China flinch with horror. They go into the country, where they may have been financially supporting a church group, and urge their foolish followers to break Chinese laws. The results are predictable; authorities clamp down on what are illegal organisations, peasants are punished and the shrill protests of the self-satisfied sect leaders lambast Beijing for a lack of religious freedom. The fact is, if people of any religion in China obey the laws and do not confront the authorities, they are usually able to pray and gather as they want without trouble.

The fact that leading converts (to Methodism) included Generalissimo Chiang Kai-shek, his widely detested wife and many other strident anti-communists who fled to Taiwan in 1949 merely reinforces Communist suspicions.

Many Westerners, notably Americans, seem to cling to the idea that they have a God-given, inalienable right to enter China and go where they wish preaching their religion and seeking converts. The fact that they are not allowed to freely do so angers them intensely. They consider it monstrous that the atheistic communist state should be permitted to restrain them.

But have a look at the other side of the coin. What would be the reaction of good Southern Baptists in Alabama or Arkansas if cadres of the Chinese Communist Party were to go traipsing through the Bible Belt distributing copies of Thoughts of Chairman Mao and urging the rural populace to rise in revolution? Can one imagine the screams of outrage if True Believers of the Party demanded the freedom to spread their doctrine in America with the same insistence that Christian missionaries press for the 'right' to proselytise in China? Just as the American Congress and people would resist the presence of Chinese communists spreading foreign political theories in their nation, so the Chinese leadership thinks it repugnant for aliens to demand to preach foreign ideas in China.

No way, padre.

## *PERSECUTION*

As China heads towards the 21st century, ancient traditional buildings arise from the rubble of the recent past. The temples are being rebuilt, often financed by money from Chinese communities abroad. Religion was one of the prime targets of the Cultural Revolution. Foreign beliefs, Christianity in particular, were seen to be alien, hostile to communism and evil forces to be rooted out.

There was dreadful persecution of all religions and any expression of belief was likely to provoke attack by fanatical Red Guards to whom Mao was akin to a god. Tens of thousands of people were slain because of their religious affiliations. Catholic priests accused of espionage were held in jails in solitary confinement for more than a decade.

In these more relaxed times, people are more likely to confess to being Christians, Muslims or Buddhists. Major Christian churches are now open in most large cities and masses in newly-reopened cathedrals as far distant as Guangzhou and Taiyuan draw big followings.

The Red Guards' frenzy saw hordes of screaming young vandals burn and smash countless temples, churches, mosques and religious shrines. The cultural destruction was enormous. The revival is equally impressive. With the swing of the political pendulum back towards sanity, the sacred places are being rebuilt, often with funds donated by generous Overseas Chinese who were appalled by the horrific toll taken of the national heritage.

At sacred Putao Shan, one of the four most revered religious mountains in China, huge amounts of money from Singapore has been funnelled into reconstructing the vast temple. The abbot, who survived vigorous prosecution, told me how boatloads of Red Guards would descend on the island during the Ten Black Years. They went to the peaceful Zhou Shan archipelago on ferries commandeered in Ningbo, Shanghai and other ports, swarmed over the island in joyful chaos, singing Maoist anthems as they ripped down the carved temple doors, smashed ancient stone pillars and crashed the mighty bronze temple bells to the flagstones that had for centuries marked the spots where Buddhists bent in prayer. Many of the monks dragged off for punishment were never seen again. By the mid-1980s, a few survivors had drifted back to Putao Shan and, amazingly, another generation of young men and women had shaved their heads and entered into the devotions of a life of contemplation.

*A young novice monk at the temple on sacred Putao Shan contemplates a life of meditation. Young people are heading back to the ancient faiths despite official disapproval. The abbot and monks here suffered dreadfully at the hands of the Red Guards.*

81

## TEMPLES

Feel free to take photographs in temples. There are no restrictions. People do not usually mind you snapping them when they are lighting joss sticks or praying. I usually smile, lift my camera and look at them enquiringly. Almost always, they smile back and nod. It's safe to work on the assumption that you can take pictures in any religious setting. Go ahead and click away. If for some reason there is a ban, some busybody bureaucrat will soon bustle up and stop you. When in doubt, shoot. Many big temples have souvenir shops attached where you can buy statues or prints of local gods. Prices are often sufficiently outrageous for the purchasers to protest to the gods.

In mosques, take off your shoes before entering. In other temples, which are common meeting places for a chat and a part of village life, don't bother. But remember, everywhere, that no matter how casual may be the general approach to temples, you are in a place of worship and should show respect and restraint.

## FENG SHUI

Central to many Chinese religious beliefs is a strong faith in *feng shui*. The words mean, simply, wind and water, and they tie together a package of folklore that can be traced back to before the birth of Chinese civilisation. Even among modern sophisticates, faith in geomancy is total. No Chinese would dream of building a house on the 'eye of a dragon' and almost all good fortune and bad luck can be traced back to benign or baleful effects of *feng shui*.

What does it mean? If you've got one or two years to sit and listen patiently, some aged sage can explain the intricacies of *feng shui* and how it influences your daily life, your bodily functions, your health, marriage, career and business. It rules your existence, dominates your life, guides your destiny. No Chinese would dream of changing the furniture in his office, no land developer would contemplate siting a building, without consulting the *feng shui* man to seek his guidance.

Based on the notion that man and nature have to exist in harmony, closely related to the concept of the yin and yang of balanced forces of every aspect of existence, *feng shui* is an entire school of environmental and cultural doctrines. Adherents firmly believe spiritual forces inhabit every spot on earth. They influence, for better or worse and for eternity, the fate of people who live there or pass by.

Hills represent dragons. To build a house on the eye of the dragon, thereby irritating the mythical beast, would obviously be hazardous. Therefore, before a new structure goes up, the *feng shui* man must be consulted to ensure it is sited in the most beneficial spot, facing the direction which reaps the most ample harvest in tranquillity and harmony with the elements. *Feng shui* men (and, rarely, women) are figures held in considerable respect in the business community and in awe by villagers.

The effect of wind and water on a building and its inhabitants can be harmful or beneficial, depending on how these influences are channelled. Hence the strategic placement of a mirror on the eave of a house can divert or reflect bad spirits. Doors in a house should never be in a straight line; that would allow evil influences to flow straight into the heart of a mansion. No, sturdy obstacles must be placed in their paths.

The laws of *feng shui* are myriad. How should your desk be placed in the office? Should it be situated so your back is to the window? The *feng shui* man will come, contemplate, study the way in which the fortunes, potentially good, perhaps threatening, look into the room. Then he will make a considered judgement. He will collect a not insignificant fee.

The forces of nature can be greatly beneficial or grossly dangerous. It all depends on how you harness the *feng shui* and channel it to your advantage. Good spirits must be encouraged. Bad demons must be placated. The elements can be encouraged to do both. Indeed, evil geomancers can be hired to plot to harm people blessed with a good *feng shui*.

During the Ming Dynasty, for instance, the city of Chaozhou in Guangdong reached peaks of spectacular prosperity. Its sons became wealthy in business and bright young men succeeded in the imperial civil service examinations for selection as mandarins. Jealous rival towns suspected Chaozhou's good fortune was caused by the marvellous *feng shui*. So they hired an unscrupulous *feng shui* expert to sabotage the wind and water which flowed so advantageously. The geomancer spied out the land. There was one significant hill in the area that he pronounced as holding a candle spirit. To put out the candle, he advised the enemies of Chaozhou to dig a well on the crest of the hill. They did so and sat back eagerly to await the decline and fall of Chaozhou. To their baffled rage, the city soared to even greater heights of power and riches. The *feng shui* man had made a mistake; the hill held not a candle spirit but the essence of a lotus. Instead of quenching a candle, the well merely irrigated the water-hungry lotus spirit, bringing even better good fortune to the town.

## *HERBAL MEDICINE*

Closely associated with the notion of *feng shui* is Chinese herbal medicine and implicit belief in its efficacy. Modern scientific research at medical institutes throughout the world show many of the old herbal potions have a strong chemical base that is replicated in Western drugs. For instance, out in the jungles of Guangxi, tribal folk still roam the mountains to collect wild nuts off vines high in the ceiling of the rainforest. These nuts are dried, then ground into powder which is said to aid rheumatism. Current research at the Chinese University of Hongkong's medical school shows the nuts have a strong concentration of the same compound which Western scientists prescribe for rheumatic treatment. Chinese herbal doctors have been administering it for well over 1,000 years.

There are many similar examples where herbal remedies contain chemicals known to modern science. Such cures were devised in rural China by trial and error over many centuries. During that time, millions of peasants must have been used as guinea pigs by untrained herbalists who administered home-made potions and hoped for the best. If the patients survived, the cure was judged a success. By such means, a vast body of knowledge has been built up and today, in many parts of China, herbal homeopathic cures are frequently used alongside Western-style medicine.

## ACUPUNCTURE

The idea that ills could be cured by sticking pins into people was at first regarded as outrageously bizarre by sceptical Westerners. Today, acupuncture clinics can be found throughout the world. This ancient discipline holds that the careful placement of small pins in strategic locations of the human geography influences how the body reacts to stress and internal forces. It has been likened to a form of *feng shui* of the human body. There can be no doubt that it works. In many Chinese hospitals, major surgery is conducted with only a couple of acupuncture injections to cut off feeling to the part of the body that is going under the knife. Worry not; any foreigner undergoing an operation will receive Western anaesthetic.

## CUTTING THE DEMONS' TAIL

If you should be driving in China, be eternally on the alert for pedestrians, particularly old folk, who suddenly leap in front of your car. If you miss them by six inches or so as they hurl themselves across your path, this will be great good fortune. You will have cut off the string of demons which follow folk about and the lost band of bad spirits, having been cut off from the nimble pedestrian, are now firmly stuck on your tail. Tough luck. Bad joss.

## FESTIVALS

Visitors will find it difficult to discover in advance when religious festivals are being held. Ask friends or hotel staff if any special event is happening in the next few days. They'll probably know but haven't bothered to tell you because it would never occur to them that you could possibly be interested.

If you should be in some suburb or town and see a crowd of people in festive mood, follow them and join in. They'll make you welcome and there's sure to be someone who can tell you in broken English what's going on.

## *Animal Years*

Based on beliefs linked closely with the body of common religion and philosophy, this endless pattern of the years flows smoothly on. Just as some Westerners believe in astrological signs, so do many Chinese pay at least lip service to the idea that they are born with qualities belonging to the animal year into which they were born.

Most Americans would not like to be a rat. Chinese born in that year, however, are held to be smart, cunning, brave and clever. The horse year child is expected to have stamina, the snake to exhibit sagacity, the ram to show good business judgement. Just as rival Western palm readers may have different opinions about one person, so Chinese soothsayers can attribute various qualities to those born in the same year. You pays your money, you takes your choice.

## *For the Ancestors*

Most major religious festivals in China are officially ignored, based as they are on old religious or philosophical beliefs. They are widely practised by the people, especially in the countryside.

If you should be in a rural area in spring and see hordes of people heading for grave-speckled hillsides, they are carrying oranges and other offerings to their ancestors. The living will sweep the graves of the dead, tidy up the tombs and pay their respects. There is a similar rite in autumn. As winter nears, you may see old ladies lighting bonfires in the streets.

This is the festival of the hungry ghosts and they are burning paper gifts to appease the uneasy spirits who may otherwise return to make trouble.

## *Feast Days*

Just as ardent Catholics find a saint to pray to every day, so can Chinese always clutch an excuse for a festival from among their wide collection of deities. Similarly, devotees normally pay homage to their special deities on their feast days, anniversary of their birth or death. (They also tend to go to temples on the first and fifteenth days of the lunar month, so these are good dates for picture-taking.)

## *Folk Festivals*

Every village has its own folk festival. These are often wonderful events. All along the southern coast and far up the rivers, the annual dragon boat races draw immense crowds. Once religious rites to offer thanks to a woman elevated to goddess status because of her piety and sacrifice for fisherfolk, these delightful races of long, narrow boats with more than a score of hardy paddlers are exciting, shouting gatherings.

Visitors are always welcome; join the mobs and scream and clap for whatever team you fancy. It's like Superbowl in every village.

One of the most fun-filled days I ever had in China was in a nameless Guizhou valley where I saw thousands of Dong tribesmen gathered in a big circle. Wandering down to find what was happening, I discovered I had stumbled across a buffalo fight.

This is a gentle procedure. One village brings its bravest and biggest buffalo to face its rival from another hamlet. Much screaming of encouragement and urging of the beasts to battle goes on. Much beer is drunk. Many backs are slapped. Everyone is vastly excited. Even the buffaloes enter into the spirit of things and clash horns, pushing against each other to show which is the stronger beast. Everyone has a great time. The fact that some weird foreign devil has joined the party only makes proceedings that much more lively.

# Chapter Five

# HISTORY

*He who reads history*
*Knows the affairs of the ancients*

*As one sees a reflection in a polished mirror*
*So can one know the present by studying ancient times*

Modern China is, very literally, built on its past. Cities like Xian and
Kaifeng stand on the same sites as grand and noble former capitals.
Throughout the Yellow River heartland where the Chinese race was
spawned, the mud of floods and the endless deposits of wind-borne

loess dust cover the ruins of cities that stood 5,000 years ago. The world knows the terracotta warriors of Xian and the impressive underground chambers of the Ming Tombs outside Beijing. These are just two of China's treasure-house of buried priceless relics of former dynasties.

Around Xian, there are scores, maybe hundreds, of mounds similar to the one which contained the kiln-fired troopers and courtiers who guarded the imperial tomb. Archeologists have identified and numbered these sites; even if limitless funds were available and armies of archeological diggers were employed, it would take decades to unearth and catalogue whatever historical riches are clutched in the deep, good earth.

The soil frequently gives up its priceless hoard. Down the River Yong from the old river port of Ningbo in Zhejiang, local peasants were digging a pit a few years ago when they came across some old charred logs and broken pieces of porcelain.

Constant newspaper and radio publicity had made farmers aware of the potential historical value of such finds. Farmers told local officials who notified provincial authorities. Academics arrived from the provincial capital in Hangzhou to take samples from the ruins near the village of Hemudu. As archaeologists dug, they found not one village but three of them, each built atop an earlier occupied site.

Deep beneath protective layers of silt laid down by prehistoric floods, they finally unearthed a sophisticated log cabin village. Amid the ruins were grains of rice. The significance of their find did not become apparent until the discoveries were carbon-dated in Beijing. The rice cultivators of Hemudu had planted their fields more than 7,000 years ago, dating those ancient farmers as the earliest known growers of grain in the world.

Today, those blackened specks of rice grains can be seen in a special museum on the banks of the renowned West Lake in Hangzhou, along with reconstructions of the village of the prehistoric farmers of the Yong River. The cultural importance of the find was immense; much of China's lifestyle is based on rice cultivation. The find was hailed as a major discovery of ethnic origin.

Much of China, especially in the north, is sitting atop rich layers of history. Dig down, and you literally are going through the dynasties, as though you are turning a massive book whose pages are metre-thick layers of earth packed with relics of past dynasties.

One splendid example of this treasury packed in the soil is in Kaifeng in Henan, capital of a dozen emperors. The overflowing Yellow River has over the ages buried this woefully-sited city time and again. The bed of the Huang He is now elevated six metres above the streets of the town. Every time the river burst its banks in the past, the thick silt settled down over the town. Sometimes, survivors dug out their homes. At others, they simply built a new town on top.

Archaeologists examining the foundations of modern Kaifeng can dig through metres of closely-packed loess earth, finding a new civilisation every few metres. In 1985, workmen laying a new duct for electricity cables and water pipes came across a marble carving. Careful excavation revealed this was part of the magnificent Bridge of Zhou, a famous piece of Song Dynasty architecture that had been lost for 1,000 years. Now restored, the carved marble bridge that has featured in many paintings and poems, is a proud historic sight of Kaifeng.

The warrior guards of Xian which have over the past decades attracted hundreds of thousands of foreign tourists were also discovered by accident. Throughout China, mysterious mounds that hide the graves of emperors and the tombs of forgotten kings stand enigmatically amid rice paddies and in northern deserts.

## THE DYNASTIES

The earliest rulers of China were men whose lives are legend. Semi-deities, they are gigantic figures who stride across an enormous historic stage. Like Solomon or Moses in the Judeo-Christian tradition, they are impossibly larger than life, personalities who merge tribal folklore with the actions of individual rulers of early flourishing county-states along the fertile banks of the Yellow River. Nevertheless, there remains a constant but tenuous strand linking the earliest rulers of China with those who followed them onto the Dragon Throne.

The earliest era can be pinpointed to roughly between 2852 B.C. and 2205 B.C. It is known as the Age of the Five Rulers (Fu Hsi, Shen Nung, Huang Ti, Yao, and Shun). As with Old Testament rulers, it seems historians of ancient times run the lives of a number of rulers into one reign. The first legendary ruler, Fu Hsi, is said to have reigned for 115 years, during which he invented writing and stringed musical instruments, organised the clan and family name system and introduced animal husbandry.

The third mythical ruler was the Yellow Emperor and patron saint of Taoism, Huang Ti, who came to the throne in 2697 B.C. Massing infantry with stabbing swords behind stout shields (like the Roman Legions 26 centuries later), he won the leadership of tribes throughout the Huang He plain. He has been credited with the invention of the bow and arrow, wooden houses and boats, and governmental institutions. His wife was reputed to have discovered silk production and taught women how to breed silkworms and weave silk fabric.

His successor, Yao, who ruled around the 24th B.C., was exalted by Confucius as a perennial model of virtue, righteousness, and unselfish devotion. He was said to have offered sacrifices and practiced divination. However, according to some old annals, he did nothing more notable than enjoy his reign playing music.

Yao bypassed his own son to bestow the kingdom on Shun. Shun is credited with the standardisation of weights and measures, the regulation of waterways. Miraculous phenomena were reported in the heavens and on earth during Yao and Shun's reigns.

By the time of the first recorded dynasty, China had reached a level of considerable sophistication that was not to be matched in the Western world for another 16 centuries.

## *Dynastic Eras*

| | |
|---|---|
| Xia | – 21st to 16th century B.C. |
| Shang | – 16th to 11th century B.C. |

| Zhou | – 1027 B.C. to 221 B.C. |
| Western Zhou | – 1027 B.C. to 771 B.C. |
| Eastern Zhou | – 770 B.C. to 221 B.C. |
|     Spring and Autumn | – 770 B.C. to 476 B.C. |
|     Warring States | – 475 B.C. to 221 B.C. |
| Qin | – 221 B.C. to 206 B.C. |
| Han | – 206 B.C. to A.D. 220 |
| The Three Kingdoms | – A.D. 220 to A.D. 280 |
| Jin | – 265 to 420 |
| Fragmentation into succession of dynasties | – 304 to 589 |
| Sui | – 581 to 617 |
| Tang | – 618 to 907 |
| Fragmentation into 10 southern kingdoms and 5 northern dynasties | – 907 to 960 |
| Song | – 960 to 1279 |
| Yüan | – 1206 to 1368 |
| Ming | – 1368 to 1644 |
| Qing | – 1644 to 1911 |

## Xia: 21st to 16th century B.C.

The first cohesive state that rose along the banks of the Huang He was the Xia. The founder of the dynasty was Ta Yü or Yü the Great, remembered and respected still as the ruler who vowed to tame the Huang He. After years of strenuous labour, he was believed to have provided outlets to the sea through dredging with the aid of dragons, thus making the world suitable for human habitation. Four thousand years later, engineers of the Yellow River Conservation Commission raised his statue atop a hill in Henan province in tribute to him. Today, the imposing likeness of Yü the Great stares purposefully across the 16-kilometre wide floodplain confined within massive dikes not far from the provincial capital of Zhengzhou, where he once ruled.

Ta Yü allegedly made the rulership hereditary in his family, founding the first legendary imperial dynasty in China. The Xia Dynasty held sway over an increasing area of the rich central length of the river for four centuries, a time when the Chinese race consolidated and combined with other early tribal groups. It was a prosperous agricultural community whose wealth was already based on grain.

### Shang: 16th to 11th century B.C.

Written records of the Shang have been uncovered in surprising quantity. This treasury of ancient literature survived because of the sturdy writing materials used in the era before paper was invented. Some records of the 30 kings of Shang were cast in bronze and describe in considerable detail the daily life and economic structure of the state. Other written remains are inscribed in ideographs on tortoise shells and flat cattle bones (commonly called oracle bones). Shamans would deeply carve their predictions on tortoise shells, then put them on hot coals. They would eventually split in the heat and from the shards of the shattered written message, the priests would make predictions. Large numbers of these oracle bones have been unearthed. They tell of millet and wheat cultivation, animal husbandry of cattle, pigs, horses, sheep and dogs, of a sophisticated manufacture of silk. Shang bronzes show the artisans of the era were both highly skilled technicians and imaginative artists.

It was during this period that a writing system developed, found as archaic Chinese inscriptions on these oracle bones. This writing was pictographic, that is, words were represented by pictures that fairly closely resembled the meaning of the word.

Alas, the era was marred by slavery and superstition. Human sacrifice to the gods was common; some graves of Shang nobles have been uncovered and found packed with up to 400 skeletons of subjects killed to accompany rulers to the next world. The Shang domains were extensive, spreading from the Yellow River down to the Yangtze and eastwards to the coast.

### Western Zhou: 1027 B.C. to 771 B.C.
### Eastern Zhou: 770 B.C. to 221 B.C.

In the first great recorded revolution, the peasants of the Zhou vassal state in the Wei River valley rose against the Shang. The legendary ruler who founded the Zhou was Qi. His great claim to lasting fame was the introduction of a new type of millet, easier to cultivate and a guarantee of survival for a growing population. He is enshrined as the Lord Cultivator (Hou Ji), the god of agriculture.

Under Zhou's rule, China emerged from the shadowy era of myth and legend to accurately dated history. This dates from 841 B.C. with the publication of the *Table of Twelve Princes*. The Duke of Zhou created scores of principalities under his realm and installed his relatives as local rulers. Constant invasion and incorporation of neighbouring primitive states enlarged the realm. Following in the tradition of their founder, the Zhou rulers improved agricultural techniques over the centuries. In 770 B.C., one of the many tribal leaders, Quan Rong, killed the King of Zhou and established a new Zhou Dynasty.

Sharing the language and culture of the Shang, the early Zhou rulers, through conquest and colonization, gradually extended Shang culture through much of China Proper north of the Yangtze River. The Zhou dynasty lasted longer than any other and it was the philosophers of this period who first enunciated the doctrine of the "mandate of heaven" and the notion that the ruler was the "son of heaven" who governed by divine right.

## Spring and Autumn Period: 770 B.C. to 476 B.C.

This period was when many vassal states fought and competed for supremacy. It was named after the title of a Confucian book of chronicles: *Ch'un Ch'iu* (which translates as "Spring Autumn"). During this period, an explosion in technology leapfrogged China out of the bronze age and into the era of iron. Better agricultural equipment could be made with the new material, which was quickly in widespread use. This led to larger crops and a booming economy which in turn encouraged the growth of cities.

During the Spring and Autumn Period, the imperial house's powers diminished as the local nobles struggled amongst themselves for power. Survival required coalitions, both political and economic, as well as the accumulation of productive wealth. To this end, many drainage operations, canals, dikes, reservoirs, roads, and the like were undertaken, often on an interstate or multistate basis. Merchants and artisans began to rise in significance. Education and intellectual life advanced with Confucius and other famous thinkers.

## Warring States Period: 475 B.C. to 221 B.C.

This period was one of the most fertile and influential in Chinese history. It not only saw the rise of many of the great philosophers of Chinese civilization, including the Confucian thinkers Mencius and Hsün-tzu, but also witnessed the establishment of many of the governmental structures and cultural patterns that were to character-ize China for the next 2,000 years.

Money was also invented when increasing trade could no longer be handled by barter. More than 200 mints have been identified from this age.

## Qin: 221 B.C. to 206 B.C.

This dynasty was originated by the martial state of Qin, one of the many small feudal states into which China was divided between 771 and 221 B.C.. Its rulers began to centralize state power, creating a rigid system of laws that were applicable throughout the country and dividing the state into a series of commanderies and prefectures ruled by officials appointed by the central government. Under these changes, the Qin slowly began to conquer its surrounding states.

In 247 B.C., the boy king Chao Cheng came to the throne. He, together with his minister Li Ssu, completed the Qin conquests and in 221 created the Qin empire. Chao Cheng proclaimed himself Qin Shi Huang-di ("First Sovereign Emperor of Qin").

Under his rule, a rigid, authoritarian government was formed which standardized the writing system and the measurements of length and weight and the width of highways; abolished all feudal privileges, built the Great Wall, and in 213 B.C., halted subversive thought by ordering all books to be burned, except those on utilitarian topics such as medicine. The emperor was also not one to take criticism lightly. If scholars displeased him, he buried them alive. By the hundreds.

These harsh methods, combined with the huge tax levies needed to pay for their construction projects and wars, took their toll, and rebellion erupted after Qin Shi Huang-di's death in 210. The Qin Dynasty did not sit long on the Dragon Throne. But it was under the brutal, intemperate, suspicious and brilliant rule of Qin Shi Huang-di – Great Unifier – that dukedoms, kingdoms, far-flung states and vassal thrones were bonded together in blood and fire into the first truly united China.

## Han: 206 B.C. to A.D. 220

Such was the glory of this era that even today the Chinese refer to themselves as Men of Han. The new rulers took the wide boundaries of the Qin and within that vast sweep of territory built an administrative system whose outline can still be seen today. The Emperor Wu, widely known as 'The State', created a vigorous bureaucracy. He was sole authority in legislative, executive and judicial branches with the nation split into small kingdoms and prefectures administered by court favourites and officials appointed by the Dragon Throne. The Han battled wild Huns across the northern borders while at the same time welcoming Buddhist teachings that seeped in from India.

The dynasty was founded by Liu Pang who adopted a Confucian ideology that emphasized moderation and virtue which masked the authoritarian policies of the regime.

Intellectual, literary and artistic endeavours flourished. This period produced China's most famous historian, Sima Qian, whose *Shiji* (Historical Records) provides a detailed chronicle from the time of a legendary Xia emperor to that of the Han emperor Wu Di. The first major stone tomb sculpture in China was created in the Han period, and the weaving of silk in rich colours and patterns of geometric designs or cloud and mountain themes became a major industry and source of export trade. The Shang dynasty discovered lacquer, but it was the Hans that brought its lacquerwork to perfection. Poetry was nurtured by the Han dynasty, and a new genre, *fu*, a combination of rhyme and prose, began to flourish.

Technological advances also marked this period. Two of the great Chinese inventions, paper and porcelain, date from Han times. After 200 years, Han rule was interrupted briefly (in A.D. 9–24 by Wang Mang, a reformer), and then restored for another 200 years. The Han rulers, however, were unable to adjust to what centralization had wrought: a growing population and wealth resulted in financial difficulties and rivalries, and increasingly complex political institutions. Hollowed out by corruption, the Han empire collapsed in 220.

### The Three Kingdoms: 220 to 280

Overlapping the end of the Han was a period of chaos during which the northern regions were largely ruled by three competing realms, the Wei, Shu and Wu. A short and bloody time of warfare and political intrigue, this was one of the favoured periods for historical novelists and other art forms. One of the most celebrated examples is the novel *San Kuo Chih Yen-i* ("Romance of the Three Kingdoms").

### Sui: 581 to 617

China was reunified by the short-lived Sui dynasty. This dynasty's early demise was attributed to the government's tyrannical demands on the people, who bore the crushing burden of taxes and compulsory labour on the Grand Canal – a monumental engineering feat – and other construction projects, including the reconstruction of the Great Wall. Weakened by costly and disastrous military campaigns against Korea in the early 7th century, the dynasty broke apart through a combination of popular revolts, disloyalty, and assassination.

### Tang: 618 to 907

What the Renaissance was to Europe, the Tang was to China. Stimulated by contact with India and the Middle East, the empire saw a flowering of creativity in many fields, it was a golden age in which art, painting, sculpture, poetry and other cultural pursuits flowered richly. Poetry was the greatest glory of the period. All the verse forms of the past were used and refined, and new ones developed. Nearly 50,000 works by some 2,000 Tang poets have been preserved.

Buddhism, originating in India around the time of Confucius, flourished during the Tang period. A government system supported by a large class of Confucian literati, selected through civil service examinations, was perfected under Tang rule. Wealthy and peaceful at home, powerful and respected abroad, the Tang forged solid links with surrounding lands and protected the borders by a series of pacts with friendly states.

The era ended in a welter of uprisings and rebellions that resulted in short-lived dynasties. In one of these rebellions, there occurred a harbinger to future anti-foreigner outbreaks; one rebel force sacked Canton and butchered 100,000 Arab traders who had settled there under the benign reign of Tang.

## Song: 960 to 1279

Huge areas of China were occupied by northern barbarians when the Song era began. The Tanguts ruled the dusty northwest while in Manchuria and on the steppes the Khitans held stubborn control. Eventually, a far more formidable enemy was to gallop down and seize the entire northern half of the nation and for most of the dynasty, the Song abandoned the old homelands on the Yellow River and retreated south to establish their capital at Hangzhou. They built it into a city of splendour.

Merchants rose in esteem in this period, sponsoring arts and supporting writers, and widespread appreciation grew of the man-made garden. The world's first paper money has been traced to this period, appearing because of shortage of copper for coinage. Song intellectuals sought answers to all philosophical and political problems in the Confucian Classics. Neo-Confucianism also emerged later in this period, combining ideas from Buddhism and Taoism. Notable inventions were movable-type printing, gunpowder and the compass.

The enemies established in the north were in turn themselves conquered by a new wave of even harsher barbarians, the Jin, who established a dynasty in the north. Soon they were to be swept roughly aside by the most horrific invaders China was ever to suffer.

## Yüan: 1206 to 1368

Led by Genghis Khan, the Mongols came into China with the fury of a fire-belching dragon. Historians estimate they killed 35 million Chinese. They swiftly despatched other barbarian kingdoms, slaughtering everything in their path as they galloped into China, laying to waste huge areas, putting cities to the torch, destroying for the sheer joy of conquest. The Song held on for decades in the south. But their time was limited and eventually the entire realm came under Mongol rule.

Kublai Khan, grandson of Genghis Khan, was regarded as comparatively mild and benevolent, efficient and incorruptible. He expanded the boundaries significantly, winning back all the territory lost by previous dynasties. The Yüan put down rebellions with utmost ferocity and when they shuffled off the centre stage of history, their rule left Chinese territory intact, although the Chinese humiliated: they were forbidden to bear arms, forced to learn the Mongolian language, and required to scrape and bow to Mongols and all other non-Chinese. The Mongols were never totally Sinicised and continued to maintain their separateness from the native poulation and utilized foreigners, such as the European traveller Marco Polo, to staff the government bureaucracy. Revolts in the mid-14th century overthrew the Yüan, making it the shortest lived major dynasty of China.

The Mongols, whilst encouraging commerce and trade, overprinted the currency, which led to runaway inflation. Their effort to stimulate agriculture was also unsuccessful, leading to widespread starvation by the early 1300s. However, two important crops introduced into China: sorghum in the north and cotton in the south.

## Ming: 1368 to 1644

Rivalry among the Mongol imperial heirs, natural disasters, and numerous peasant uprisings led to the collapse of the Yüan dynasty. The Ming dynasty was founded by a Han Chinese peasant and former Buddhist monk turned rebel army leader. The nation largely rejoiced when a Chinese emperor returned to the Dragon Throne. Nationalism had been making impressive strides during the last years of the Yüan and there was a feeling that all would be well with the world if Chinese ruled China. For a while, that seemed to be the case.

Following the example of their brutal predecessors, the Ming were ruthless autocrats. Punishment for misdemeanours was impressively savage; in some cases, the bodies of chastised officials were stuffed and left to hang in their offices to remind new occupants of the need for honesty and efficiency in government.

The Ming reached the zenith of power during the first quarter of the 15th century. Chinese armies reconquered Annam, as northern Vietnam was then known, in Southeast Asia and kept out the Mongols, while the Chinese fleet sailed the China Seas and the Indian Ocean, cruising as far as the east coast of Africa. Foreign trade boomed and internally the empire was largely at rest and prospering. Long wars with the Mongols, incursions by the Japanese into Korea, and harassment of Chinese coastal cities by the Japanese in the 16th century, however, weakened Ming rule, and the Manchus invaded China easily.

### Qing: 1644 to 1911

In 1644 the Chinese capital at Peking was captured by the bandit leader Li Tzu-ch'eng, and desperate Ming dynasty officials called on the Manchus for aid. The Manchus took advantage of this opportunity to seize the capital and establish their own dynasty in China. By adopting the Ming form of government and continuing to employ Ming officials, the Manchus pacified the Chinese populace. They adopted Chinese dress, cuisine, language and customs and for more than a century ruled the nation with laudable efficiency. To guarantee Manchu control over the administration, however, the Ch'ing made certain that half the higher level officials were Manchus.

There was always much internal opposition by Chinese to Manchu rule, today the subject of many romantic novels. It was from this resistance to foreign rule that the triad movement sprouted. For centuries it was a patriotic democratic ideal, only to degenerate into an international criminal conspiracy long after the Manchus finally tottered off the throne at the beginning of this century.

## HISTORICAL REMAINS

When it comes to history, China has an awful lot of it. A vast amount has been destroyed. There are two reasons for this. Much of the monumental work – palaces, temples, administrative buildings – were constructed of wood. Over the centuries, it has rotted or burned, leaving little to admire. The tumultuous changes of rule in China saw enormous and widespread destruction. Many emperors, jealous of the glories of their predecessors, deliberately destroyed the physical evidence of earlier grandeur. Then there were the waves of invaders whose troops saw China as a vast treasury which they could plunder at will. Periods of local uprisings were times of anarchy when chaos reigned and cities burned.

Take the last century or so for an example of how the treasures of China have been laid to waste. The Taiping rebellion destroyed a sizeable section of the south. One of the most wonderful architectural legacies of all time, the Summer Palace of the Qing Emperors, was wilfully smashed and pillaged by British and French troops who saw the act as a punishment for the Chinese emperor breaking an agreed peace treaty imposed after the Second Opium War. Local civil wars and uprisings in Guizhou, Gansu and Xinjiang saw much destruction. The Yellow River broke its banks several times (once when retreating nationalist generals deliberately blew up the levees), swamping huge historic areas.

There was the warlord era which saw the nation divided, the Japanese invasion, the civil war; all of these conflicts resulted in much of the past being lost. Above all, there was the organised, state-controlled vandalism of the 1960s when for a decade, gangs of hysterical young fanatics roamed the land, encouraged to smash the Four Olds.

They did so with remarkable efficiency, pounding priceless artifacts into rubble, pulling down temples which had stood for centuries, laughing as they smashed precious relics.

It is a wonder that so much of China's past has survived.

*Unswept eaves of traditional architecture can be seen in every town, but liks one in Guizhou capital, Guiyang, they are likely to be modern structures.*

## *The Museums*

Once grim, grey and attractive only to serious scholars, the museums of China tend now to be modern and interesting. As always, it depends totally on local initiatives. If a city government is inspired by forward-thinking leadership and a positive approach, the museums will tend to be bright with items properly displayed. Without such spurring, idle staff will take little pride in showing the treasures of the past.

As so often happens, Shanghai sets a sparkling example. Its new museum, largely financed by Hong Kong billionaires and shaped like a vast incense burner, is a wonderful example. Its array of paintings, sculptures, maps, banknotes, clothing, stamps and other artifacts are breath-taking. To walk the display floors is to stroll through the nation's history.

Sadly, such imaginative use of space is not universal. There are many museums in China where fascinating legacies are on display but their surroundings are often dim and drab. The lack of any information in any language other than Chinese detracts from the allure; why would a tourist stare with wonder at something which he cannot understand?

On the other hand, "improvements" can be disastrous. In central Shanghai the house was once preserved when a band of young revolutionaries met on 1 July 1921,to found the Chinese Communist Party. This was a humble but honest display. There were snug rooms where the men who would change China spoke of their dreams, with pictures of the idealistic crusaders on the wall. It was intriguing to imagine what would have happened if they had not slipped out the back door and escaped into the canals and backwaters of Shanghai; a traitor had tipped off the French Concession police to their meeting. If they had been captured, they would have been turned over to Chinese authorities which would have meant swift decapitation.

This appealing old house has, to my dismay, been demolished to be replaced by a monstrosity of concrete, marble and carpet. Imposing? Maybe. Impressive? Not to me; the old, cramped house where the underground conspirators met seemed much more genuine.

Having said that, there are magnificent museums in many cities. A visit gives glimpses of the past. Maintenance in many of them is rudimentary and often there is no non-Chinese printed information available.

## *THE CONSTITUTION*

It is important to remember that China is in many ways a schizo-phrenic nation, at once 5,000 years old and 50 years young. The intense national pride in the immense and ancient cultural heritage is balanced by constant declarations that the People's Republic was founded only on 1 October 1949, when Mao Zedong stood at Tiananmen Gate and proclaimed, "The Chinese people have stood up. Now let reactionaries at home and abroad beware."

This pride in the revolutionary tradition can be seen everywhere. Many buildings and organisations are named with the first two characters Xin Hua, meaning New China.

Guidelines for governing this New China are laid down in the constitution of the People's Republic of China. This is possibly the most inspiring charter ever written. It guarantees freedom of speech, religion, assembly and many other rights.

While the document itself is the very model of an advanced, liberal society, things do not work quite as well in practice. People seeking to exercise many of the rights guaranteed in the constitution are likely to find themselves in a thought correction centre for a couple of decades where they can ponder the error of their ways.

Even today, to the astonished horror of the world community, China persists in prosecuting, convicting and jailing mild dissidents. True, they have broken Chinese law. Many Chinese find nothing objectionable at all in the prospect of someone calling for a peaceful change in the system being jailed for 15 years for treason.

When one of these unfortunates was incarcerated for 10 years for mildly criticising the regime, an aged friend of mine, a charming, smiling man who spent 30 years in London, shrugged it off. What did the critic expect, my pal enquired? If you challenge the dragon throne, the serpent will crush you mercilessly. Stupid to protest. About the same time, a minor labour leader that few people in the world had ever heard of was refused permission to go back to China, his homeland, after a trip abroad. The man was stuck in limbo, stateless in Hongkong, where he swiftly reaped vast headlines with attacks on his own nation which would not let him back. Another friend of mine, a civil servant in the Hongkong government, was enraged – at the hapless dissident who had enraged Beijing. "Serves him right," the public servant said. "It's like a child going outside and insulting his parents to other people. Naturally, they will not let him back into the house."

Chinese justice may be harsh. But you find few people who do not support rigorous, strict punishment for comparatively minor crimes. This has got nothing to do with communism. It's part of the wider Chinese heritage. In Hongkong, polls show 95% of people favour capital punishment. In Singapore, the government policy of flogging vandals and violent criminals is widely supported. And, above all, children are expected to dutifully do as they are told.

# Chapter Six

# GETTING ABOUT

*If a man makes himself friendly wherever he travels,*
*Where can he go and not find a friend?*

Old timers (e.g. foreigners who were in China before 1985) love to sit down with a well-chilled Qingdao beer and swap horror stories about travel in China. All these stories are true. The trouble is, nobody who didn't live there before 1990 is ever going to give any credence to such bizarre tales; they sound too incredible. Believe me, most of them are true.

These days, travel in China is – with some notable exceptions – more or less similar to the rest of the world. The appalling, creaky old national airline CAAC (fondly known through its initials as Chinese Airlines Always Crash!) was long ago broken up into smaller regionally based companies. Now China's aviation industry is being restructured into three large modern airlines, providing the nation with a logical aeronautical foundation. They have stocked up on an entire new generation of modern aircraft, for which Boeing shareholders should give thanks, that are well-maintained and flown properly trained pilots. So what, you ask? So you should have been around in the Bad Old Days when you took to the air, if you were lucky, in a rattling Russian-built propeller-driven aircraft that was riveted together when Uncle Joe Stalin and Chairman Mao were the best of buddies. Transport throughout China has been through a revolution as significant as the political changes. Indeed, the unbelievable improvement of infrastructure from bridges to highways to mass transit schemes to new airports is a core part of dramatic overall national development.

There are still hassles, most of them caused by either language problems, over-crowding, unhelpful tourism officials or the sorts of problems that crop up all over the world. Twenty years ago, about the only way to get about in China, unless you were a troublesome type like a Hongkong reporter, was in a group tour. Some of these were most enjoyable, others were dull and boring. It depended largely on luck; if you got a keen, interested and knowledgeable guide, you could have an enjoyable and educational trip. If you were unlucky and drew an irritable and bored guide, the visit was likely to be disastrous. Tour planning and guide training have both improved, so your chances of enjoying a planned trip are now much better.

The best way to go, however, is by yourself. Language problems? Sure, but if you don't speak Chinese there is invariably an English speaker who is only too delighted to leap to your aid. You make some delightful friends in unexpected places; I still write to a waitress named Swallow who as a 15-year-old came to my aid at a small restaurant alongside West Lake in Hangzhou in 1986.

## *PUDONG TAKES OFF*

China tends to carry out projects with little fanfare. While Hong Kong was transfixed for years by the construction of its super-airport at Chek Lap Kok, an equally ambitious aviation hub was being built without headlines on the banks of the Yangtze north of Shanghai. Pudong was to be lynchpin for China's air traffic, but there was comparatively little fanfare until it opened.

Negotiations with German combines over a planned rail link between Shanghai and the airport were discrete. The 450kph trains would be levitated by magnetism and make the trip in six minutes. What's more, this was to be a test for a city-to-city railway which would run from Shanghai to Beijing, making the trip in four hours.

Such huge infrastructural projects that would in the West be debated for years are decided in quiet by senior officials in China, then go ahead. Of course, the public have little if any say in what's going on. That may not be democratic, but it certainly seems effective.

## *DON'T RUSH CHINA*

As with everything else in China, getting about the countryside has undergone vast changes in the past decade, almost all for the better. But travel in China frequently remains hard work. This applies particularly if you don't read or speak Chinese and intend to travel independently and not with an organised tour group.

Be prepared to take time. Be prepared to waste time. And be prepared to give a dazzling smile when confronted with baffling inconsistencies and what seems to any sane person to be ridiculous and wasteful procedures. That's the way we do things, the answer will be. This is China. That explanation covers every situation.

## *GETTING TICKETS*

Standing at the transport desk of the Ritz-Carlton Hotel in Shanghai, one of my favourite hotels in China I watched a common scene. A bustling, brisk young American finance executive was on his first trip to China and had not confirmed his return flight. The smartly-dressed girl at the desk was patiently trying to help him. He demanded to get on the first possible empty seat to Hongkong. He tapped his finger impatiently on the desk as the helpful hotel staffer called all the airlines. The first available empty seat was ... three months in the future. "Three months!" he wailed. "You've got to be joking." She wasn't.

That was a couple of years ago. Today, things are much easier. There are a lot more flights and they are a lot more reliable. The advent of Hongkong-based Dragonair with its flights to a score of cities is welcome; it has helped give Chinese airlines something against which to compare their services.

China is on the move. Everyone wants to travel. Domestic travel inside the country is enormous, with business and leisure travellers cramming every seat on every flight, tram, bus and ferry. It is essential to book, confirm, reconfirm and check again that you are on the passenger list. Then make sure you are early to board your flight or climb the gangplank. Otherwise, the seat will have been reassigned. Don't bother complaining. This is China.

## LITTLE EMPEROR SYNDROME

Despite enormous improvements, transport booking offices sometimes remain chaotic, confusing and inefficient. Tourist industry staff who are supposed to help tourists are often the least helpful people in the land. They often suffer extreme cases of the Little Emperor syndrome; give them the most modest positions of power and authority – even waitresses – and they lord it over other mortals. Put them in charge of a train station booking office and they are as dictatorial, inflexible and authoritarian as the Dowager Empress.

Veteran travellers shake their head; the only people they met in China who are not helpful and friendly are those who are paid to be just that. But to really get around the country, despite the headaches, nothing can beat going by yourself. It may be frustrating but it can also be a tremendous amount of fun. Change here is also obvious; travel industry staff are now grasping that people who pay for tickets, tours and beds are the people who pay their wages. Three free market economy has made service staff really give service. About time.

## *SHEEP AND SHEPHERDS*

Before mass tourism exploded in the late 1970s, foreigners going to China were treated like some rare and delicate form of life. They were herded together like sheep and flocked obediently behind their minders as they shuffled past temples, went into the obligatory kindergarten, snapped their Nikons at the dutiful happy peasants on a model farm and tramped through a factory where the machinery was clean but obviously unused. The aim was to segregate the cash-paying foreign nuisances from the people and to show them only what officialdom wanted them to see.

No longer. I have not had to go to a kindergarten for the past decade. And thanks for that; an endless display of well-scrubbed kiddies with glowing faces singing about the glories of the New China is something that swiftly palls. The age of being trotted around socialist projects is thankfully over.

Earlier eras saw visitors being escorted by eagle-eyed officials whose main concern was to prevent them seeing anything less than perfection. The political cadres were frequently bored and hostile; they didn't see why they had to waste their time trotting about with some ignorant foreigners. Today, escorts are like tour guides anywhere else. Some are terrific, some are useless. Generally, standards are quite high. As China develops a proper tourism infrastructure, guides are becoming more professional. Standards of English are frequently excellent; linguistic education in China is very high and students toil mightily to succeed.

## *VISITORS CHANGE THE NATION*

Tourism has changed the face of Chinese cities as much as industrialisation. Most of the country is now open to foreigners who can travel freely by themselves. It's now comparatively hassle-free. But wherever possible, book in advance.

In the past, individual journeyers who made solo adventures prayed halfway through their odysseys that they had stayed at home and watched a travelogue on television. Once having braved the solitary traveller's road in China and survived, the new Old China Hand could congratulate himself. It was rather like the fellow who kept belting himself on the head with a hammer; it was so nice when he stopped. That's how some Westerners felt when they departed China.

Today, the excitement remains but many of the problems have gone. From zero visitors in 1971 – apart from drab party faithful from such tiny communist fanatic-lands as Albania – a massive tourism industry has developed. Like everything else in China, the figures are astonishing.

In 1995, China was the fifth most popular destination for global visitors, greeting about six million "foreigners". This did not include huge numbers of Hongkong, Macau and Taiwan Chinese. Tourism revenue topped US$9 billion; that's the reason for those towering new hotels, the unlikely theme parks and the near-desperate scramble to "improve" beauty spots at waterfalls and mountaintops. Every local government wants to get its share of that gigantic tourism bounty. In 2000, China earned US$54.5 billion from tourism. There were 10 million foreign visitors.

The largest "foreign" contingents are Americans, followed by Australians and British with Germans, French, Italians and Singaporeans.

Money used to be the bane of going to China. You used to have to carry immense bundles of cash. Until comparatively recently, credit cards were novel pieces of plastic, to be admired by storekeepers and

111

hoteliers who then returned the useless articles to you and demanded renminbi, US dollars or Hongkong currency. As in so many other ways, China has caught up with the rest of the world. The credit card is king. Not long ago, to the rage and frustration of travellers, they were an exotic novelty that held mystical powers, but which couldn't be used.

I frequently used to return from some backwoods area filled with regret. I may have seen a painting or a piece of art that I would dearly have loved to buy, but didn't have enough cash.

What sort of cash? There used to be two very different kinds, and they were segregated with extreme strictness. For the people, the renminbi with its socialist-realism artwork of ardent workers and strong intellectuals used to be the norm. This is renminbi, or People's Money. The people with any brains didn't use to want it. It could be used only to buy Chinese goods. Until the late 1980s, there was a parallel currency called FEC, or Foreign Exchange Certificates. Armed with this, you could buy imported goods, go to luxury hotels (locals without FEC were banned) and do all sorts of other interesting things, like leap into the flourishing blackmarket.

On any street corner in any sizeable city, the visitor could swap FEC for RMB at double the official rate. You could spend your RMB on what you wanted – Chinese food and wine and beer and taxis – and the blackmarket dealer could buy what they wanted, colour television sets and Scotch whisky. Everyone was happy and for years the dim officialdom which presided over such nonsense didn't seem to care. The basic idea, of course, was to preserve China's hard currency, to get tourists to pay in foreign cash (US dollars preferred) and for those greenbacks to get stuck in the greedy maws of the official banking system. Finally, China grew up and scrapped the FEC, much to the relief of everyone except the blackmarket traders.

## TIPS

Tourism has not yet eroded the general custom of not tipping. Don't bother. When visitors first started visiting China, tipping was widely discouraged as a filthy capitalist ploy to bribe the proud proletariat. Times have changed. Gratuities are still not sought openly. However, waiters and bartenders will not be insulted if you offer them a tip. They're not mad!

As for taxi drivers, guides, doormen and other service staff, tipping is neither expected nor requested.

Beggars are few in China, but some professionals have started to appear in places where tourists are common, like the railway station concourse in Guangzhou. Most likely, those who approach you are cheeky children trying their luck on notoriously stupid foreign devils. Smile and wave them away.

## MOVING AROUND

Travel guides used to be surly and indifferent. Sometimes, they were outright hostile. This was because they were ordered to do jobs they hated. For the past 15 years, Chinese colleges and universities have been running specialised courses up to degree level to train a new generation of travel guide, as well as the other specialists needed to run a booming tourist industry. The result is predictable; travel guides are now efficient, reliable and know what they are doing. "Service" is the key word in their training, which was a concept totally unknown in the travel industry before 1985. Here's another field where advances and improvements have made China more like the rest of the civilised world. Unlike some areas, here the changes are welcome.

In the old era of the Iron Ricebowl, counter staff at places like hotels, airline offices and travel agencies were often arrogant and deliberately unhelpful. This was caused partly by ignorance – they didn't know anything and were not keen to see this proven – and by the Little Emperor syndrome that saw any spoiled offspring of a minor party hack given a toady's job where he could wear a uniform, sit inside, do nothing and bully the public. The idea was to show that you were the boss. Give such a person a position of minor power and they love to throw their weight around. I refused always to put up with such rudeness and spent years writing letters of complaint to senior officials, none of which achieved anything except to make me feel better.

Such attitudes, thankfully, have gone. Now that people are expected to work for a living and good jobs are hard to find, there's a welcome change in attitude. No longer do young people regard a job in the hospitality industry as a troublesome interruption to their lives. Today, it's a highly regarded career with a pathway to success.

This welcome change in attitude means far better treatment for visitors.

Local tourist guides will help you discover that every city in China has interesting old environs. You may even strike it lucky and find a brochure outlining these attractions. Armed with a map, you can probably find the way about by yourself.

Local buses cost a few fen for long distances and there are always active fleets of private enterprise mini-buses going on main routes. Taxis have exploded in number in the past five years. Public transport can be fun, if you don't mind being jostled and pushed in overcrowded conditions. This gives you the chance to rub shoulders with the 'broad masses' as the people are referred to in leftist propaganda. It's fun. Once people realise you are not some haughty grandee and are approachable, they are eager to make friends. It's astonishing how often you find someone with a grasp of English, even in the most remote areas.

Escorted tours are best because guides can fill you in on the history of tombs, temples and old buildings. Don't let their absence put you off from exploring on your own, however. It's a lot of fun rambling around old back streets. And it's perfectly safe.

## *TRAVEL ORGANISATIONS*

Ten years after China's door creaked uneasily open, the organisations that ran mass tourism were roundly condemned by those unfortunates who had to depend on their services. Every single last word of abuse was well deserved. I must confess I was one of those who bellowed most loudly about the grudging ineptitude of reluctant, ill-tempered and incompetent officials.

That was in the 1980s. Today, the big tourism bodies are slick, impersonal and competent. There's several reasons things were so bad. Firstly, tour companies handling huge numbers of visitors had to start from scratch. They simply didn't exist before 1972 because there were no tourists. Secondly, many early recruits were reluctant and unwilling guides. Some were foreign language students who had hoped to be diplomats or journalists; it was not their idea of fun having to tramp about curio shops with gawping, camera-adorned drapers from Kansas on their heels.

Not now. In 1994, I was standing in a bar in the old ceramic city of Foshan in the Pearl Delta when I bumped into a Manila-based German businessman. We had, naturally, a Zhu Jiang (Pearl River) lager. How had he got to Foshan? By bus from Hongkong to Guangzhou and then on to the fertile and swampy delta, all fixed by China International Travel Service. Bad luck, I said. No, he quickly answered. No way, CITS were terrific.

This took me aback. I usually travel by myself and get my own tickets. I did some checking on people travelling through China's plethora of agencies and booking offices. All were enthusiastic about the sophistication and slickness of the expanding official agencies. This is a far cry from the past when these hapless organisations were renowned for hostility, haphazard service and a lack of care for customers. The travel services have caught up with booming tourism, although over-the-counter attitudes can still be sloppy and uncaring.

China Travel Service fixes visits in China for Overseas Chinese visitors. China International Travel Service does it for foreigners.

China Youth Travel Service handles young people on a tight budget. These organisations all have something in common; they are all too big. Usually visitors have no option but to deal with the big official bodies. It's still a good idea to depend more for local trips and excursions on the concierge desk at your hotel.

Ask the assistant manager, with a smile, if they can aid you. If they have time, hotel staff usually like to chat. Ask them what local maps or guidebooks they have and where they think is a good place to visit. They will often go to the in-house tour booking desk to help you make your reservations. To confirm outward flights, always do it when you are checking in. It doesn't matter if you are going to be in China for a couple of weeks. Reconfirm at every hotel you go to.

Incidentally, in 2001, the Hong Kong-Guangzhou traffic is enormous, with tens of thousands of people passing between the two cities daily. There's an enormous fleet of moderned airconditioned buses going from a dozen points around Hong Kong and stopping at major hotels in Guangzhou. You do immigration-customs at the border, painlessly, then speed on the super-highway to the City of the Five Rams (a legend that roughly rivals the wolf cubs of Rome). Trains are also a great way to skip the 150 kilometres from Kowloon to downtown Canton.

## GUIDES

Some big travel departments may still lack a positive service outlook, but the chances are much better than even that individual guides will be delightful. This is especially so if they have a genuine interest in their job. The previous system worked against this; in the old era before the open market was introduced, a young person sent to university to study a language was then more or less forced into the travel industry.

Many disliked it. Many were simply not cut out for such jobs. Others who had been forced into serving as guides hated the compulsion – and showed this in their attitude.

The new freedoms eliminate most of these problems. Guides and escorts are now doing the jobs for the same reasons that tour companies elsewhere in the world find staff; it's work they like. Most guides in China welcome the opportunity to meet people from abroad and to widen their perspective of the world. I still get letters and Christmas cards from tour guides I met a decade ago. And they are totally overwhelmed when they receive postcards or pictures back from people they have escorted. Be nice; if a guide has shown you a good time, send them a holiday snap when you get home. This will pay dividends to other tourists in future.

## BE PREPARED

Make sure you are ready for China. For almost everyone, a visit to the country is a significant investment. You are throwing half this money into a paddy field if you do not take sensible, basic preparations.

Before you leave home, buy a couple of decent guidebooks. There are plenty about. Also, read some modern history; libraries and bookshop shelves are crammed with volumes on China, many of them far too scholarly and tedious for the first-time visitor. My tip is that you read two books. *Red Star Over China* by Edgar Snow is the true account of the grim birth and struggle for survival of the early Communist Party, culminating in the incredible story of the Long March. Without understanding the sacrifice and bravery of the soldiers and peasants of the Red Army, it is impossible to grasp the moral ethos at the core of the New China. How that victory in the civil war was used – and how the fine vision was eroded – is explained in *The New Emperors: Mao and Deng* by Harrison Salisbury. This masterly American journalist sketches what happened to the proud dreams born at the Gate of Heavenly Peace in October 1949, when Mao Zedong and the marshals of the People's Liberation Army proclaimed the birth of the People's Republic. These two are essential reading; they are also thrilling accounts of living history.

When you book your tickets, ask your local travel agent what material they have about your itinerary, hotels and cities you will visit. Probably not much. Roam the Web and cruise through excellent educational and travel China homepages. Write to the nearest Chinese embassy or consular office, asking them for the address of the city or provincial tourism offices of places you plan to visit. Then write to them asking for promotional material. If you are staying at a big hotel – say the Hilton in Shanghai, the Sheraton in Beijing or the Holiday Inn in Guangzhou – call the local hotel of that chain and ask their public relations staff if they have any brochures on the property.

Go to your library. Read your paper and see what the foreign pages report on China (but don't believe all the anti-China propaganda you read in the foreign press). In short, do whatever you can to read and study before you leave home. You are going to be in a very different environment. Do what you can to prepare yourself for the experience.

## *TAXIS*

In many parts of China, taxis are a disgrace. Often like chicken coops on wheels, they are usually tastefully decorated inside by crushed watermelon seeds and stamped out cigarette butts. In the south in summer, they are like moveable saunas. In the freezing north in winter there are two dramatic alternatives; the cab will either be superheated by dry air or be cold as the North Pole in midwinter and have a window which will not close.

Not all taxi journeys are so bad. Some cab drivers in major cities now even speak a few words of English. But do not trust this.

Never, ever, get into a cab unless you are confident you can tell the driver in his local dialect where you want to go. Never. Otherwise, you can end up driving expensively through miles of dreary industrial estates, the meter ticking on and the driver puffing on cigarettes and shrugging his shoulders.

Always ask your hotel doorman or concierge desk to write the address for you in Chinese. If you are using a map, make sure the

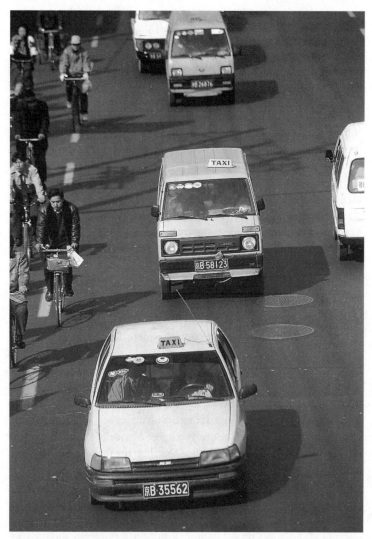

*A cavalcade of brightly-coloured taxis compete with cyclists for road space in China's capital city, Beijing.*

address in Chinese can be read and that local landmarks are prominently displayed. Never get in a cab until you are sure the driver knows where you want to go. I've got to admit that during hundreds of taxi journeys in China, I have only had a couple of instances where cabbies deliberately tried to rip me off. Almost all misunderstandings can be avoided if you make sure the driver knows exactly where he is to take you. Don't rely on him having a map because that's about as likely as him having a Ph.D. in nuclear engineering. Never pay a taxi driver until you have been inside the building and found that he has delivered you to the right address.

It is always a matter of some wonder to me that I end up in cities all over the world directing local cabbies to take me where I want to go. This doesn't only apply in China but happens also in Manila, San Francisco, Sydney, London and in my hometown of Hongkong.

Is there some universal law that states taxi drivers must be totally ignorant of the city in which they drive?

## *COMPLAIN*

Tourist officials are well aware that bad taxi service is a major complaint by visitors as well as businessmen. There are always hotel limousines, but these are expensive. Taxis are supposed to have meters that work and to display photographs of the drivers. Good luck to finding either. The state of some cabs would astound Henry Ford. Many are tiny, tinny vehicles. It's difficult to get two normal-sized adults into the dirty back seat. If there is no meter or – more commonly – if it does not work, make sure you agree a price before you roar off into the unknown. Always offer less than half the fare drivers demand. You'll still be paying too generously.

Like so much else in China, there has been a marked improvement in recent years. And it's fair to admit police in Hangzhou, for instance, are as frustrated at taxi malpractices as are their counterparts in Cleveland. I always report bad or dishonest service; so should you. Write to the local newspaper and they will translate and print your letter in Chinese. This is one way of letting the local authorities know what sort of service you are getting.

If I feel I have been overcharged too outrageously, I call a policeman or one of the special uniformed tourist officials you sometimes find.

'But this will get the driver into trouble,' some people protest. Bad luck, I respond. If the thief had not tried to rob me unreasonably, I would have happily paid and given a tip. It's not that I mind paying the money, but I do object strenuously to being treated like an idiot.

Have no mercy on unscrupulous taxi drivers. If they try to con you, don't pay them – report them.

## DIRECTIONS

Getting about in China poses problems. Most people don't speak English and attempts by visitors to speak basic guidebook Chinese, while appreciated, will probably not be very successful.

So when you venture outside your hotel, always take a hotel card with you that gives the name and address in English and Chinese. At least you will be able to get back.

If I am going to see someone, I always ask them to fax directions – written in Chinese and English – to my hotel, with a map showing the local pagoda, police station, hotel, railway station or some other prominent landmark that even a taxi driver will recognise.

## SECURITY

When exploring a Chinese city, wander freely. There are no closed areas any more (apart from a few clearly marked military installations where photography is forbidden) and getting about the old core areas of ancient cities is a fascinating experience.

In any sizeable city, street maps are available at hotel book kiosks. They cost a few dollars and are a very worthwhile investment. Make sure before you set out on your first jaunt that your hotel is clearly marked in Chinese on the map. That way, you can point to it and no matter how far you wander, someone will be able to direct you back.

Bear in mind that everyone you meet in China will be friendly and eager to help a wayward tourist who has lost his way. But they can't help you if they do not know what you want or where you wish to go. So make sure you always carry the address of the place you are staying and, if possible, a simple map.

## STREETS

When it comes to naming streets, the present regime has got a lot to answer for. Old names, such as the delightful Bubbling Well Road in Shanghai, have replaced by more utilitarian ones. It is now Nanjing West Road. There is no city in China, as far as I know, which does not have a major artery named Zhongshan Lu and Jiefang Lu. Zhongshan is the birthplace of Dr Sun Yat-sen. Jiefang means 'Liberation'. Lu, of course, means 'Road'. Anywhere in China, you're pretty safe if you get in a cab and shout Zhongshan Lu. The driver will head to the middle of town because that's where the street is sure to be. (Zhong Shan means Central Mountain, although it is located in the flat, swampy Pearl delta.)

In most big cities, the names of streets are in the pinyin version of Latin spelling. This is a great help in finding your way about with the aid of a map.

## TRAFFIC

Prosperity has meant a huge increase in cars, trucks, motorbikes, taxis, mini-buses and anything else that coughs, bumps along the road without being towed by a horse and coughs out noxious black fumes. So, hello to the world's capital of traffic jams and diesel pollution.

Major cities have thrown up circular ring roads, triple-decker flyovers and all the other concrete paraphernalia of the vehicular age. Chinese cities are beginning to resemble Los Angeles, including the smog but without the gratuitous crime and violence.

Chinese drivers like to drive fast and, wherever possible, in the middle of the road. This is fun for nervous tourists, quivering in terror in the back seat. Road accidents are comparatively new in China; 30 years ago, there was virtually no vehicular traffic. So how could there be traffic accidents? Since then, the rare buses, army vehicles and state-owned cars have been joined by millions of modern trucks, buses and tractors built in China's own booming auto works and by huge imports of Japanese vehicles which are used by the tourist industry and for local transport by joint venture companies. One result is a rocketing road toll.

Passengers who wander – eyes carefully averted from the traffic – over streets and major highways are as much to blame as lunatic drivers.

Getting a driver's licence in China is an agonising business. For a Chinese, it requires many months of theoretical study and endless practical tests including stringent health examinations. So how come, after such effort, the standard of driving is so appalling?

In the cities, it is not so bad. The newcomer is likely to stare with a horrified fixed grin of fascination out the window as his taxi weaves through a sea of cyclists.

It seems the norm that a bicyclist on a Chinese street refuses to look sideways to see if a car is aimed straight at him over an intersection. This is apparently on the grounds of what you can't see, won't hurt you. So pedallers blithely proceed directly across intersections. Needless to say, they frequently end up under the wheels of trucks. And that's just the start of the fun. Huge crowds gather to look at the crumpled figure and traffic comes to a dead halt.

At night, the situation is much worse. I have never seen a bicycle in China with a light. And outside the centre of every city, the suburbs stretch in a dim, unlit maze of wide, tree-lined streets. Out of the gloom, cyclists appear suddenly. Their vehicles have no reflectors and they are hard to spot. Cars go through city streets dodging cyclists (who seem to be on the road 24 hours a day.) This is made much more fun by the universal Chinese practice of turning off the lights. The reasoning behind this seems to go as follows: Putting on the lights makes the engine tired and uses up more fuel. Therefore, if you don't need to see, turn the lights off. Only turn the lights on when there is a positive need to look where you are going – for example, when a cyclist is about three metres in front of you or when the car is going around a dark bend at 80 kph and another vehicle without lights is coming from the other direction. And both are, of course, firmly in the middle of the road.

With an increasing number of foreigners living in China, the former practice of hiring a driver to be on permanent duty is on the wane. People are going to the huge amount of trouble necessary to get a Chinese driving licence. Brave folks. If they are ever involved in an accident, which is highly likely given the customary standard of driving, the foreign devil is always going to be held at fault. There will be instant, inflated demands for compensation. People without a scratch will immediately fall victim to agonising, unspecified pains (the Chinese version of crying 'Whiplash!') and getting things straightened out will be a protracted agonising task. I have one friend whose departure from Beijing was forbidden until teams of doctors had made lengthy, week-long investigations of a person who collided with her while both were on bicycles.

My advice to visitors is: Don't even think about driving. If you choose to do so, fully balance the odds. Is it worthwhile to take the risk of going out in a car by yourself or should the independence and freedom of self-travel be weighed against the strong possibility of an accident and the resulting endless bales of red tape this will certainly involve?

Visitors find themselves inevitably trapped in situations where they are captive victims of lunatic drivers. There is no safeguard against this. Up in mountainous Guizhou once, I was in a small bus going over a scenic nightmare of steep ravines and eroded limestone escarpments. The driver seemed to think himself a close relative of a Macau Grand Prix driver; he swung that vehicle around sharp corners, tyres screaming, and roared down unguarded roads with the bus leaning wildly over the side of steep cliffs falling hundreds of metres onto the jagged rocks of wild rivers. The minority folk of the highlands seemed to think this was barrels of fun – more exciting than their cultural gathering of water buffalo fights – and beamed in approval as the vehicle yawned sickeningly on the curves. Not me. I was pale with terror. Coming down into one valley, I spotted a clutch of rooftops. *"Teng, teng!"* (Stop, stop!) I called. The vehicle came to a halt with a screech of brakes and the smell of burnt tyres.

I tottered gratefully out, paid and looked for the local beer stall. Sipping a warm ale in the pale winter sunshine of the mountains, I nodded amiably at the local Dong tribal folk and waited for the next bus. And waited. And waited. Eventually, a couple of hours on, another vehicle hove into view coming down the mountain. Thankfully, I climbed aboard to be greeted by the customary looks of astonishment a foreigner finds in rural China, then by welcome grins as I said hello. I wasn't smiling for long because the bus got off with a start like a fighter bomber taking off from an aircraft carrier and commenced rolling around the frightening corners over the gorges at twice the speed of the bus driven by the former maniac. "Oh my God," I said, clutching the seat in front while an aged mountain grandmother beamed at me in approval.

The horrors of road smashes in China are easily witnessed. Most seem to be head-on disasters. Given the popular habit of driving right down the middle of the roads, this is not surprising. On most stretches of road, pedestrians keep to the side. Then come the cyclists. Then there are small puffing tractors converted to small trucks (taking the part of the water buffalo or draught mule). Swerving past these slowly-travelling road users, heavy trucks swing out to the middle of the road. Passing them on the wrong side of the road are buses and cars. Every vehicle is honking incessantly. So on one narrow lane, you have up to five classes of travellers all going in the same direction at various speeds. Coming in the other direction, the traffic flow is likely to be identical. In the middle of the road, the swiftly-moving cars and buses jostle for position. It is a situation designed for disaster and the end results are frequently seen where two vehicles have slammed into each other head-on. The sights are horrific. So there is ample reason for my fear on the roads; I have witnessed a lot of the end results of this haphazard transport mess.

If the situation is bad in the cities, in the wide open spaces of the country it is far worse, if only because there is comparatively less traffic and the flow is faster. China is supposed to be an atheistic country but any passenger in a car driven by a man in a hurry soon becomes a convert to some belief; you are likely to spend a fair amount of time praying that something is not coming around the blind corner which you are screaming around at 120 kph. It is pointless to ask a driver to slow down or drive less dangerously. He will ignore you. It's his job to drive and drive he shall, just the way he wants to. In past times, it was probably safe to overtake a lumbering truck on a rural road on the crest of a hill or on a sharp blind corner. Chances were, nothing would be coming the other way. These days, with a lot more traffic on the highways, the possibility that another vehicle will be swinging equally wildly around that corner towards you is much more likely.

## *ROADS*

Roads in China are generally pretty bad but getting better. They differ from province to province. Shandong prides itself on the new series of highways linking its major towns into an economic network. They claim with justification these are the best in the nation. Indeed, the four-lane divided highway system would not be out of place in Europe or America.

In other spots, roads between major centres can be atrocious. The 'highway' between Shanghai and the old cultural city of Suzhou is a case in point. It is a potholed, rundown shambles of a stretch of macadam. In most countries, it would take 40 minutes to cruise down a road between two such great cities. Here, the journey normally takes about two and a half hours with cars, tractors, horse-drawn carts, trucks, buses and cyclists all fighting for their share of the narrow, two-lane track. Other surprises await in the provinces. In some remote, hilly areas of the southwest, the roads sweeping over mountains and through steep valleys can be excellent.

The superhighway between Guangzhou-Hongkong-Macau is excellent, except that it seems to be constantly dug-up for random reasons, squeezing traffic into one lane. Of course, this was built by private enterprise, which is possibly why it is so good.

When travelling by road in China, it is not much point asking the driver how far it is to your destination. Rather, enquire how long the journey will take.

## TRAIN TRAVEL

When China travels, it does so mostly to the clank of the Iron Rooster. Trains still carry the bulk of the people on their intercity journeys. For the visitor, a journey by train can be the highlight of a trip to China. In the crowded hard-class compartments, you sit crammed grubby-cheek-by-bearded-jowl with the common people. It's one of the best and swiftest ways to meet the normal man and woman from factory and field, the average Chinese people.

In recent years, China has invested gigantically in railway infrastructure. Lines have been improved dramatically and rolling stock – most of it made in China's own impressive workshops – speed smoothly along newly laid tracks. The last great steam trains which were made in Manchuria, clanked majestically out of the railway factories a decade ago. Most trains are now reliably powered by diesel and many of the lines surrounding cities are dual-tracked and electrified.

The busy service from Hunghom in Hongkong to the new Tien He station in sees a dozen trains daily linking the twin cities, running in competition with speedy super-bus services. Add to that fast hydrofoils and turbocats linking the growing cities in the Pearl River Delta and you have a public transport system probably unsurpassed anywhere. With Hongkong's return to the Motherland, the former British colony's internal railway and underground links are now been wedded to the neighbouring city of Shen Zhen, something which should have happened a decade earlier if it had not been for blind intransigence on both sides of the River.

Trains are fun. Don't let people talk you out of making at least one lengthy train journey.

Tour guides and government officials will be horrified if any foreigner older than an adventurous back-packing youngster indicates they wish to travel anything but soft (first) class. Indeed, it will be hard for you to persuade a ticket clerk to sell you a hard-class ticket. And I wouldn't advise it for a lengthy journey.

But for a trip of two or three hours – from Shanghai, say, to Ningbo or Suzhou – it can be fun. And it's an adventure. Once aboard, no matter how crammed the carriage, people will squeeze to make a seat for a foreigner. Cigarettes, biscuits and fruit will be offered with a shy grin. Within a couple of minutes, the inevitable English speaker will have come forward and the questions will begin.

Where do you come from? Where are you going? What do you think of China? Why is a rich foreigner in the hard class? By the time the train wheezes out of the station and starts clattering along the tracks, you'll be firmly part of the travelling circus that is the Chinese railway system.

With more than 55,000 kilometres of track covering every province and linking the far borders of the nation to Beijing and other great cities, the National Railway Administration is a vital cornerstone of the Chinese economy. It is also one of the most efficient organisations in the land.

This does not mean the visitor can go to a railway station and without difficulty buy a ticket. As with every other aspect of Chinese officialdom, that would be far too easy. Railway service staff are rude, abrupt, incompetent and lazy. As with so many other aspects of 'service', they seem to think the jobs have been provided for them as a rostrum from which they can abuse the public.

Fares for Chinese passengers are kept deliberately low. Foreigners pay three times as much. From Beijing to Tianjin costs US$20 and from Shanghai to Wuxi US$11 – far cheaper than by hire car.

If you are buying tickets for yourself, be prepared to stand in line for a minimum of an hour, to face a slothful, slow and idle clerk and then to go through agony before he or she reluctantly produces a ticket. Make sure you have the seat you wish to purchase written out clearly in Chinese, preferably on a railway timetable with the appropriate train marked. Better still, spend the few extra dollars needed and have your hotel buy the ticket for you.

Realistically, any foreigner travelling as a tourist in China on anything more than a short day trip is well advised to pay to go soft class. At night, if you are travelling alone, this means you will share a four-berth car with three strangers. It's a good way to make friends. The bedding is warm and clean and as the train rattles through the dark Chinese night, sleep comes easy.

Restaurant cars in most Chinese trains are best avoided, if possible. Most look like mobile pigpens and as you examine tablecloths which appear to have been used to wipe the floor of a public toilet, the thought of hepatitis springs instantly to mind. If possible, have your hotel prepare you a hamper. (My best meal on a Chinese train was across Shandong with fresh German sausage and bread packed by the Huiquan Dynasty Hotel in Qingdao.) But if you are on a lengthy journey, like the three-day Beijing to Guangzhou trip, cross your fingers, point to what looks appetising on other tables and hope for the best. Surprise! There are now English menus.

One delight for the foreigner on the rails of China a few years ago was to see the enormous variety of railway engines. The piercing wail of a steam engine, the chuffing locomotive with its plume of dark smoke, was a common sight. Alas, this romance of the age of steam has now largely disappeared, replaced by modern diesel electric locomotives. It's another sign of progress – don't knock it – but for nostalgia buffs, times ain't what they used to be.

## *TOILETS*

For the newly arrived Westerner, going to the toilet in China can be a traumatic experience. Looking back, it can provoke a laugh once safely home. It is seldom so humorous at the time.

The state of Chinese public toilets is normally disgraceful. Even in some large cities, the stand-up urinals for men consist of large upright ceramic jars in which one aims as best one can. The resulting precious liquid is taken away to the nearby fields.

Newcomers are frequently appalled by the standards of hygiene, or lack of any apparent standards, in public toilets. This is partly caused by the Chinese attitude of 'I'm alright, Wong' that reflects a lack of consideration to anyone else. In their homes, Chinese are spotless and so are their toilets. Why should they worry about what sort of mess they leave behind in a public lavatory? How is it their business? They don't intend to go back.

No other single subject fills tourists with such horror. This revulsion is mystifying to many Chinese. What's the problem? they ask as some white-faced American matron stumbles in shocked disarray from a streetside lavatory. Inside, she may have had to use a simple hole in the floor that since its last cleansing had been occupied by a few hundred others. The saving sanitary grace is the Chinese-style toilet. In modern hotels, railway stations and a few government offices, Western-style 'sitters' may be found. Elsewhere, the 'squatter' is universal.

For the novice, this may at first be awkward. You have to be reasonably adroit. Practice swiftly makes perfect. A word of caution; remove all money, wallets and other valuables from the trouser pockets before attempting to use a 'squatter' for the first time. Otherwise, you may find yourself attempting to prise your passport or traveller's cheques out of a noisome mess.

### *'Hey, Harry!'*

Years ago, I was at the bustling railway station at Hunghom in Kowloon where the express train to China picks up its eager loads of tourists for the Middle Kingdom.

The splendid station was overwhelmed by a human tidal wave of visitors as soon as it opened. Planned for the days before China opened its doors to the world, when the Bamboo Curtain suddenly swung wide, the new station was instantly packed. The Hongkong authorities had built for large crowds. Besides restaurants, bars, bookshops and banks, there were also adequate toilet facilities.

These offered a choice. Those whose cultural bent was towards 'sitters' could use a Western-style loo. For those more used to 'squatters', this variety was available.

Two elderly American retirees wandered into the toilet. Urinals were in the middle. On one side were cubicles of 'squatters', on the other, similar cubicles held 'sitters'.

One of the Americans headed for the Asian-type section where there was a hole in the floor with a flushing mechanism above it. He had obviously never seen anything before remotely like this equipment. He blinked, scratched his head, looked again, then called to his friend.

"Hey, Harry," he shouted. "Get a load of this. Somebody's stolen the john."

## *SPITTING*

Health authorities throughout China have engaged for years in public health campaigns aimed at stamping out this highly regarded social custom. They have failed. Walk down any street in any town in China and you are likely to hear a rumbling, throat-clearing hawking that precedes an explosive expectoration.

Persuasion and education over the past decade has had little obvious impact in reducing the incidence of spitting. So those caught by police and health workers are now given on-the-spot fines. In addition, enthusiastic cadres in the anti-spitting corps are likely to pull out microscopes and require the spittee to go down on his hands and knees to examine what he has just lodged on the pavements.

*Beijing Daily* and other papers also regularly print the names of those convicted of spitting in public places. But there is little public opprobrium in being known as a spitter so the effect of this move is dubious.

Advice for travellers; try to close your ears but watch your step.

## *CROWDS*

In any city in China, there are hundreds of thousands of people standing around doing nothing. Any free entertainment, anything out of the normal mundane flow of life, can produce huge numbers of them at an instant's notice.

Two cyclists collide and exchange angry words; it is street theatre in the raw and the idle flock to listen, take sides, sit in judgement on the rights and wrongs of the incident. A truck hits a bus and it is immediate cause for a gathering that looks like the Superbowl.

A foreigner stopping a policeman to ask for directions with the aid of a map can swiftly become the focal point for a gathering of hundreds. In rural areas where Westerners are still rare, the mere sight of a foreigner sitting down at a streetside stall sipping a beer and eating a bowl of noodles is sufficient to cause children to come running.

The natural curiosity of people and the blankness of their everyday lives combine to create crowds. Let three or four people stop to look at something and soon others gather around. Seeing a clump of people, passers-by at a distance drop their hoes or jump on their bicycles and come pedalling to see what others find worth staring at.

Once, in Guizhou province, where I was the first foreigner to penetrate some isolated areas for many years, I went into a toilet in a small town. Five minutes later, I emerged to find myself confronted by a silent crowd of several hundred Dong, Miao and Bouyei tribesmen and Han townfolk who had gathered to look at this weird apparition of a foreigner. "*Ni hao*," I said, slinging my camera bag over my shoulder. This earned enthusiastic applause.

Such spontaneous rushes of people to look with wonder at the most minor incident can cause apprehension and claustrophobia to the stunned Westerner caught in the middle of a human crush. Just say '*Duibuqi*' (Excuse me) and push out of the throng.

## *FICTION*

There is probably more nonsense written and believed about China than any other nation. The old, baseless myth about Chinese being inscrutable is one example. Take the Cantonese. Go to a football match and see them shouting, screaming, yelling as they urge on their team. They are about as inscrutable as Sicilians.

Wander through the old brick houses and courtyards that make up the core of most northern cities. If you are a Westerner, you will be a curiosity, especially in towns off the tourist beat. People will look at you curiously – why not? You're different. But if you smile, they will flash you a brilliant grin. Say '*Ni hao*' and they will want to chat. Where are you from? Ask at your hotel how to say the name of your country in Chinese. If you are American, learn the name of your state as well.

Soon you'll be surrounded by shy but friendly folk and the chances are some old lady will urge you into her home for a cup of tea. At times like this, language barriers don't mean a thing.

Relax. Enjoy. Smile.

Inscrutable? Don't make me laugh.

Always remember one thing; the Chinese may be proudly different from the rest of the world but, first and foremost, they are people, just like you and I and everyone else. Treat people politely and the chances are they will do the same to you. A smile costs you nothing. It is worth a million yuan.

Good manners are the same in any country. When you are touring in China, you will meet many people. Greet them the way you would back home. Smile, say hello and shake hands.

## *NEVER SAY NO*
Chinese people do not like to say NO. They will squirm with embarrassment as they try to find a more diplomatic, tactful and considerate way of expressing the negative. Sometimes, this leads them to great lengths of circumlocution.

This reluctance to say a simple 'No' may seem strange to Westerners. But it is part of the Chinese notion of politeness. It is not thought right simply to deny a visitor a request. So instead of just saying 'No' they will go to great lengths to hint that something is not possible, hoping behind the bland smiles that the thick-skinned, hopelessly stupid foreign devil will take the hint.

As an inquisitive reporter with a skin like a Mongolian pack camel, I sometimes find myself pressing officials for an answer about a question. Over on the Liuzhou Peninsula once, I started to wander away from an organised group visit to an oil refining installation. A few hundred metres away, there were rows of new apartment buildings and I wanted to see what the living standards were like for local people in the 'Houston of China'.

Alarmed, an official came running after me.

Where was I going? To have a look at those buildings, I explained. But, he said, clearly worried, this was not on the programme. It had not been arranged. There was nobody to escort me.

Quite okay, I said. I would just stroll over by myself. Being in the south, people spoke Cantonese, the lingua franca of Hongkong, so I'd be okay. No, he pressed. He gave the standard excuse for explaining the impossible in China. 'It is inconvenient.'

This covers a wide variety of impossibilities from 'It's too much bother' to 'It's punishable by a long jail term'. If you press, as I did, the matter becomes vital. The official became agitated.

Why the hell not? I demanded. I was sick and tired of seeing showplace oil refineries and wanted to see how the people lived.

Out he came with another old chestnut that in China is normally sufficient to end all argument. "It is not the normal procedure to allow people to go there by themselves," he explained.

I pressed on over the paddy field dike. He clutched me by the arm. "Please," he said. "It is not permitted."

It was obvious that if I kept going, he was going to be forced into the position of dreadful embarrassment of telling me bluntly that it was forbidden for me to stray. He was a reasonable fellow and a happy travelling companion so I reluctantly gave in.

As a casual visitor to China, most tourists will probably not encounter the difficulty of forcing someone to say 'No'. But if you make a request to your guide to go somewhere and he seems reluctant, take the gentle hint. Don't put him in a position of having to say 'No'. It will make him lose face and make you unreasonable in not understanding that what you asked was impossible.

## *HEALTH*

Standards of medical care vary widely in China. In the great teaching hospitals in Beijing and Shanghai, they are excellent. So are those in the private, semi-secret hospital in Beijing reserved for the top brass of army, party and government. If you are a normal citizen, however, best of luck if something is wrong with you.

For tourists, the best bet is to hope for the best. No vaccinations are needed for visitors to China but my medical friends advise me to take the shots aimed at preventing hepatitis which is endemic. In 1988, when Shanghai people indulged in their annual gastronomic orgy of eating hairy crabs caught in the lakes upriver, more than a million people came down with this liver disease. Stay away from shellfish, is my advice. And get anti-hepatitis shots before you leave home.

If you break a leg, you will get swift, competent medical care anywhere in China. Anything more complicated is a great deal more problematical.

If you feel seriously ill, contact your embassy in Beijing. They may be able to get you to a reliable doctor. But bear in mind that it is standard practice for all Western embassies and foreign companies in China to evacuate sick staffers and their families. At the first sign of trouble, they are on the next jet heading down to Hongkong where medical facilities are excellent. I advise you strongly to follow this example.

In many large cities with expatriate communities, hotels now have modern clinics staffed by foreign-trained doctors.

## BASIC IMPROVEMENTS

My wife teaches rehabilitation, and spends a lot of her time in Chinese hospitals and medical universities far off the beaten tracks. She has great admiration – indeed, love – for her Chinese colleagues. I am very proud of the incredible work she and her academic colleagues from the Department of Rehabilitation Sciences of the Hong Kong Polytechnic University have performed in China. They have made very real differences to the way in which the health profession and the public regard disabled, handicapped and crippled people. They have brought hope and a new life to millions.

Part of this was done with a generous grant by the Hong Kong

Rotary Club and Rotary International. This enabled Kit, my wife, and her colleagues to produce a package of electronic and printed material in Chinese to show modern techniques in rehabilitation. This has been reproduced by the thousands and distributed to professors and doctors in hospitals and universities. They teach they colleagues who in turn train their professional therapists.

As a result of this, I have been to a lot more hospitals than a normal person would care to visit. It has given me a deep admiration of the under-paid and over-worked Chinese medical professionals. They strive in unhappy circumstances. But I had rare joy when I went to the Shanghai Children's Medical Center; back in 1990 I was involved on the fringes of helping to raise money for this splendid institution. Today, it takes in doctors and nurses from all over China and trains them in modern medicine.

Hospitals in China, as with so much else about the nation, are improving. There's still room for criticism, but the advances are stupendous.

## *Emergency, Doctor*

Out on the Zhoushan Islands off the coast of Zhejiang province, I was having dinner one night with a gregarious bunch of local winery staff, fisherfolk and officials. It was a merry night for myself and a group of Hongkong-based correspondents and diplomats.

The local wine was sweet red stuff but the first dozen glasses were the worst and after that, along with a couple of cleansing ales and a few toasts of *mao tai*, the evening progressed well. There was much good fellowship, back-slapping and, at the end of the night, song as people of assorted nationalities stood around the tables and sang national folk songs. All very jolly.

The next morning, however, much of the joviality had worn off and as the bus lurched over hills and around sharp bends, I was feeling distinctly unwell. 'Oh, my God,' I groaned.

What was wrong, one of the local escorts asked.

'I'm never going to drink again,' I vowed. 'I think I'm going to die.'
Never speak literally to a person unfamiliar with a language.

At the next town, we were filing into a hall to hear someone talk
about fishery joint ventures with Japan when a doctor, two nurses
and a couple of fellows carrying a stretcher suddenly appeared on
the scene.

What's up? I wondered. Then they came over to me, sat me down,
took my temperature, blood pressure and pulse. 'Why do you think
you are going to die?' the doctor asked, through an interpreter.

It took a bit of explaining until I persuaded him the only medicine
I needed was a cold can of Qingdao beer.

## HYGIENE

Standards of hygiene in China are different from those in the West.
The contrast between the gleaming, spick public areas of Japan, the
startling cleanliness of Tokyo restaurants and the ingrained filth and
dirt of China is striking.

Why? It's hard to explain. Basically, a Chinese looks after himself
and his family. Clean your house thoroughly and sweep the dirt out
onto the street. Once there, it's not your concern. Why bother?

Newcomers eating in a local restaurant can be disconcerted by a
diner at the next table noisily hawking and spitting on the floor. There's
not much you can do about it except pray that his aim is good. In restaurants, if you are nervous about the state of the chopsticks, take a paper
napkin and wash the eating implements and your bowl with hot tea.

## WATER

Better safe than sorry. In every hotel and guest house in China, room
staff will bring in a large vacuum flask of boiling water as soon as you
check in. Use this. Unless you want to spend a good part of your time
in China on the toilet, do not drink tap water.

If your water supply runs out, just take the flask to the desk on the
floor of your hotel and give it to the girl or boy on duty. They'll fill

it up for you. Chinese don't drink tap water and this is a wise piece of advice to follow.

## XINHUA

In every town in China, usually on the main street, there is a Xinhua Foreign Language Bookshop. In bigger cities, these are large and impressive places with an astonishing range of titles in English, German, French, Arabic and many other languages. Most of these books are of such approved 'progressive' authors as Sinclair Lewis, Charles Dickens or John Steinbeck. They are cheap, the quality of printing and binding is excellent and they make impressive presents for young nieces and nephews who need to study good works.

The bookshops also have an incredible array of how-to and technical books. Changsha, capital of Hunan province, is one of the great printing centres on earth and the variety of titles you can see at their annual book fair is truly astonishing.

Xinhua shops (run by the government's international news agency cum propaganda arm) also run to a good selection of maps, posters exhorting you to have one baby and to support the armed forces and to very good inexpensive stationery. Usually close by there is a shop that sells old stamps and in smaller towns where foreigners are not so common, you can snap up some great collector's pieces.

## QUESTIONS

When it comes to sex and morals, Chinese are surprisingly coy by Western standards. The simplest questions like 'Do you have a boyfriend?' will result in furious blushes and protestations. (Official sanctions advise girls to wait until they are 25 to be married, men to hold off tying the knot until they reach 28.)

On the other hand, Westerners will be disconcerted by Chinese bluntness on financial matters. How much do you earn? How much did your watch cost? Your camera? Does your wife work? How much does she get? How much does your home cost?

Chinese are quite happy to answer these sort of questions and expect foreigners to do the same.

My advice: Tell the truth. But explain when doing so that although your salary may be enormous when compared with theirs, you have to pay taxes, medical bills, rent or mortgage, school fees and many other expenses which in China are taken care of by the various layers of the state.

## THE SEXUAL REVOLUTION

Sex in China … you could write a book about it. Several books. Thousands of volumes. It's a big subject. Customary attitudes to sex have changed over the years. In old rural China, it was a blunt farmer's attitude. Sex was natural. You did it. In most villages, for 1,000 years, marriages were arranged and lasted for life. This was the way things were done.

Even in today's Hong Kong, there are couples in villages close to my home where the bride was escorted from one village to meet her husband-to-be for the first time on their wedding day. Six decades later, such marriages still flourish. It was the rural norm.

City life has always been faster. In the early days of the revolution, the ardent young socialists who wanted to overturn the established order had a similar disdain for existing social mores. Free love blossomed, briefly. Then they gained power and became as bourgeoisie in the bedroom as any other middleclass politicians. (Well, there were exceptions and Chairman Mao's vigorous exploits until well into his 70s have been well documented.)

Of course, the birds and the bees are universal and romance, love and sex always existed, although officially frowned upon. But it's true to say that until about 1990, China was largely puritanical.

Goodbye to all that. TV, money, fashion and, above all, the feeling among young people that life holds more than perpetual revolution means an enthusiastic breaking of old bondage. Sexual customs are not as relaxed as in the West, but it's my impression that the old lore has gone forever, that love and lust are on the rise.

Certainly, commercial sex is open and blatant. Stroll down any major street and a young lady is likely to approach, smile widely and ask if you want a friend. It seems universal and foreigners who indulge these days do not seem to run into trouble, apart from the usual medical, social and financial penalties that accompany prostitution anywhere else.

In 5-star hotels and bars throughout the country, I have been approached by girls and women. "No thanks," I say, with a smile. Many of the women you encounter in bars seem pleasant as well as pretty. It's just not my scene.

## Gay Life

Just as sex as come bursting into the open, so has gay identity for the first time begun to more discretely come out of the closet. Once again, it's important to realise that the Chinese – though they may protest this – are human and like every other national or ethnic group have their own foibles and customs. Hypocrisy is well developed, as it is in other societies. For a long time in modern China, the existence of homosexuality was totally denied. It was "not Chinese." However, doctors and academics who have studied the subject say that about the same percentage of people in China tend towards homosexuality as anywhere else.

Certainly, Chinese gays are now leading open lives, although acceptance is nowhere near the levels of tolerance in the West. Discrete and unprovocative behaviour seems not to cause any trouble. There doesn't appear to be systematic gay bashing, either by the authorities or the public, although public opinion polls in reasonably socially advanced places like Hong Kong still show discrimination against homosexuals. I suppose you'd find exactly similar opinions in Manchester or Dallas. Incidentally, on a recent visit to Shanghai, I discovered the leading gay bar in town is a very popular joint named – Kevin's. Thanks a lot, fellows. Once again, it's not my scene.

## *Self Denial*

In 1969 I was working for a Hong Kong paper when a crusty old billionaire politician (they were appointed by the British in those days, without any of the pesky inconvenience of being elected) made an astounding statement. This elderly Northern Chinese proclaimed in outrage that sex, gambling and drinking were all Western sins and not part of Chinese custom.

I sent a cameraman to follow this cynical old clown. We published pictures of him – aged 72 – with his 26-year-old mistress and also pictures of him leading his race horse into the winning stall. If Chinese don't drink, gamble or have sex, how come there are 1.2 billion of them, how come more money is bet on horses any Saturday in Hong Kong than in all of Britain in Ascot Week and how come seven million Hong Kongers enthusiastically gurgle more 3-star cognac every year than 55 million Frenchmen?

Just goes to show there are silly old fools everywhere.

## *LANGUAGE*

It's impossible to learn to speak passable Chinese in a few hours. But you can learn a few simple phrases and the efforts you make to speak Chinese will be greatly appreciated. It will also provide a few laughs, for you and the people you attempt to address. China is a land of many tongues. The Chinese language itself is as diverse as the country. Dialects abound. The Cantonese speaker in the south cannot speak to the Northerner talking in Mandarin.

Since 1949, the regime has made great efforts to unify the country by making Putonghua (literally, Ordinary Language) official. It is taught in every school in the land and no matter what language or dialect children speak at home, they learn standard Chinese at school. This is based on the language of Beijing and the north.

The minorities have their own languages which are preserved carefully. But everyone—Tibetan, Mongol, Manchu, Zhuang, Uygur, Yi, Miao, Dong and all Han Chinese—go to school in the Ordinary Language.

*A newsstand decked with the latest local and international magazines never fails to draw eager browsers.*

For the first time in history, Chinese from every province can now speak to each other. In the past, and until now in many Overseas Chinese communities, even well-educated professionals had to write in characters to make themselves understood by people speaking another dialect.

On the other hand, Chinese is a very simple language. It stands to reason. After all, tens of millions of children aged three or four years old can babble away in Putonghua or other dialects and if they can do it, surely you can, can't you?

The quick answer (for short-time tourists) is: No, you can't.

The first thing to remember is that Chinese is a tonal language. One sound, pronounced in various tones, can have many different meanings. Take the sound 'Ma'. It can mean 'mother'. Said with a different inflexion, it can mean 'horse'. Hence the baffling and hysterical stories of foreigners trying to ask someone 'How is your mother?' and, instead, saying to a city dweller who lives in a tiny 6th floor apartment, 'Have you fed your horse?' Ma can also mean hemp, numb or to scold. Mandarin has four tones. So a sound like Gu (pronounced Chu) can tell you 'to go', can mean 'a region', could be exhorting you to 'work hard' or may be referring to a musical score. Take your pick. And good luck.

You think that's difficult? Well, down south in Guangdong, Cantonese has a tongue-twisting nine different tones. Think of the embarrassing situations you can easily babble your way into trying to express yourself in that dialect.

## *Pinyin*

There are about 5,000 characters used commonly on a daily basis. There are an estimated total of 230,000 written characters and compounds, many of them used in technical, scientific or medical terms; no one person can possibly know them all. But just consider the 5,000 common characters. There are only about 400 syllables which the human voice can make to express these 5,000 ideas. So the same sound, in different tones, is used. High tone, low tone, rising tone, falling tone ... the way you say a sound determines what it means. A professor at the Beijing Number Two Foreign Language Institute once told me that one sound could be used for 100 various written characters.

In an attempt to try to translate the characters and tones into understandable Latin characters, scholars have for centuries been battling with the baffling tones. There have been many attempts. Most have now been scrapped in favour of the universal Latinisation system known as *pinyin*.

This seeks to translate as nearly and neatly as possible the way Putonghua is spoken into Latin words. It is heavily burdened by legacies of the past when many words and place names were rendered in English under a system used a century and a half ago by well-meaning missionaries. Thus, familiar places like Hongkong became

Xiangkang in pinyin. Canton turns into Guangzhou. The port of Amoy reverts to its real name of Xiamen.

If you think *pinyin* has no rhyme or reason, explain to an earnest young Chinese student of English why 'koff' is spelt c-o-u-g-h.

## *Speaking*

In *pinyin*, the universal welcome is spelled *ni hao*. You pronounce this 'knee how'.

To thank a host for a dinner or a waitress for serving you a drink, you use the common expression for 'thank you', xie xie ni. This is pronounced 'shi shi nay'.

*Qing* is how you say please. Try saying 'ching' to rhyme with 'sing'.

When it's time to go, you bid people *zai jian* or goodbye. The closest you can come to writing this is dzai jee-an. But don't worry. It's a lot easier to say (once you've heard it) than it is to write.

'I'm sorry' or 'excuse me' is *duibuqi*, pronounced 'doi bu chee'.

*Pinyin* may at first look awkward and difficult to you. It's not easy. But a couple of days of listening to people speak gets you into the rhythm and sound of Chinese patter. The written system may appear clumsy and needlessly complex, but linguists and scholars spent decades perfecting it and it renders spoken Chinese as closely as possible into Latinised script.

## *Writing*

Some bemused visitor once remarked that Chinese writing looked like what snails left behind after they crawled over a flagstone. Anyone with a simple grasp of the language sees the convoluted characters as things of beauty.

Basically, the system of ideographs was based on pictures. Every idea had a picture that expressed it. Gradually, the pictures became more stylised and simplified, a process that continues today as Chinese scholars strive to make common characters easier to read and write.

Take the symbol for sunrise. It was once a complex picture of a sun with beaming rays rising over the horizon. Now, it is shown as a box with a line through the middle. It is also, incidentally, the first character for the name of Japan, Land of the Rising Sun.

The first character for China, is similarly simple. It is a box with a line through the middle, but up and down instead of side to side. This character means 'central', and is the first character of Zhong Guo or Middle Kingdom.

The commonly seen character *shan* or mountain began as a picture of a range of mountains and developed over thousands of years to the simple sign used today. Many other characters have also changed in this fashion.

When it comes to new characters for new ideas, especially in technology, the awkwardness of written Chinese becomes obvious and only experts can recognise many of the very complicated characters used in science, computers, medicine and research, which are completely unknown and virtually indecipherable to most laymen.

A tip for tourists: Buy yourself a simple book on written Chinese and try to learn two characters a day. You'll be surprised at how soon you pick up some of the basic ideograms and the history of how the written language has developed is a gripping intellectual jigsaw puzzle that can provide much enjoyment.

## *A GOOD LAUGH*

The Chinese people have a sense of humour that can sometimes be baffling to Westerners. They laugh uproariously, slapping their thighs with deep appreciation of things which would leave Europeans either unmoved, mystified or appalled. The sight of someone falling down a flight of stairs can provoke outright laughter. Often, this mirth covers embarrassment.

Having said that, laughter is universal. Go to a movie theatre and watch a Chinese comedy – Hong Kong super-star Jackie Chan is my favourite – and you raise a smile even if you can't understand the dialogue.

# Chapter Seven

# DOING BUSINESS

*Amiability begets riches.*

With an extraordinary lack of fuss and fanfare, China over the past 15 years has dramatically altered the way business is conducted. Under the direct supervision of Premier Zhu Rongji, who will go into the history books as one of the great builders of 21st century society, the sprawling, chaotic, inefficient state-owned corporations have been demolished. These were states within the nation, virtually independent baronies with their own rules. They could employ tens of thousands of people, many of them doing nothing but collecting a miserly monthly pay. Zhu broke up these appallingly ineffectual legacies of Marxist thinking, dragged them either into the marketplace as slimmed-down companies that made a profit or let them go to the wall. It was one of the most significant, and under-reported developments in post-revolutionary China. It laid the solid foundations for rapid expansion.

It was not easy. Taking the jobs of tens of millions of people is a nightmare, but at least skeletal safety nets were in place. The deep surgery that sliced into manufacturing, distribution and other basic business may have hurt the patient, but it rejuvenated China's industry.

For any newcomer starting a business or a new job in China, the obvious adage is: Take care!

As with so many other aspects of life in China, doing business has changed dramatically in the past decade. But in this case, it's a matter of the more things change, the more they remain the same. There are pitfalls of which foreigners could never be aware.

Misunderstandings are frequent because of the vast gulf in common business practices. Never forget that modern Chinese "business" is at most 20 years old; before that all commerce was clutched jealously in the prejudiced and inept hands of zealous communist officials. They were blinded by twin misconceptions. Either they suspected all foreign devils were hellbent on plundering China (often not far from the truth) or they believed truly that all the world wanted to sign sweetheart deals with the Mainland because China deserved special favours. Their grasp of the realities of business was weak, to say the least.

This confusion was often compounded by the behaviour of many Western businessmen, who seemed to the Chinese either demented or impossibly optimistic. As the bamboo doors creaked open in the early 1980s, there was a frenzied rush in China. It was like the last days of the Klondike; everyone wanted to stake a claim before the gold ran out. It was a replay of Western merchants' attitude of a century earlier when the cry of 'oil for the lamps of China' summed up the outlook of foreign traders. That gigantic market was a mouthwatering temptation. Well, in the 19th century, most Chinese didn't have lamps and couldn't afford oil. In the late 20th century rush, Western firms blinded by the sheer magical figure of 1.2 billion potential customers paid little heed to economic reality. They wanted to put colour TVs in every Chinese home, cars in every non-existent garage and to clad the lithe thighs of a hundred million teenage girls in blue jeans. Few seemed to realise that the average pay in 1980 was about 68 RMB (or US$8) a month. In they blundered, chequebooks waving, eager to do deals, sign contracts; little wonder there was mutual astonishment when the eager go-getters came face to face with their inexperienced counterparts. Credit? What's that? Oh, you give me machinery and I pay you later. Thank you very much. Oh, you want me to pay you money? So sorry, no money. It seems incredible now, but that's how many deals were done.

Gradually, the frenetic pace slowed down. Westerners began to realise that doing business in China required investments in time, not only money. Many of the commercial nuggets seized so easily by eager newcomers turned out to be fools' gold. Contracts were signed with keen state entrepreneurs who had no clue about what they were doing, nor the authority to do it. Corruption, the curse of China in earlier times, swiftly made a revival.

With no rule books and few guidelines, the officials who had suddenly been thrust into the unaccustomed role of commercial trader inevitably made gross mistakes. Westerners who thought everyone played by their well-known rules were aghast; was every Chinese dishonest? No. They were merely playing the game using different rules.

## WHO'S TO BLAME?

In a normal society, when a business deal turns sour, the matter is dealt with by the law. One partner sues another and a judge decides who is right and who is wrong. If it's a criminal case, a report is made to police and if there is sufficient evidence, the wrongdoer is charged and appears before a court which weighs the evidence and makes a decision.

Not in China. The country has a lot of laws and rules and regulations, most of which seem to be ignored when it suits the powerful. Foreign businessmen, particularly Overseas Chinese, are held accountable for the firms they represent. At one period in 1998, there were at least 12 Hongkong businessmen held in various places of detention or confinement – simply because their firms owed money. In none of these cases was there any suggestion that the people being held prisoner had done anything wrong. No, their firms owed money.

## *CORRUPTION*

The weather in 1997 was vile. As the British prepared to leave Hongkong, the heavens opened. It rained solidly for months, swamping the former colony and much of southern China. Rivers swept over their banks. Some people said the heavens were crying to see the Union Jack come down over The Peak. Others said it was a joyous indication that the city-state, now embraced in the warm clutches of the glorious Motherland, would be blessed by unprecedented prosperity; in Cantonese, the word *shui* (water) can be used for 'money'.

The next year, it was worse. This time, it was north and central China that recorded heaviest rains in history. The huge levees that protected the agricultural heartland of China along the Heung He (Yellow River) and the Yangtze, as well as other great waterways in Manchuria, were breached. Millions of soldiers rushed to defend the soil, slogging through rising mud to desperately heap sandbags on crumbling dykes.

Prime Minister Zhu Rongji went to inspect the threatened banks. He found out that iron and other materials that were supposed to have been used in building the dykes had never been purchased. Instead, the money had drained away into the pockets of grafting officials and business cronies. Totally furious at the spectre of China's wealthiest farmland being ruined because of corruption, Zhu ordered an immediate investigation.

In every dynasty for 20 centuries, graft has been a major problem. The present regime is determined utterly if not to eradicate graft completely, at least to wipe out the worst excesses, and to wipe out the guilty. Anti-corruption forces operate at every level, from city police forces through specialised provincial bureaus to the national government. These ardent battlers against corruption have reaped a noisome crop; although statistics are difficult to find, at least 10,000 officials at various levels have been charged and taken to court in recent years. Hundreds have been executed for economic crimes against the state. These are no mere clerks. The roll of dishonour goes to the very top of the party hierarchy; the mayor of Beijing was disgraced and convicted along with senior officials from almost every ministry of state and provincial planners by the score.

Foreigners doing business in China used to complain that they had to pay bribes or were locked out of deals. There is a temptation to go along with the flow and pay kickbacks. Take my advice; don't do it. Sooner rather than later foreigners who pay bribes are going to find themselves in the dock along with their co-conspirators. They should not expect any more mercy from the rigorous Chinese courts than local crooks get, and that's precious little.

## THE THREE GOLDEN RULES
A wise old hand once gave me his three prime rules for doing business in China.

1. Be Patient
2. Be Patient
3. Be Patient.

"Stick to these rules and you can't go far wrong," he advised.

## FROM REVOLUTION TO COUNTING PROFITS
"Revolution grows out of the barrel of a gun." So wrote Chairman Mao Zedong and it was a lesson he practised all his long life. From the formation of the first Jiangxi Soviet in the 1920s through the appalling Cultural Revolution he launched on the Chinese people in 1966 right until his death in 1976, the Great Helmsman was an advocate of violent, wrenching change.

Out of the turmoil that is customary for a change of leadership in Beijing came the diminutive powerhouse Deng Xiaoping. He saw things differently. "To grow rich is glorious," he proclaimed. After

*How about a cool pair of shades for you? Thanks to Deng Xiaoping's new economic policies, the entrepreneurial spirit is well and alive today in China.*

three decades of uncertainty and political frenzy, after the ceaseless campaigns for class purity and revenge against the landlords and enforced poverty for all (except party leaders and their privileged offspring, the so-called princelings) the people heard him.

Since he laid down the new economic policies in 1978, China has changed more significantly, more profoundly, than in the entire broad and rich sweep of her 5,000-year history. The nation has been transformed. It was a comparatively simple tactic; Deng Xiaoping first relaxed the strict rules governing agriculture, permitting the artificial commune system to collapse and allowing 800 million peasants to grow what they wanted and to sell it on the open market. The effect of this economic freedom was startling and dramatic. Agricultural output doubled in five years. Farmers became rich, leading the vanguard of Deng's monetary revolution.

Reassured by the realistic, sound new policies, a tidal wave of investment flowed into China. First it came over the southern border from the incredibly wealthy colonial enclave of Hongkong. Feverishly, the billionaires from the British-ruled territory poured money into hotels, conference centres and tourism infrastructure. Entire factories were uprooted from the high-rent territory and transported across the border to take advantage of cheap land and an inexhaustible supply of eager labour. As China became rich, the same hugely-wealthy entrepreneurs built palaces of shopping centres for them to get rid of that fast-growing disposable income.

Hard on the heels of the speedy Hongkongers came other Overseas Chinese with big bank accounts and a renewed faith in the revival of the ancestral motherland. From Singapore and Thailand, from Malaysia and Indonesia and the Philippines, ethnic Chinese ploughed vast cash investments back into the newly fertile economic soil.

First it was to the southern provinces, to Guangdong, Fujian and Guangxi from whence their ancestors had sailed to settle Nan Yang, the South Seas. Then the investments started flowing to the capital, to Shanghai and to other coastal cities. Eventually, that tide of investment cash lapped into the interior.

Coupled with renewed natural vigour of the Chinese people, freed from the shackles of Stalinist dogma, China awoke.

## *THE CHINESE MANNER*

But there are still major, significant differences in striking a deal in China than anywhere else. The country still does business in a very Chinese manner. You had better swiftly get accustomed to this and change your ways; China is not about to change for you.

Ask why something which elsewhere on the planet is simple and yet is extremely complex in China – like trying to find out who is in charge at a joint venture factory – and the answer is bland. "That is our procedure," comes the answer. Don't bother trying to argue. You will not succeed, especially if you are a foreigner. Despite the vast changes of recent years, China does things its own way. If you want to succeed in China, you must bow with the wind, like the bamboo. Submit to the inevitable. Do otherwise and you get ulcers and the result will be the same.

### *'Have a Rest'*

I used to catch an aircraft in Hongkong for the 20-minute hop up the Pearl River Delta to the old trading port of Guangzhou. Immigration and customs were swift and pleasant. Stroll out of the new terminal and there was the young official from the Foreign Affairs Office. He was polite, friendly, knowledgeable and had my best interests at heart.

His job was to escort me to my hotel. Once there and checked in, he would shake my hand and leave. What about the interview with the Mayor or the factory manager I was supposed to see?

Oh, no, it was explained. I had come all the way from Hongkong. I had to have a rest. But, I didn't want to rest, I would protest. I wanted to work. He would give me a patient smile. Work later. Rest first.

So this was the normal welcome to China, wasting half a valuable day.

Well, things have changed. Today, there's a much more brisk attitude as the new generation take over. Meetings are conducted much faster, much more efficiently, as Chinese commercial practices begin to conform to those of the rest of the world. But there remains a Chinese friendliness and courtesy, which is still accompanied by hidden suspicion that the foreigner must only be there to make a profit out of China. Well, of course he is. That's what business is about.

Basically, businessmen will find the new breed of businessmen are switched-on entrepreneurs. They don't have time to waste, like their predecessors to whom time was not money; they had plenty of the first and no idea about the second.

In the crumbling state-run enterprises, however, the former slack habits and overmanning are still alive and well. It's hard to know what the solution will be. If all unprofitable or inefficient public businesses were shut down, as many should be on strictly cost-effectiveness grounds, then tens of millions of people would be thrown out of work. Despite the explosive growth, there are not enough alternative jobs.

## FOOTING THE BILL

There used to be an irony confronting every foreigner to China. On the one hand, communist propaganda held capitalism oppressed the workers. On the other, every single foreigner, particularly Western-ers, who went to China was thought to be sufficiently wealthy to pay huge bills for everyone. This was an accepted fact of life. All Westerners were rich. If they were not personally rolling in dollars, francs or marks, then their companies have unlimited wealth and the visitor to China has a personal spending budget and expense account that allows him to spend like a drunken sailor. Try to explain that you cannot afford to foot the bill for lunch in an expensive five-star hotel – with prices higher than Maxim's in Paris – and your Chinese friends will smile knowingly. All foreigners are rich. Everyone knows that.

This was the view up until the early '90s. Now the roundabout has made a few circles and sometimes the business visitor finds the Chinese businesses and government agencies with whom he is negotiating are eager not only to pay for lunch but also pick up hotel and travel bills, if it helps to secure a contract.

It's been a swift adaptation. In past years, before setting off on a business trip to China, you had to know precisely what you were going to be paying for. The fax machine has made a big difference here. If you are going to visit a factory in, for instance, Wuhan, people there will make the arrangements. Before you go, check with them the cost of a car from the airport, hotel rates, location of the factory and how you get there and ask what other costs may be involved. In the not-so-distant past, arrangements for the visiting barbarian were often made – without consultation – in accordance with the notion that the visitor had as much disposable cash as a Texan oil billionaire. Cost was not counted by those making the arrangements; they weren't paying so why not get the best? This sometimes led to lavish receptions and travel in a fleet of costly limousines, with the shaken visitor at the end of the trip being handed a vast bill.

In most parts of China, growing sophistication has seen an end to all that. Today, visiting executives are treated more reasonably. As in every other area, China has learned very quickly. The welcome and friendly greeting is still there, but so constant has been the flood of foreign businessmen seeking to open trade with China that foreigners are no longer strangers in a strange land. They are familiar, and the business climate in which they find themselves has adopted a semblance to the rest of the world.

This welcome change brings China more into line with the rest of the world. But there is still the idea that foreigners are all rich – and in comparison with most Chinese, of course, they are. So to avoid surprise, embarrassment and a massive bill, check by fax exactly how much essentials will cost.

## *A PIECE OF THE PIE*

A thick strand of greed runs through the weave of China's history. The most austere mandarin in many dynasties was expected to add to his miserly salary by squeezing those he ruled. Most did so with grasping enthusiasm.

The Kuomintang was defeated largely because its officials and generals were inextricably up to their armpits in graft. The sober and strict functionaries who marched into government offices in 1949 to run the New China were dedicated believers in serving the people. Their outlooks were rather like monks who had taken a vow of poverty. But as the revolutionary fervour faded, the bad old habits of the ages came back. And when the invigorating economic policies of Deng Xiaoping made farmers and entrepreneurs millionaires overnight, many cadres were only too eager to leap in to clutch their share of the new riches.

The result was conspicuous corruption on a grand scale. Officials asked themselves why they should miss out on a fair slice of the pie? No reason, they felt. So the problem rampaged out of control like a cancer, especially when provincial and city government agencies got into business for themselves. As well as administering towns and cities, they were running construction companies, hotels, supply firms and transport organisations. The opportunities for easy money were abundant; many cadres plunged into the mire like pigs into a watering hole. One problem was a total lack of experience. Accustomed to living on tiny state salaries with fringe benefits coming from the bureaucracy, most simply could not see any difference between public ownership and private benefit. Well, after all, they were representatives of the people, weren't they?

Lavish dinner banquets costing more than an entire village could earn in a year became commonplace, often hosted by cadres who work units owned the hotel where the feasts were thrown. *Mao tai* and wine flowed freely with costly delicacies on the menu. Life was fine for those with a place at the trough, but muttered discontent began to come from the public. Even the muzzled local press began to snipe salaciously about the prodigal expense and newspapers outside China held up the extravagant lifestyle as an obvious example of unfairness.

Money from public enterprises that should have gone into official coffers was wasted, misspent because of inexperience or simply stolen. Eventually, the central government (whose senior officials do not themselves mind being supported like emperors) clamped

157

down. In 1992 and again in 1995 there were sweeping anti-corruption campaigns. Some of the more obviously thieving officials were swiftly found guilty and publicly executed. Others, right up to the level of provincial governors, went to jail for lengthy terms. Strict guidelines were laid down on when dinner parties could be thrown, how much they could cost and even the number and type of dishes that could be ordered.

For foreign businessmen, this helped clarify doing business in China. No more did they have to sit through long and expensive official banquets, then be expected to respond by ordering a competitively-priced feast.

Chinese hospitality, in all its warmth, still exists, but the ridiculous extravagance of earlier years in the first blush of wealth has now given way to more sober and serious relations.

## DOUBLE STANDARDS

China's rulers get enraged – and with good reason – with the double standards arguments of outsiders. Take the issue of video piracy and invasion of intellectual copyright, something United States trade negotiators have used for several years to belabour Beijing. Okay, fair enough, it's a problem. In a thousand factories, the new generation of canny free enterprise industrialists are making products that get constantly more sophisticated. In doing so, they fling down an export challenge to global competitors. The concept that a piece of computer software or a movie video or a taped song should not be instantly copied and sold is an exotic novelty to China's new generation of manufacturers? Are you joking? Pay some writer or programmer or singer for copying his work? No way. So factory bosses rip-off artists and investors. The foreign firms which have the international rights to such products are, very understandably, outraged. They put pressure on their governments which in turn demand that Beijing instantly halts all such activities.

The Chinese government has passed laws and imposed regulations that make such piracy of ideas a crime. It has trained and deployed many thousands of customs and trade officials to find such factories, seize the goods and destroy them and jail the owners and dealers. Yet such are the huge profits, the illegal use of foreign material continues. China tries to play by Western rules because to do otherwise could see trade doors slammed shut; remember the country was refused entry to the World Trade Organisation largely because of this issue.

What angers China is the government is held to blame for individual acts. Some Americans point the finger at the Central Government and make meaningless threats. "If China does not stop exporting pirated goods, America will impose trade bans." The implication is the Chinese government is directly involved in making or encouraging fake goods, stealing the intellectual copyright of others. This is simply untrue. Beijing and the provincial governments have taken serious steps to wipe out pirates. They have received no recognition for so doing.

There is an odious comparison. The United States has for many years been fighting alongside other governments to stem the flow of narcotics into America. All such efforts have been fruitless; the inner city ghettoes and swank nightclubs of the United States remain awash with drugs. So is it fair to say that because cocaine and heroin and marijuana are freely available – albeit illegal – in New York that the government and administration in Washington is engaged in drugs trafficking? Of course not, it's ridiculous as well as grossly offensive. Yet this is the same kind of reasoning that many Western trade negotiators use in accusing China of not stamping out copyright criminals. No wonder the Beijing leadership gets upset.

## CHECK THE CHEQUE

Still, the first-time visitor can be in for a nasty shock unless he enquires exactly what he will be paying for on a business trip.

In the airport arrival hall, you will almost certainly be met by someone from the enterprise with whom you have been corresponding. Hands will be shaken, greetings extended, cards exchanged and the new arrival will be ushered into a luxury car (probably Japanese) for the trip to the city centre where arrangements have been made to lodge you in the finest (foreign joint venture) hotel.

All well and good. What you have not been told, and what you must check before you arrive, is that you are being charged for every last cent. The car is on your bill, sometimes costing as much as it would in New York. It may sit in the shade with the driver snoozing all day long. Even if he never puts the key in the ignition, it's going to cost the same. The car has been hired (it may belong to your host's company, anyway, but you will still pay) not for your convenience but for that of your putative partners. These days, with free enterprise as well as publicly-owned taxis ubiquitous, it's usual to grab a cab.

A decade ago, in the era of extravagance, the people you had travelled to visit may well have checked into the same hotel as you; the reason they give is that they are there to 'assist' you. You would find yourself footing the bill, even if you seldom saw them. This sort of behaviour used to infuriate many foreign businessmen who raged when they got an outlandish bill. They thought they were being treated like honoured guests only to find when it was time to book out that they were charged for every last item ordered by their 'hosts'.

The message that Westerners are not all rich and cannot all afford to support huge teams of hangers-on while trying to fix a workable deal has now penetrated Chinese bureaucracy.

But to be on the safe side, always IMMEDIATELY on arrival ask what you are paying for. Is the car on your bill? If you don't want it, say so. Who is your escort officer? Are you being charged for his time by his department? How much? What exactly are his duties? If you are doing business in a city centre and do not want a car, say so. Taxis in many cities are now reliable and cheap. But always find out – preferably before you go to China – precisely what it will cost you.

Don't be a cheapskate. Be prepared to spend for a banquet and for a similar level of entertainment of contacts as you would in any other country. But do not let yourself be taken for a sucker. Be exactly as generous as you would in any other society where you are doing business.

## *ORIENTAL MAÑANA*

To the go-go Western executive and entrepreneur who wants to get things done quickly, working in China can be a frustrating experience.

The motto is similar to the old army adage: Hurry up and wait. Until 1986, the after-lunch snooze was a standard feature of Chinese business life. Most offices had cots on which civil servants could sprawl for two or three hours to regain their strength after an exhaustive morning of reading *People's Daily*, drinking tea and making a few phone calls.

The deep sleep lasted at least two hours and could easily, in the sultry summer months when the deep, humid heat settled on the cities, extend generously past this. Rousing reluctantly from this badly needed siesta, the cadre would stretch, go to the toilet, have some more tea and ponder the possibilities of dinner.

This sedate pace of life was shattered rudely in 1986 when that bustling octogenarian Deng Xiaoping declared the afternoon siesta outmoded in the era of faxes, satellites and China rushing towards modernisation. There was much muttering among the paper shufflers of the vastly overstaffed bureaucracy. No sleep in the afternoon? Impossible!

Even today, a deep and impenetrable hush settles over many a government office from noon until mid-afternoon. First it's a hurried lunch in canteen or noodle stall. Then it's back to work for a sleep. Officially, government offices and most companies work an 8 a.m. to 5 p.m., six-day week.

Things are not as bad as a few years ago when a post-prandial snooze was almost compulsory. But if you should arrive for a mid-afternoon appointment and find the cadre you are supposed to meet rubbing sleep out of his eyes, don't be surprised.

## *GETTING RICH*

By some estimates there are now a million RMB millionaires in China. Making those fortunes did not come easy. First, the Chinese people had to rediscover their ancestral work ethic, something that had been beaten out of them by four decades of stifling socialist policies.

As the new Deng era dawned, one of the great mysteries of the east is why Chinese societies outside China were invariably so vastly efficient, successful and profitable while inside the People's Republic, the giant slumbered slothfully on.

There were many theories.

Look at Singapore where Overseas Chinese have helped to create a gleaming financial city-state. Observe Taiwan, penniless in 1949, where the standard of living now rushes towards that of Japan. Cast a fearful eye at Hongkong where six million workaholic Cantonese have made toil and conspicuous consumption the popular state religion. Chinese dominate the commercial life of Thailand, the Philippines, Malaysia and Indonesia. They are heading the same way in California, Australia and British Columbia.

So what's wrong with the Chinese who stay home? Nothing. It's the system. The past four decades have crushed the initiative and enterprise out of the entrepreneurial nation. Under communism, if you were wise, you kept your head down and were as inconspicuous as possible among the other billion fellow citizens of the New China.

You didn't make waves. And you certainly didn't try to make money.

With the new reforms of 1978, things changed suddenly. The shackles of outmoded Maoist theory were broken. People could work for themselves.

The Chinese urban middle class reacted hesitantly at first. They had heard many glowing promises in the past of economic reform, only to have them nipped swiftly in the bud. But this time, things were different. Comrade Deng meant what he said. Slowly at first, then with swiftly gathering impetus, the Chinese people hurled themselves into business.

## THE IRON RICEBOWL

Enshrined in modern Chinese life as deeply as a state religion is the concept of the iron ricebowl. Put simply, this means a commitment by the state to provide a job for life. The pay is not good, the position may be humble, the task may be boring – but come hell or high water the system means that you've got a guaranteed job until the Yangtze runs dry.

Well, the river has dried up, to the astonishment and consternation of millions. State economic planners ushering in the open market system smashed the iron ricebowl. Millions of make-work jobs in inefficient and vastly overmanned state enterprises were abolished. It was a painful, but necessary, surgery. It was essential if China was to adapt and prosper.

The guaranteed job-for-life system under which everyone was paid about the same – manager or toilet cleaner, toiler or idler – simply didn't work. A generation of frustrated foreign businessmen discovered the system had in-built faults that invariably result in lost production, delays, breakdown of equipment due to lack of routine maintenance and factories missing deadlines for orders.

For anyone who has been in a factory or workplace in the West, going into a Chinese state-run enterprise under the old structure was vastly illuminating. China's appalling productivity could be easily understood. Most factories had scores of useless mouths with a half-

163

dozen slackers assigned to a job which could be handled easily by one efficient worker.

In a steel factory in Guangdong a few years ago, I was being shown around by some senior cadres. We walked through the foundry and scores of 'workers' were loafing around the plant. Those who were not sitting around reading newspapers, sipping tea or chatting with friends had spread newspapers on benches or floors and were sleeping the just slumber of the exhausted. After all, they had turned up to work, hadn't they? What more was expected of them? Not a great deal. In another society, such on-the-job laziness would have meant dismissal. Not in revolutionary China. The workers took no notice at all of the cadres, who in America or Europe would have been the equivalent of members of the board and chief executive officers of the company. They knew they could not be sacked.

## *Breaking the Ricebowl*

Seeking greater efficiency, trying to boost the wealth of the country, the new policies introduced in 1978 called for a revitalisation of industry. The old slack habits of the Maoist past could not be tolerated in modern plants, especially when foreign investors were asked to pour in millions of dollars.

As new management techniques – a fair day's work for a fair day's pay – were introduced, the most dishonest, idle and lazy of workers were sacked. This came as an enormous shock to a workforce which for 30 years had come to think of going to work as an opportunity to relax.

The iron ricebowl system had inherent faults. Why should Comrade Wong work arduously and conscientiously if Comrade Chan spent the day reading the *People's Daily* and Comrade Li played cards and Comrade Tsai crawled into a corner and dozed? All got exactly the same pay and privileges. Each of them had a tiny apartment that was virtually rent-free, enjoyed the same subsidised food and got the same miserable pay. So why should one person work while a dozen did as little as possible?

All this ended when the responsibility system was introduced, although it took 15 years for the new work disciplines to seep through the ranks. Then diligent Wong got promoted and earned more pay, Chan got paid on piece work only for what he produced and Li was criticised by other members of the workforce because his slackness was affecting overall productivity and eroding the value of bonuses paid for production. Comrade Tsai was warned to work or be sacked. The results were astonishing. In factories where workers were paid on piece rates or where staff enjoyed profit-sharing bonuses, production immediately soared.

## *QUALITY*

In its headlong rush towards industrialisation, Chinese industry has made many basic mistakes. These are admitted by central government planners who frankly confess the country was overwhelmed by the pace of development.

The basis of many complaints by foreigners doing business in China is the lack of quality control. They complain that the attitude 'near enough is good enough' is widespread throughout the country. But goods produced using this work philosophy are certainly not good enough for most end-users.

Examples abound. A hopeful American who signed a multi-million dollar contract for rubber surgical gloves went broke because the material had microscopic holes that would allow the deadly AIDS virus to penetrate the gloves. His Western customers refused to accept them.

When an American automotive company established a joint venture with China to produce the Beijing Jeep, every single part produced by local plants had a fault. The American on-site manager complained. To no avail. Then he took the unprecedented step of writing a personal letter of complaint to the then party boss, Zhao Ziyang.

He explained the situation, described in detail how his Chinese joint venture partners had broken promise after promise and said that if things were not made good promptly, he was going to pack up and American Motors would simply cut their losses and pull out of China – forever. Results came as swift as a summer lightning blast. One of the nation's top economists (a can-do bustler named Zhu Rongji, now prime minister) was sent to sort things out. The money owed to the Americans flowed in, the plant was saved.

The moral of this story is simple; if you are in a deal and it is going sour, do not grimly hold on and keep losing money. State your cases plainly to the most senior official. Then, go to the press, both local papers and international publications that circulate in China. Call press conferences in the city where your factory is sited, and in Beijing and Hongkong. If the worst comes, cut your losses and pull out. In the post-1989 climate, with China desperate to attract and retain foreign investment, tough talking works wonders.

Do not allow yourself to be strung along by lying, incompetent and dishonest cadres. Be firm. Stand fast. Insist they meet their end of the agreements. And if they don't, scream loudly to the press.

The same thing happened to McDonald's, whose Beijing outlet was said to be the biggest dispenser of burgers – at a vast cost on a Chinese budget – in the world. They had negotiated a steep but agreeable rent for a set period, then were suddenly given orders to move out. It turned out another agreement had been subsequently reached with a Hongkong business group to rip down the premises and develop a skyscraper (incidently, totally against city building regulations.)

Instead of Ronald McDonald clowning about, the company howled foul play. They protested to Chinese officials and the world press. This was a stab in the back, a betrayal, the breaking of an agreement. Beijing authorities were astonished; how could a company publicly accuse the authorities of bad faith just because they had a better deal. Didn't these foreigners realise they had to do as they were told?

No, McDonald's didn't realise it and refused to accept it. The national government was startled. What was going on? An investigation started. A deputy mayor of Beijing was found shot dead, a suicide. The mayor was deposed. A total of 18 senior officials and party leaders were charged and disgraced.

Do not be bullied. Do not be robbed. If you are treated wrongly by Chinese officials, complain to the highest in the land, and above all, to the local and international press. If they hear your cries, the national leadership is almost certain to order an inquiry, if only to shut you up.

## DISPUTES

In a large industrial undertaking anywhere, there are likely to be disagreements between partners. In a country long addicted to strict Marxist theories, short of foreign currency and believing that the world owes it a living, this is particularly so. When the foreign partner is a hard-headed, tough, shrewd capitalist who refuses to bow to blackmail and threats, such disputes are likely to be spectacular. Take the case mentioned above of Beijing Jeeps and American Motor's Don St. Pierre.

Because of shoddy workmanship of parts and lacklustre management, not to mention labour idleness, this man's promising licensing venture came perilously close to disaster in 1986. The Chinese had no money during one of their periodic economic slow-downs. They refused to pay for the American kits needed to assemble the vehicles.

Infuriated by constant delays and arguments, the forthright Canadian had a personal letter delivered to then premier Zhao Ziyang. If the cash was not forthcoming, the Yanks would go home, he said. As well as taking the dispute to the top ranks of the Chinese leadership, he also took it to the press. Hurriedly, a senior negotiator stepped in and after a week of tough negotiations the Chinese paid up. The project was saved and is now a success.

The result of the face-to-face confrontation was surprising. Suddenly American Motors began to get full cooperation.

The lesson is obvious, say veterans of China's growing business scene. Foreigners should be as cooperative as possible but when a situation gets to crisis point, it should be made absolutely plain that things are so unsatisfactory that it is time to pack bags and head home – and that the situation will hit the headlines in the international press.

## A BILLION CONSUMERS

When ping-pong diplomacy swept aside the Bamboo Curtain in the early 1970s, international businessmen poised ready to swoop on what they saw as the greatest commercial prize in history. In front of them, hungry for Western consumer goods, were a billion potential buyers. They saw a bonanza.

Trouble was, as many multinational executives and ambitious entrepreneurs were soon to discover, that enormous marketplace was populated by paupers. The five million striving capitalists in Hongkong had more money to spend than the vastly numerous compatriots over the Shenzhen River.

Many of those who dived so eagerly into the frothy waters of the newly opened Chinese market emerged sodden and sad.

In the treaty port era, the slogan that guided businessmen was 'oil for the lamps of China'. If the Western oil companies could corner the market and provide the kerosene to provide light in millions of Chinese homes, it would add up to big profits. The same sort of philosophy guides many modern-day businessmen. If every Chinese could just be persuaded to buy a Japanese bedside clock or a pair of Italian shoes or a pair of American jeans, all would be well with the world.

They forgot that the Chinese peasant had scant few yuans with which to purchase such consumer goods. And the Chinese government was not keen to see people fritter away currency on such fripperies. No, what Beijing wanted was the West to invest in modern plants that could use Chinese materials to make goods that could then be sold to the outside world, bringing hard currency into the national coffers.

There was a fundamental difference in perspective.

## *A Different Market*

A few years ago, standing in the Corner Bar of the China Hotel just across Liu Hua Road from the Trade Fair Building in Guangzhou, I fell into conversation with two American traders.

Both men had gone to China's biggest fair to sell, not buy. What they were selling and the success they had illustrates how China is a very different market to the rest of the world.

One man was selling used bus and truck tyres. Under American regulations, these had served their safe life's work and were destined for the scrap heap. By Chinese standards, the tyres had tens of thousands of miles of use left on their treads. He sold the lot to enthusiastic officials from many provinces and got agreements stretching far into the future to sell a lot more. He was jubilant.

The other man was not so merry. He had journeyed all the way to China to sell cheap but reliable and efficient electronic gadgets. You attached one of these to your garage door and put another in your car. When you drove home, the garage door automatically opened so you could drive straight inside. Terrific! Except that in 1983 there was not one single private car in China and nobody had a garage. He didn't make a single sale.

## *EXCHANGING CARDS*

If you are in China as anything except the most casual of tourists, you must carry business cards. And plenty of them. Even if you are travelling as a simple sightseer, the possession of a bundle of cards saying who you are, what you do and where you come from will come in very handy and smooth your passage. If you are there on business, cards are absolutely essential. Without your *ming pian* (business cards) you scarcely exist. If you don't have them, you certainly are not a person of any importance.

Cards should be simple. If your company or association has a logo, this likeness should be carried on the card. Then there should be your name, title and position, a mailing address and a telephone.

The card should tell what sort of work you do. For instance, if you are sales manager of a company named John Brown and Sons, the card should indicate if the company makes wine, builds ships or buries people. On the reverse side, the same information should be in

170

Chinese. Remember that a lot of the people you meet may not be able to read or speak English. Most sizeable towns in the Western world can now arrange to have bilingual cards printed. If not, you can have them done swiftly in Hongkong, Singapore, or any other Asian city you pass on route to China. If you go direct to China and find yourself without proper cards, your hotel can probably have some quickly whipped up for you. The cost will be worthwhile; proper cards will oil your introduction and help you in your initial steps to doing successful business in China.

When introduced, shake hands, say '*Ni hao*' and then hand over your card. The card should be passed over, held in both hands. You should also use both hands to accept cards offered to you; that's the polite way.

## *MAKING ACQUAINTANCES*

Basically, introductions should be made in China in the same way as in the West. Introduce most senior members first. If your company has a delegation, the highest-ranking member on your side should be introduced to the senior representative of the Chinese side.

In an informal setting, the oldest people present should be introduced first, reflecting the traditional Chinese respect for age. All else being equal, a woman should be introduced to a man first. 'Miss Wong, I would like you to meet Mr Smith.'

As anywhere on earth, younger people are likely to be far less formal than their elders. But to be on the safe side, when introduced to a Chinese of any age, shake hands, smile and say 'Hello' in Chinese or in your own language.

## *TABOOS*

Chinese men often hold hands with other men. There's nothing sexual in this, merely a show of friendship. Western men in China are sometimes embarrassed when a Chinese to whom they have just been introduced casually pats their thigh or drapes an arm over the shoulder. It's not meant to be offensive, merely a relaxed demonstration that you've been accepted as a pal.

Much greater care has to be taken between the sexes. The Western practice of kissing a newly introduced person of the other sex on the cheek is shocking to Chinese mores. Never do it. Shake hands instead in welcome or farewell.

## *NAMES*

Names are serious things to Chinese, especially the family name. It's polite to remember them. Mr Wong will be distressed if you call him Mr Lee.

The Chinese way with names is simple and logical. The family name is given first. Hence, Mao Zedong is Mr Mao. In the case of the late chairman, Zedong, the given name, means Very Clear East. The given name is the equivalent of the Western Christian or first name. Thus Chan Mei-ling is Ms Chan. (Mei-ling means Beautiful Intelligence.)

Unlike Chinese communities in the West, and in places like Sarawak or Hongkong, very few Chinese in the Mainland have adopted Western names. Those who have probably work in a Western-run hotel or some other organisation connected with tourism.

In such cases, you might come across a person with a name like Irene Wong Chan Mei-ling. This can cause confusion to a newcomer to China who wonders what on earth he is supposed to call her.

Here's the explanation; Chan Mei-ling is married to Mr Wong. She also has adopted a Western name, Irene. So she is Mrs Irene Wong. Or Ms Chan. Or Mei-ling. Or Irene.

So what do you call her if you want to be polite? Either Madam Wong or Miss Chan. In China, unlike most overseas communities, Ms Chan when she is married remains Ms Chan.

And you will normally call business contacts by their surname even if you have known them for a long time. If you stick to calling Vice-Director Li, Mr Li, you can't go wrong. Trying to use his given name, Kwok-wen, for instance, can lead to needless misunderstandings. Keep it simple.

## *COMMUNICATION*

Facsimile machines are ubiquitous in China. The reasons are simple. While it is extremely awkward and time-consuming to transmit a message in Chinese characters by telex, it is easy as pie to do so by fax. To send a telex, every ideogram in a message has to be looked up in a translation book and the appropriate number noted down. Then the message, in the form of a long string of numbers, is telexed. At the other end, the message is studied by a postal authority staff member who consults a book that lists numbers and characters. The message is then written out in Chinese characters. If you want it in English, it has to be translated.

Given the slackness and lack of any sense of emergency by most Chinese junior bureaucrats this is a system that could have been custom-designed to ensure frustration and rage. Hence the joy and delight with which the facsimile revolution has been welcomed by Chinese and foreigners alike.

The Chinese mail system is excellent. Why? This is yet another of the Great Mysteries of the Orient. Most Chinese public services are a disgraceful joke but the posts are swift, efficient and certain.

Telephones are another matter. The IDD system that now links most modern hotels to the outside world is superb. The interior telephone system is ramshackle, unreliable and tends to operate at the whim of telephonists on hotel switchboards and city exchanges.

Telephone manners take a bit of getting used to. Say you call a factory and want to be put through to the manager. The telephonist demands to know who you are and what you want. Then you get put through to some other nameless functionary. A similar telephonic interrogation is held.

Finally, you get the great man's secretary. Where do you come from? What is your name? What is your company? Why do you want to speak to Mr Wong? Does he know you? Is he expecting your call? After a grilling that makes the Grand Inquisition seem like mild,

173

child-like whimsy, Mr Wong eventually comes on the line. He is debonair, helpful, pleasant. When you get to know Mr Wong over a banquet and a couple of glasses of *mao tai*, you query him about the barriers. Why is it so difficult to get him on the phone? He professes astonishment. No such instructions have been given. Is it nosiness by impertinent staff? Is it overzealous secretaries trying to protect the boss from unwanted callers? Is it sheer stupidity? I suspect a combination of all three, plus a healthy dollop of snooping by underlings.

And remember, any telephone number in China is treated as a state secret. Obnoxious secrecy is not confined to China. I once tried to fax the manager of an Asian airline based in Hongkong. His secretary flatly and persistently refused to give me the fax number on the grounds that maybe her boss did not want to get my fax.

## *THE RECEPTION OFFICE*

They are identical all over China. The bleak layout is the same, the furniture looks as if it was mass-produced for the purpose in a factory that has not changed design since the 1940s, and after a dozen meetings in reception offices all over China, the visitor begins to swear the same tea is being poured from the same pot by an infinite variety of twin sisters.

Be it government office or manufacturing plant, the welcome for the foreigner is warm and genuine. The Reception Officer (surely, he must have some other duties in addition to welcoming guests?) shakes hands, exchanges cards and escorts you to the Reception Room. Almost invariably, this is up a flight of concrete stairs to the third or fourth floors. If there are lifts, chances are the electricity is turned off or the operator is out for lunch. Up you trudge.

Once inside, there is a familiar scene. Around all four walls are arranged low-slung, soft sofas. In front of these, arranged with the precision of a People's Army parade in the Square of Heavenly Peace on National Day, are equally low tables. The sofas are usually covered in uniform green material. The tables have glass tops with embroidered doilies underneath. The cups are traditionally handless with matching covers to keep the tea warm.

You sit. The cup is filled. You wait. Sooner rather than later, the official you have come to see arrives. You are introduced by the Reception Officer, you go through the etiquette of exchanging cards. The VIP sits on the couch, usually directly opposite the door. The visitor sits next to him, on the right. The interpreter gives a welcome speech.

## THE BRIEF INTRODUCTION

Then comes the infuriating waste of time of The Brief Introduction. This can be a lengthy ramble through history, geography, climate, agriculture, habits and other facts, figures and fantasies. The visitor is often treated as if he is an illiterate and the very basic facts of life have to be patiently explained – yet another example of how Chinese treat backward outsiders. If you have done your homework, the endless litany of The Brief Introduction can be agonisingly boring.

Most people who travel to a specific destination in China, especially for business, have done their ground research. Local officials, especially in provinces off the commonly beaten track, take no chances. In 1989, I was in Taiyuan, capital of Shanxi province in the north, to research and write a series of articles on coal, power, minerals and industry in this resource-rich area which is also one of the cradles of Chinese civilisation. We had more than a dozen meetings. The start to each was similar. In would come an official. Hands would be shaken, cards exchanged, welcomes extended. Then would come The Brief Introduction.

Every official – at three or four meetings a day! – would commence by pulling out a handwritten brief obviously copied laboriously from a textbook. He would then proceed to ponderously read. "Shanxi," he would announce with great satisfaction, "had an area of 156,266 square kilometres and a population of 24.76 million people. The capital, Taiyuan, was at an altitude of 800 metres above sea level and was in the exact centre of the province, which occupied the high loess plateau". On they droned. And on. And on. And interminably on.

There was no stopping them. First time, it was bad enough. By the 12th performance, both of us could almost chant along in Putonghua, with a strong Shanxi accent, the statistical account of the province, its peoples and its industries. Only after each official had got to the end of his own personal version of The Brief Introduction, could we begin asking questions.

It is a tactic familiar all over China. Local officials want to introduce their area, be it a small town, a city, a regional district or a province. They are trying to be helpful. They have gone to some trouble to gather the facts and figures. It is no use taking the Reception Officer aside and hinting discreetly that you have heard it all before; you are about to hear it all again. The chances are, you have amassed all these details as routine background before you left home. No matter. The Brief Introduction rolls on as certainly and as inexorably as the Yellow River rolls down to the sea.

Grin, sip your tea, nod periodically and pray for it to come to an end.

## INTERIOR POLLUTION

If you want to make yourself a figure of derision, go to a Chinese restaurant and ask for a non-smoking table. Hey! Here's proof that foreigners are indeed insane.

Cigarette addicts are unrepentantly puffing away in China. The health fad that has had nicotine fiends stubbing out the evil weed in other parts of the world has not affected China. The result is decided discomfort for those who don't like sitting in a smoke-filled room.

On one trip to a Chinese provincial capital, I went to a briefing by top officials. When I arrived on time at 2.30 p.m., the 15 men who awaited me had evidently been in the reception room for some time; I walked through the door and the smog had me groping for my seat.

All 15 men were chain-smokers. They would light up cigarettes made from the powerful local tobacco and happily puff away. As soon as they finished one coffin stick, they put it aside to smoulder in the ashtray and lit another.

The room was choked in smoke. The windows were tightly sealed to keep out the winter chill. My eyes streamed. I coughed constantly. The fumes continued.

It is no use whatsoever asking Chinese not to smoke. You will be considered very rude if you do so. The only solution is to try not to breathe, to cut the interviews as short as politely possible and to stumble out for a lungful of clean air.

## WHO'S IN CHARGE HERE?

This is a good question. Sometimes, nobody seems certain. Partly this is because of the jobs-for-the-boys syndrome so richly beloved and deeply entrenched in Chinese life. At other times, it is because of the confused power structure in which a corporation manager may have equal status with the factory's party secretary. Sometimes one of them answers a question, sometimes another.

If you are a businessman seeking a session with the top man who can make a vital decision, you are likely to spend a couple of days speaking to officials of various levels. Your first contact will be with the local government or corporation's foreign affairs office. Then you will meet the economic and export officials in charge of exports.

Finally, you will meet a person whose title on his business card will probably announce him to be the Deputy Director or Assistant President. Don't be fooled by this. It is similar to the Vice-Chancellor of a British university. The Chancellor is a respected figurehead; its the Vice who's got the clout.

Same in China. The deputy or assistant is probably the top decision-maker. The man who enjoys the prestige in the top slot could be some aged veteran of the Long March who has never been to the factory or office, apart from turning up to head the table at welcoming banquets.

I recall once down in the Liuzhou Peninsula in southern Guangdong toasting the President of a 2,500-room luxury hotel for foreign oil workers. We were at the same table eating a 16-course banquet of local specialities. How long had he worked at the new hotel in Zhangjiang? Eight months, he said. Where had he worked before? For the government. What part of the government, I persisted? In the army? Doing what? I rudely kept on. It turned out, he was a venerable old general who had been given the hotel job as a communist equivalent of a golden handshake, a plush retirement benefit near his home county. The hotel was being run on a day-to-day basis by a 29-year-old Hongkonger.

## *THE ELEVEN COMMANDMENTS*

Negotiating a deal in China can be an agonising procedure. The Chinese have been doing business for a long time and are often prepared to talk for weeks, months – sometimes years! – before signing an agreement. Time is on their side and they will hold out for the best deal they can get.

To cope with the endless, frustrating sessions of negotiations, visiting entrepreneurs have to prepare. Veterans have drawn up a list of suggested rules to follow:

1. Patience
2. Perseverance
3. Stamina and persistence
4. Friendly sincerity
5. Firmness to press your point
6. Flexibility
7. Tact and a sense of humour
8. Technical knowledge of the product
9. Simple clear language to ensure accurate communication
10. Honesty and frankness
11. Ability to sit through endless banquets, drink gallons of tea and toast your potential business partners with such potions as snake wine, *fen* (herb) bamboo spirit and the dreaded *mao tai* (strong local liquor).

## MUTUAL BENEFITS

Traditional Chinese business philosophy holds that all parties involved in a commercial agreement should be happy and should make a profit. In am ideal world, this would be a laudable aim. In reality, it doesn't always work like that.

When China first opened its doors a decade ago, there was wild enthusiasm for doing deals, not only from the West but also from hundreds of state corporations who saw the prising open of trade doors as the opening of a treasure trove. The attitude of many Chinese officials reflected that ancient outlook of the rulers of the Middle Kingdom; foreigners should think themselves richly blessed because they were permitted to trade with the celestial realm.

The notion that the world owed China a living and special generous terms should be extended by Western businesses was not one that appealed to entrepreneurs whose only political and social concern was focused on the bottom line. Overseas Chinese, especially, were expected to scrap all normal rules of commercial acumen and extend open-handed terms to state corporations. In particular, members of the Chinese diaspora who had become wealthy abroad were looked at as philanthropists who had a duty to fund factories in their ancestral provinces.

As the initial enthusiasm began to wane, a more realistic approach to investment returned. The traditional idea of mutual benefit was once again embraced. Any businessman in China today will hear the phrase uttered again and again. It should be a welcome refrain. It means the state corporations and other bodies with whom they are signing agreements realise that a businessman has to make a profit.

## THE CHINA CONNECTION

Another phrase that is not so welcome in the new atmosphere is *guanxi* or connections. In modern parlance, this is an undefined linkage of close friends, old comrades, relatives, workmates, the Asian equivalent of the Old Boy network.

If you are 'in the loop', to use another Western expression, you are going to get special treatment. Your contract will be signed without great loss of time in negotiations. You will find raw materials provided and deadlines met. All problems will be smoothed over.

Based mostly on friendship and close relationships, guanxi also comes with a strong element of bribery. This is more in the form of luxury gifts, banquets and invitations to trips abroad than in hard cash. Those who cashed in most on connections in the past were high-ranking officials in state corporations, their family members and the children of top cadres in Beijing and provincial governments. They became known as 'fixers' who could cut through the smothering bonds of red tape that otherwise made doing deals so difficult.

Most of those who could extend the benefits of guanxi were Chinese and the beneficiaries were largely Overseas Chinese setting up shop in China.

After the student upheavals of the late 1980s, connections have been regarded with great suspicion and as part of the general corruption which sparked off the popular rising. But they are still invaluable, the invisible glue that holds together many of the business deals struck in China today.

## *PRESENTS*

Never offer cash. It is quite acceptable for foreigners doing business in China to take along small gifts to distribute to those they meet for discussions. But handing over money is crude, could be misunderstood and – in the worst possible scenario – could lead to an affronted Chinese official claiming some capitalistic Westerner was attempting to bribe him. Such items as pen sets, solar calculators, transistor radios, Walkmans and other relatively cheap items are the favoured small presents. Cigarettes (any leading American brand) are always welcomed. I generally prefer taking books.

Just as anywhere else in the world, what you give depends on how well you know the recipient. If it is an official you have met on some former trip, you know whether he smokes and drinks, in which case a carton of cigarettes or a bottle of brandy may be appropriate. In the case of new acquaintances, a degree of care is needed. While gifts may be appreciated, they should not be distributed in a way that can give offence. The best way is to say, through your interpreter, that you appreciate greatly the help and hospitality you have received and would like very much your new friends in China to accept a small token of thanks. Mention also that if any of those present are ever in your town, you would very much like them to contact you so you can return their hospitality. This gesture will be greatly appreciated as a sign of friendship.

The ideal present is something tasteful. It should also be comparatively small so you can carry gifts in your baggage without too much trouble. Items like pens, desk sets and other mementos with your corporate logo are presents which are very suitable.

My own personal choice for close contacts are books. But here you have to know the person. Obviously, giving a book in English to someone who doesn't read the language is not an ideal solution. If you have met someone on an earlier trip who has been helpful and know he has a child, it touches the Chinese heart if on a return trip you bring

181

a small token for the kid. It doesn't have to be big or expensive – Western T-shirts are ideal – but it will be a gesture that warms any relation.

In other words, good manners and politeness are universal.

WARNING: Do not take cameras to China to give as gifts. Chinese customs officials are paranoid about cameras. You have to list each one by make on entering the country and be prepared to show it to Customs on the way out.

## NEW FRIENDS, OLD FRIENDS

Sometime on your first business trip to China, one of the cadres to whom you are talking will mention that you are welcome to the country as a 'new friend'. When you depart, the chances are you will be welcomed back in an elevated status.

'You came to our country as a new friend,' the ranking official will say as you prepare to leave his city or province. 'When you return, you will be an old friend.'

To Chinese, the difference is significant. A new friend, while welcome, is a person who comes to China on a visit. An old friend is someone who knows something of China. As an 'old friend', one receives preferential treatment.

## OPEN CITIES

China's drive towards business modernisation was initially spear-headed by Guangzhou. Then Special Economic Zones (SEZs) were started, mostly clustered around Hongkong. The idea was that a symbiosis would grow between the world's most capitalistic city and the communist monolith. This idea worked; by 1988, more than two million people in Guangdong province worked in new factories owned by Hongkong companies which had invested a few miles away just over the provincial border. The Hongkong people had moved their plants over the border to take advantage of cheap labour, plentiful land and generous tax holidays offered by a government eager to attract manufacturers. These breaks more than offset the inbuilt burdens of doing business within a bureaucratic maze.

The SEZs were so successful that China later extended the welcome mat. Fourteen major coastal cities, from Zhangjiang on the Liuzhou Peninsula up to Dalian in Manchuria, were named as zones which officially welcomed foreigners. These blossomed commercially as each city strove to make more generous offers to attract business. The ground rules were laid down by the central government – ten-year tax holidays, permission to hire and fire staff and guarantees of being able to take out profits, to name a few – and bolstered by local efforts to make it easy for foreigners to set up shop.

These days, all China is 'open' to business. In general, the further one gets from the coast, the more welcome the potential investor becomes. In go-ahead Qingdao and prosperous Xiamen, a manufac-

*Playing catch-up with the rest of the world: The mobile telephone is fast gaining popularity with prosperous businessmen in the big cities.*

turer wanting to start a small television assembly plant might be greeted with a polite but distant handshake. Out in Anhui province or the backwaters of Guangxi, someone with a similar proposition would be hailed as an economic saviour.

## *The Guangzhou Trade Fair*

When the Rattan Door of trade inched cautiously open in the early 1970s, the twice-yearly Guangzhou Trade Fair was China's main business window to the West. Today, the spring and autumn sessions of the fair still give merchants, especially newcomers, a vital and exciting overall picture of the national trading pattern. All 30 provinces put their goods on show.

There are would-be wheelers and potential dealers from every industrial city in the land. Rug merchants from Central Asia rub shoulders with men who launch satellites from China's space bases, technicians demonstrate sophisticated medical electronic equipment and Sichuan officials demonstrate the intricate arts and crafts of mountain minority tribesmen. It is a place of great fascination and a week at the trade fair is equivalent to a couple of years studying China's business profile at a Western university. It's also enormous fun.

Not only does the novice meet state traders from all over China and officials from the great ministries in Beijing, he also has the invaluable chance of having a drink with men and women who have been doing business with China for decades.

The old hands gather in the bar of the Dong Fang (East is Red) Hotel across the road from the glass-shrouded trade fair headquarters. There, they swap tales of the bad old days of the Cultural Revolution when import-export men from abroad were closely confined to the hotel, awakened at dawn every day by loudly-broadcast trumpets squealing the Maoist anthem (The East is Red which gave the hotel its name), then escorted across Liu Hua Road to do business through a gauntlet of hysterical Red Guards screaming anti-Western hate slogans. It was, the old timers say over a Zhu Jiang (Pearl River) lager, a lot of fun.

Today, these canny merchants who stayed on despite the rigours of doing business with fanatics are enjoying the pay-off. Today, they are the most respected of Old Friends. Listening to them, the new tramper of the Silk Road can pick up tips on doing business with China that the entire staff of the Harvard Business School would never dream of.

## WORKING HOURS

Officially, Chinese government offices and most companies work 8 a.m. to 5 p.m. six days a week. If you believe this, you'll believe anything. Be prepared for all business to stop abruptly at 11.30 a.m. or 4.30 p.m. – the cadres are called away for the most sacred business of all, lunch and dinner.

Officially, China has four holidays a year: New Year's Day (January 1), Labour Day (May 1), National Day (October 1) and the three-day break in late winter (depending on the lunar calendar) known as Spring Festival but celebrated with riotous good humour as Chinese New Year. Unofficially, many who try to do business with some slack Chinese concerns reckon that some Chinese bureaucrats and executives enjoy a 365-days-a-year holiday.

## LET'S DANCE!

As China's doors hesitantly creaked open in the 1970s, some monstrous notions penetrated the land. One of these was that a sure sign of advanced thinking, liberal ideas and readiness to do business with the rest of the world was to have a disco in town.

Help me, boys! How many times have I been in some quiet backwater deep in the interior where, after dinner, the local mayor or party secretary has gripped me firmly in a hammerlock and marched me determinedly to a darkened room in a hotel or meeting hall where a few tawdry coloured lights revolved and 1960s rock music blasted my eardrums. In the midst of this dim cacophony, a couple of girls would be coyly dancing together, watched by an approving mob of the

185

local version of the Chamber of Commerce, factory supervisors and party functionaries, all eager to show their modernity.

Outside China, I went to a disco once. This was in Hongkong at the height of the 'Saturday Night Fever' frenzy when I was enticed into one of these hellish places. I stayed 15 seconds. But in China, I must have been to a score of discos. While I am in no position to judge their quality, they seem to me sad, inappropriate places. Nobody there seems to know what to do or quite why they are present.

It's considered to be a sign of go-ahead local administration to have a disco and while officials seem to be as ignorant as I about what you do at a disco, it's just about compulsory for every village to have one and for the luckless foreign friend to be hauled into it.

Have fun.

*Young Chinese partying away at a Beijing disco. Hundreds of such discotheques have sprouted up in cities and towns all over the country in recent years, a nightly beacon for the restless and energetic.*

## *NARROW VISION*

China can be a narrow, blinkered place. Unless two people are assigned to the same work unit or have some other strong common bond, there seems little drive to meet people and make friends. Even within the same organisation or in the same factory, people do not mingle as they do in the West.

I have a good friend in the New China News Agency (known universally as Xinhua) and on a trip to Beijing I asked another Xinhua staffer how he was. The woman I asked looked at me in astonishment. He was in the English language section of the big organisation and she was in the Spanish-speaking section. So how could she possibly know anything about him? He was in a different section and therefore totally out of her ken.

You sometimes get the feeling that people who work in the same building but in different departments are as cut off from each other as you and I are removed from the Queen of England. This compartmentalism of Chinese life is not caused by the communist system, although the rigid bureaucracy of the system certainly reinforces the cultural isolation. If the other person doesn't have any direct impact on your life, why would you waste your time getting to know him?

Don't think this is being deliberately secretive. It's not.

## *HOTELS*

In 1991, China had more than 3,000 hotels with 300,000 rooms catering for foreign visitors. By the start of 1996, this had grown to 4,500 hotels with 450,000 rooms. From the opening of the first joint venture hotel in China back in 1980 – the stunning White Swan on the banks of the Pearl River in Guangzhou – the nation and keen foreign investors have erected hotels that can compare, often very proudly, with the best in the world. By 1999, there were yet another generation of modernistic hotels in China and surveys showed that by 2020, there would be 137 million tourists visiting China annually. So even more hotels will be needed in future.

It's been an astonishing transformation. In many ways, the provision of five-star properties that rank more than favourably with London and San Francisco is a shining symbol of China's progress. It was not easy. In the early 1980s, adventurous Swiss and German hoteliers charged with staffing and running those new hotels found themselves on a certain collision course with ulcers.

In 1983, I went to Shanghai to witness that vast city emerging from the gloomy morbidity of the Cultural Revolution. I stayed in the best the city had to offer, an imposing brick and stone mansion with an interesting history. It had been built for one of the great taipans of a foreign trading house when Shanghai was an international treaty port. During World War II, it had been occupied by the Japanese military governor and, to my utter thrilled distaste, I occupied the enormous room – with a bathroom bigger than my flat in Hongkong – where the dreadful Jiang Qing (Madame Mao Zedong) had lived when she presided over the horrors of the purges. The hotels that then existed in China's biggest city and greatest trading port were relics of the Victorian era, rundown, antique, glum and operated for the benefit of their huge, unseen and lazy staff. In this majestic structure, guests had set times for meals; if you were not promptly at table at 6 p.m., you went without dinner. The door to the kitchen was locked and staff gathered to play cards, smoke and sleep, which in those days, Chinese hotel staff seemed to do 18 hours a day.

What a change! Today, stand on the 48th floor of the Portman Shangri-La Hotel and you look at a skyline studded with hotel towers. Over the Huang He River, a spire soars 88 storeys, the top 35 floors occupied by a gleaming new Hyatt. The flags of most international hotel groups fly over China's cities.

They have spearheaded the transformation of Chinese city life. This has happened in two ways. First, the influx of tourists has opened Chinese eyes. It's very easy to forget that before 1972 China was a totally closed country, an imprisoned xenophobic society taught to hate and loathe the outside world and to mistrust foreign barbarians. In 1971, there were zero tourists. By 1995, there were 35 million overseas visitors; the average Chinese urban dweller could see they didn't have horns and a forked tail. Secondly, those 4,500 hotels not only earned a big slice of the US$26.8 billion foreign currency that came from tourism in 1995, but also played an enormous – although largely unrecognised – educational role.

It was like having an additional 4,500 vocational schools and universities. The year the White Swan opened, all locals were forbid-den entry because local government was jittery they would pick up vile foreign customs and be exposed to anti-revolutionary thoughts. I recall wandering from the spectacular bar that over-looks the frenetic Pearl River with its busy traffic, down to the toilet. It was occupied. In every cubicle, urinal and hand basin, staff were washing socks and doing their personal laundry. The young men and women recruited to work in the new generation of hotels were peasant boys and girls or youths from city schools who had studied languages. They came from homes without toilets or piped water and where the notion of hot water from a tap was an outrageous novelty. To them, those toilets in the hotel were as unspeakably glamorous as the Doge's Palace would be to a feudal serf in Europe.

Two decades later, schooled rigorously by demanding European, Singaporean and Hongkong hoteliers, staff in China's expanding hotels were universally skilled, polite, outward-looking and helpful.

*— Chapter Eight —*

# LIVING IN CHINA

*To have done a thing oneself is better than watching others do it;*
*To have made many mistakes in doing it is better than simply doing it once.*

Foreign companies used to classify China as a hardship post. There's no justification for that these days, at least in the big cities. Shanghai, for example, is as exciting a place to live as Chicago. It's got Western-styled apartments (although at outrageous prices) and foreign schools. It's got its Hard Rock Café and a plethora of beer bars, karaokes, discos and restaurants of every ethnic persuasion. Want to find out more, go to www.shanghai-ed.com and read all about it. This website, run by famous journalist Graham Earnshaw who was once the Reuters news agency's service chief in China and who is totally fluent in Cantonese, Mandarin and written Chinese, is a great way to explore the city. Other cities also have sophisticated websites.

It's still very helpful to go to China as a diplomat or as a staff member of a large conglomerate; those warm sheltering arms that arrange movements, provide apartments and do all the other work that self-employed individuals have to do for themselves eliminate much of the hard toil.

Life in a big Chinese city today is more like a Western city than China 20 years ago. Then, life could be spartan, unpleasant, lonely, cold (or hot) and barren. It could also be harsh. There were few phones, no Western-style grocery shops, little contact with the outside world and no such exotic delights as Scotch whiskey, baked beans or chocolates.

The glittering shopping malls in China today – take a look at some in Guangzhou! – are as well stocked as any in London, Paris or San Francisco. You are no longer an exile cut off from the outside world.

## PLAY BY THEIR RULES

If a foreigner is going to live in China, he has to play by Chinese rules. If you are determined to keep comparing conditions and practices in Shanghai to what is done back home in Omaha, you should catch the next plane heading back across the Pacific. China is not about to change for you, pal.

Don't keep carping about human rights and democracy. The Chinese idea of human rights, broadly, is that if you behave yourself, you'll be okay. If you err from the politically straight and narrow or verge over in criminal ways which harm others, you are in for the high jump – or down on your knees in a sports stadium with a rifle butt at the nape of the neck – and nobody is going to have a lot of sympathy.

The rule is simple. Obey Chinese laws. You might not like them, but that's the law. If you can't stick with them, get out.

## *GETTING BETTER*

All the basic necessities of modern life – and many of the unwanted frills from karaoke to traffic jams – can now be enjoyed in China.

It was not always so. Life for a foreigner in China (and for hundreds of millions of Chinese, come to that) was, in the recent past, drab, dreary, uninspiring and narrow.

Here is a very brief list of some of the things you could NOT get even in Beijing or Shanghai in the early '80s: a cold beer, English-language novels (except for the politically approved writings in government foreign language book shops), baked beans, a shortwave radio, a fax, edible non-Chinese food, outside newspapers, French wine, lamb chops, air conditioning, bread, hotel room service, cable TV, an apartment, a car ... the list goes on.

The nation has been truly transformed.

I remember the icy winter of 1986 when Beijing students were marching in the snow in an early harbinger of the massive demonstrations that were to erupt three years later. I was staying in the Minzu Hotel, which in those days was a truly horrific dump. Huddled in bed fully dressed in my dim-lit room, with my PLA greatcoat piled atop the blankets, I listened to the BBC World Service (and praise God for the Beeb!) through long frigid nights. There was nothing else to do. The restaurant closed at 6 p.m., the uninviting and unstaffed bar had insipid local beer or *mao tai* that would strangle a yak.

Why in the name of sanity would anyone in their right minds want to live in this country?

My last trip was to wonderful, transformed, Shanghai. The museum is a masterpiece. The opera house is even better. I danced with a 73-year-old grandma in a sunny square, to the immense amusement of all concerned. The streets are pungent with pollution and dust from the rising skyscrapers and the new highways cutting through the city. The energy of relentless change is everywhere; it is racing towards its true role as the greatest city in Asia.

Other cities, likewise, are pressing forward, transformed from drab sprawling slums into modern metropolises.

Civilisation has dawned. In hotels, staff are smiling, clean, courteous and professional. Wine lists include vintages from Chile, Australia and California in addition to China's own fast-improving Chardonnay from Shandong province.

If you have the inclination and the energy, you can dance till dawn or karaoke the night away.

What does it mean? Basically, China has caught up with the rest of the world. Apart from the more sordid and open commercial sex available in many countries, a resident of China can live pretty much as he would anywhere else. Some may lament the 'old' China of proletarian values. They are people who never had to live in a faceless world where monotonous uniformity in dress, food, customs and outlook were impressed forcibly on a vibrant and energetic people.

## Benefits

If you are sent to China by a well-established company, you face few problems. Your employer will have furnished apartments on tap, telephones are already installed and there is probably an office car and driver. Living is easy.

It's not so sweet for a small businessman attempting to set up a one-man office in China. That's when the fun starts. Or try being a technician sent to a regional centre to advise on how best to use modern machinery. Even today, in some remote centres, you are an exile cut off largely from many of the facilities that the rest of the world takes for granted.

## Changing Times

Visitors going to China for the first time cannot begin to imagine what things were like a decade ago. Then, going to China may have been exciting. It was also like a swift trip backwards in a time machine to an era the rest of the world had forgotten. There is no point in dwelling on the esoteric miseries of those times. But for old business hands, progress in the past decade has been magical.

Fax machines, IDD telephone systems, copiers, business centres in hotels, access to foreign newspapers – these are all recent developments. So when Old China Hands regale you with horror stories of the not-so-distant past, grin and bear it. You might even learn something.

## *LIFELINES*

One piece of advice for any businessman, student, adviser or Foreign Friend who is to be stationed away from the largest cities on the tourist track: take plenty to read and arrange before you go to China for a lifeline with friends outside the country to send you a steady supply of books. This is probably the best opportunity you will ever have to catch up on reading the classics; there is precious little else to do in many of the backwater towns.

Whenever I go to China, I am accompanied by one of my most prized possessions. This is a small Sony shortwave radio, the size of a paperback novel. Using normal batteries obtainable anywhere, this electronic wonder plugs me into the outside world. During long northern nights when darkness plunges most of the nation into silence like a mausoleum, I whip out the antenna and am in contact with the world. This machine has a 'seek' command that scans all shortwave and medium-wave frequencies. After a couple of days roaming the airwaves, you have located Voice of America, Radio Australia, Radio Japan, Radio Moscow or stations broadcasting in German, Spanish, Indonesian, French, Hindi or a score of other tongues.

The best of this plethora of news and views of the airways is the British Broadcasting Corporation's magnificent World Service. This has news on the hour, interviews with topical figures, chat shows, book reviews and in-depth research profiles on top news items of the day. Many a long, icy night I have spent huddled under the down cover of a rural guesthouse bed with my radio tuned to distant London as I awaited the dawn.

You can also tune in to Radio Beijing and hear the news according to the Forbidden City. This often gives a quaint viewpoint on the world. More usefully, you can spend the insomniac hours of the night with your ears glued to the first-class Chinese language classes offered by many English-language broadcasts. I have always found Radio Australia – which sends a very strong signal to Northern China – to be the best of these. But Radio Beijing's excellent programme 'Follow Me!' which teaches an estimated 100 million people daily how to speak English is also well worth listening to.

In major cities, you can now buy Hongkong's excellent English language newspapers (and Chinese, of course) the same day they are printed. Ironically, although it is impossible to buy foreign press in more remote areas, I often arrive back in my hometown of Hongkong (where there are 68 daily newspapers and the best communications links on earth) with a better grasp of global news and current events than many of my newspaper colleagues. This is because I have spent up to eight hours a night listening to radio stations broadcasting from every continent on earth. These days, in all but the smallest hamlets, there is also cable television.

## Staying in Touch

A decade ago, when the foreigner entered China he strode nervously into an information vacuum. There were the local newspapers, all tightly controlled by the propaganda department of the party, and radio and television under a similar vice-like grip. All were in the national tongue, of course, with no Cantonese broadcasts even in the great southern metropolis of Guangzhou. (Now Guangdong TV broadcasts in the local dialect, as do other stations where languages other than the national tongue are commonly used in the home.)

The only reading matter were dreary publications like China Reconstructs and similar publications in a variety of languages which endlessly proclaimed in breathless prose the great strides being made under the wise leadership of the regime.

As with so many other aspects of Chinese life, things have, happily, changed. Now, in tourist hotels in big cities, you can buy international news magazines, a selection of paperbacks, guide books and novels. In big cities like Beijing, Shanghai and Guangzhou, that morning's Hongkong newspapers are on the stands by the time you are heading for the bar for a 5 p.m. glass of Qingdao beer.

The English language *China Daily* is put out by the Central Government in Beijing and, naturally enough, follows the party line. It also contains readable and topical features. *The Daily* (pronounced *Zhongguo Ribao* in Putonghua) is well worth reading, if only to get a look at the world through an official Chinese perspective.

## *HOLD THE MEI-YOU*

One of the first phrases foreigners in China come to know and hate is *mei-you*. Intoned normally in a high-pitched whine, it means, literally, "don't have". It can also mean, depending on pronunciation, time of day, the bad humour of the shop assistant or the indifference of the clerk, anything from "It's too much trouble" or "Don't bother me with your problems" or, simply, "beat it".

*Mei-you* – it's the song of modern China. You want a cold bottle of beer in a hotel and you approach the barman who is busy watching television. *"Mei-you."* You try to book a ticket on an aircraft at a CITS office and the bureaucrat is reading the paper. *"Mei-you."*

A cash customer is eager to buy a sweater in a state-run shop and the size he wants is not easy to hand on the counter. *"Mei-you."* You try to board a taxi when the driver doesn't feel like driving. *"Mei-you."*

Chances are, it will be the first word with which you become fully proficient. It covers every eventuality in which the foreigner finds himself. If in doubt, shrug, turn away and mutter *"Mei-you."* It's the answer for everything.

A few years ago, a disgruntled young American at a language university in Beijing became so irate at the continual chant that greeted his every request that he asked a friend in Hongkong to have a few hundred T-shirts printed. They bore an outline of the Great Wall overprinted with the English slogan: "China – Hold the *mei-you*." No Chinese could understand the motto but the shirts became an instant success with Beijing's growing foreign community, all of whom had suffered an overdose of *"Mei-you."*

## PACE

One of the frustrations for a foreigner living in China is the pace at which people move. Generally, they resemble a snail on holiday. This is visibly apparent at service desks in government offices where as a matter of face the staff make the customers wait – just to let them know who is boss. The painful, slow pace of work in what in the West would be the public service would make the slackest, most bloody-minded British socialist look like an Olympic sprinter dosed with steroids.

The difference is obvious in the increasing number of shops run

*Visitors can discover a whole new shopping experience among the unfamiliar selection of goods along busy streets such as this in Beijing.*

by private enterprise. Here service is swift and friendly, staff are eager to help, keen to get out the goods and assist you to try on clothing. The contrast is stark.

## SHOPPING

Going shopping for residents of China is a lot different than for visitors. Tourists want to pick up bargain-priced antiques or mementos of their trip. Residents have to buy their daily necessities.

Until just a few years ago, if you lived in China you ate what was on sale at local markets. You had FEC of course, so you could go to the Friendship Stores and purchase things like mackerel in tomato sauce. Big deal. There was nothing else.

Here's another big change. The large foreign-run hotels in places where there are sizeable foreign communities have delicatessens where French bread, American chocolates and fresh-made German sausages are available.

In Beijing, the Lido Holiday Inn has nine butchers making an enormous array of smoked meats, sausages and wursts that could have come from a Bavarian farmyard. This Teutonic gastronomic lifeline connects to every city in North China with German communities. Up in the Mongolian steel city of Baotou, German technicians look forward to the plane from Beijing that comes bearing bratwurst.

Hongkong supermarkets have now opened branches in Beijing; similar organisations selling Western groceries and basic necessities can be found in a few other big cities. Elsewhere, you either shop at Chinese stores or go without.

## *Culinary Revolution*

As China's middle-class grows by the millions, the nation is getting a taste for Western cuisine. Those Chuppies have got pockets full of yuan and want to dispose of it, often as quickly as possible. This has created a culinary revolution; instead of the familiar hot stuffed dumpling of the north, a stylish teenager in Beijing is now as likely to be chomping on a cholesterol-choked hamburger.

Many people don't realise that China is a significant food exporter, not merely of basics but of luxury items. Hold down a French chef over a hot stove and under torture he will grudgingly admit that 90% of snails served in Paris come from the warm, moist paddy fields of Guangxi. It's the same with monster mushrooms; China is the source for Italian classical varieties.

Although it's a common belief that Chinese don't eat lamb (and Cantonese often find the smell unpleasant, true) remember there are 100 million sheep in China, mostly on the rolling northern steppes.

The traditional street markets, with their customary unhygienic conditions and the caged birds and animals awaiting dispatch on the footpath (which causes foreigners to cringe with unabashed horror) are still to be found everywhere.

But around the corner, you are likely to find a modern supermarket with Kelloggs cornflakes and most of Heinz's 57 varieties.

## Arts and Crafts

The visitor sometimes asks himself, where is the legacy of 5,000 years of culture? Where are the arts and crafts on which China so endlessly prides herself? Often, this is a very good question to which no logical or easy answer can be found.

Take the city of Chaozhou, old cultural centre of the wealthy Shantou region on the Guangdong coast. This district prides itself intensely on its ceramic heritage. Famed also for brocade and lacquer work, it is the centre of a region with a distinguished history of local crafts. Every tour guide and public official discourses at length on the cultural heritage of the region. Having listened to such talk for a couple of hours over lunch, now venture out onto the street of this once great port (heavy siltation of the river now places it far inland) and attempt to buy something. Good luck.

The shops are full, that is true. The shelves are stocked with modern manufactured cloth, plastic buckets, imitation leather jackets and brightly coloured cheap clothing.

Where is the gold embroidery? A shrug. "*Mei-you.*"

The ceramics for which you are famed? "*Mei-you.*"

The paintings? "*Mei-you.*"

Or try Shandong. You've heard of Shandong silk? Of course. It's renowned. I have tramped for hours around the streets of the provincial capital, Jinan, along the 10-kilometre circumference of the park where the city walls and moat once stood and through miles of downtown streets.

Shandong silk? "*Mei-you.*"

What's that brilliant scarf? That's silk, right enough, but it's imported from Turkey!

Where can you buy Shandong silk? Try the Friendship Store in Beijing.

In Taiyuan, in historic Shanxi, the biggest antique shop boasted three carpets which had been there for years and couldn't be disturbed because junky plastic goods had been piled atop them for a decade.

In Hangzhou, home of the Southern Song dynasty which made the city a glorious artistic imperial capital, there are some nice ceramics to be found. But the shop shuts on the dot of dusk so staff can collapse after a weary day spent reading the papers and dozing.

Shopping in official China can be a disappointing business.

## THE PROFIT MOTIVE REARS ITS WELCOME HEAD

Increasingly, small family businesses are opening in China to take advantage of the yawning commercial opportunities created by the slothful incompetence of official outlets. These are places normally located close to private enterprise restaurants in areas where tourists are likely to stroll.

The difference between the eager, friendly service one encounters here and the idle, couldn't-care-less attitude that is universal in state-run enterprises provides a stark lesson in economics. The benefits of the profit motive would be obvious to the ghost of Mao Zedong. Stacked with cheap ceramics, these shops, like one I found in friendly Xiamen, often contain a few old pieces. Spend a few minutes browsing. Admire what you want. Ignore what you can find back home.

## PICKING THE BADDIES

It started a couple of years ago in Xian where a go-ahead shop manager decided to do something about his staff. He instituted a 'Nominate the Most Lazy Shop Assistant' contest. Customers were asked to write down the most useless, rudest and incompetent worker in the store and slip their selections into a locked ballot box. More people voted in this election than in picking the Party General Secretary in Beijing. It unveiled a near-universal discontent with the way the shop was run. When the votes were toted up, the least popular staff members were named and their portraits pinned up on the store's entrance hall. They improved their performance.

The idea caught on and one can now write in complaints in many stores throughout the country. Needless to say, I am an enthusiastic voter in these polls. There are thousands of candidates from whom to pick.

I also write to local Chinese papers. If I encounter bad service, I buy the local paper on the street and when I get home write to the editor and explain what happened. If I meet someone friendly, helpful and pleasant who gives a good impression of their hotel or restaurant or shop, I do the same thing. I figure this is my minor contribution to try to improve the nation's service industry.

## *STRIKING A DEAL*

Unlike the vibrant Chinese communities abroad, there is little bargaining in shops in China. In the state-run enterprises, prices are fixed. Things are much freer and easier, and pleasant, in the increasing number of private enterprise shops. Here, the natural Chinese genius for making a deal, striking a bargain, is once more flourishing.

My rule of thumb is to offer a quarter of the price the shopkeeper demands. This gives plenty of leeway for both sides to come to an agreement. Always smile. Set a pleasant tone. Have a look around a shop and if you spy a teapot without which you cannot possibly live, pick up another item and ask the price.

The shopkeeper will look at you, sizing up your IQ and wallet. If he thinks the first is suitably small and the latter disgustingly fat, he will make an inflated suggestion.

"One hundred yuan," he might say.

I slap my hand to my forehead, reel backwards in shock and outrage and, still smiling, protest. "You must be the richest man in all Jiangsu province," or wherever I might be. "I am a poor worker, exploited by the capitalists."

If you're with a Chinese friend, this translation will bring a hearty grin. There will be a bit of conversation; where are you from, is this your first time in China, etc.

Then you make a counter offer for the item you do not want.

"Thirty yuan."

It is the shopkeeper's turn to loudly lament and proclaim his poverty. Down he comes to RMB70. You weep. You throw your hands in the air. How about if you pay in Hongkong dollars? you query. Or American dollars?

The shopkeeper takes this bait like a hammerhead shark in a feeding frenzy. So, roughly calculating, you offer a red Hongkong $100 note. At the official rate of exchange, this is about RMB110. You don't want to be too greedy so you tell the shopkeeper you will buy two items for HK$100. Done! he says.

But not what you were bargaining over, you say. Then you point to the teapot that you really want to buy and, having established the value of the Hongkong dollar, start serious negotiations.

A while ago, in the old port city of Shantou, I bought a marvellous large glazed porcelain vase for the equivalent of US$4. I was so stunned by the price asked that I didn't even bother to negotiate. The shopkeeper in turn was so surprised not to have a pleasurable and lengthy argument over the price that he pointed out to me an invisible flaw in the vase. We were both happy.

In the cavernous main crafts outlet in Beijing recently, I got something for nothing. One stall had a collection of old badges from the 1960s with the golden head of Mao Zedong embossed on the facade of Tiananmen. The shopkeeper came out and began chatting. No thanks, I said, I had plenty at home. He asked me if I knew what the badge meant. I stunned this fellow – and everyone else – by singing that stirring anthem of Maoism, *The East Is Red*, in Putonghua. "You good," the old fellow bellowed. "You good!" And he pinned the badge on me, refusing payment.

## *GIFTS*

When you're onto a good thing, stick with it. Years ago, I discovered The Friendship Store in Shanghai, down near the Bund close to the river end of Nanjing Road. You can't miss it. Having been frustrated on so many trips trying to buy small presents, it was with some joy that I discovered this huge department store stocked with an enormous array of arts, crafts and silks.

What caused my enthusiasm to soar even higher was the plump and jolly lady who staffed the silk counter where they accepted foreign credit cards. I swiftly instituted a system with her that works to this day.

Get to Shanghai, unpack my computer and head downtown. Into The Friendship Store (one of the few that deserves to bear the name) and up to the third floor to the silk lady. "Ni hao!" we grin at each other. I then dash down the counter pointing to a dozen or so bolts of different silk. She whips them out and I depart, leaving her my credit card.

Over the road and around the corner to the dim and dusty old bar of the Peace Hotel. A quick Qingdao beer, then back to the store. When I return, the silks are all cut into three-metre lengths and my bill is waiting to be signed. "Many thanks," I say, bidding her farewell and striding out, deeply satisfied. Here I have just completed my Christmas shopping in 60 seconds, having bought dress lengths of silk for four sisters, a mother-in-law, a daughter and assorted friends in various countries.

But do not tarry in the Shanghai treasure house. It is stocked with extremely tempting goodies. One trip, I took an English couple with me and instead of my normal blinding 60-second shopping foray we had to hang around while the wife admired carved wooden horses, lacquer ware, gold rings inlaid with semiprecious stones and other items. I got talking to the fellow who runs the carpet section and when I emerged from the shop I was the proud owner of a silken prayer rug woven by Turkic tribesmen out in far Xinjiang province. At US$2,600, it was a pricey visit. But a couple of years later, a friend who is knowledgeable about such matters spotted the rug and raved about it. Apparently, I had got a bargain. But I still prefer the 60-second forays.

## *MONEY*

A few years ago, I was in a restaurant in Zhengzhou, capital of historical old Henan where the Yellow River comes flooding out onto the North China Plain, and the talk moved to the inevitable subject of the future of Hongkong.

Mrs Thatcher had just been up to Beijing (where Comrade Deng Xiaoping enquired of an aide "Who is this dumb woman?") to negotiate the pact which sealed the future of the colony and consigned its six million people unwillingly to a political future within China.

"What did I think of the agreement?" party leaders asked.

In answer, I reached into my hip pocket, got my wallet and extracted a Hongkong $100 bill.

"The people will resolutely follow the red banner of Hongkong," I said, waving the scarlet note aloft.

There was much laughter all round and we had another flask of the famed Dujiang wine, a particularly noxious brew with heady effects.

On a more serious note, having a few Hongkong $100 notes in your pocket when shopping in China can be a lot of use.

Do not change money with street black marketeers – that's illegal and with the demise of the FEC and freely interchangeable currency, no longer necessary. But you can legally spend Hongkong money in shops. So if you are bargaining in a free enterprise shop and make offers to buy in Hongkong currency, you often get extremely good prices. The familiar red notes are devoutly admired throughout China.

## *SEX*

Customs change. And sexual habits in China have swung through a near-total reversal. The prudish old socialist morality has given way to a much more relaxed view of sexual relations. Those strict moral codes were preached but not practised by lusty leaders like Mao, who was not adverse to a rollicking good time with a series of shapely young revolutionaries. But largely speaking, China before 1980 was a land where you married late, had one child, and stayed married for life. No more, except for the one-child family policy remaining firmly in place.

There is not the level of casual sex that you find in the West. Chinese are still more moral and chaste, with both boys and girls coming under close parental scrutiny. But the sap rises... in parks and along riverbanks in any city or town, you see lovers cuddling, kissing and sometimes getting almost embarrassingly personal. There seem few illegitimate children, although such statistics are impossible to obtain.

Sex and personal relations in China are now far closer to the international norm. But I warn friends to use not only common sense, but caution. Going to bed with a foreigner probably means a greater commitment to a Chinese than a casual one-night-stand means to a European or American. Your partner may think that a night of bliss is the curtain raiser to a lifetime relationship. Be aware. Beware. Be careful.

In 1984, the late Dr Ma Haide had to take China's doctors back to school. The medicos had to learn the symptoms of diseases that doctors in China had not had to treat for a generation.

With the opening of the bamboo curtain and swarms of tourists going to China, the inevitable had happened. Sex had reared its ugly head and the result was the reappearance of venereal disease. So Dr Ma, an American born as George Hatem in Buffalo, New York, had to instruct Chinese doctors what to look for if patients went to them with a problem. Ironically, it was Ma Haide who after 1949 had led the medical drive that eliminated the widespread prostitution in cities such as Shanghai and which, to all intents, had wiped out VD in China.

The new liberalism which accompanied the advent of foreigners and wealthy Overseas Chinese saw a reversal from the strident puritanical attitude that ruled Chinese morals when Mao Zedong was alive. Boy met girl and the result sooner or later was love.

This did not go down well with many of the Old Guard. Lusty as they may have been themselves in their revolutionary youth a half century earlier, they were not keen to see sex blossoming in public places like the park in the Bund in Shanghai. To stamp out such practices as kissing in public (and the other shameful symptoms of what was seen as Western moral corruption), a campaign was launched against 'bourgeois pollution'. It created a lot of headlines but didn't do much to stop people doing what came naturally.

## Silver Bullets

When the idealistic communists took power in 1949, they were appalled by the immensity of the problems facing them. They were determined to change many things and close to the top of their list of essential moves was to stamp out prostitution.

This was not only on moral grounds. There were also ideological reasons. For centuries, many Chinese women and girls had been casually sold into concubinage or sexual slavery. They were treated not so much as human beings but as commodities. The communists were determined to stamp out the trade in women; most of the soldiers of the Red Army were peasants and it was peasant women who were sold when the crops failed.

In Shanghai, estimates were that one house in 12 was a brothel. They were staffed by many thousands of women and girls, some of whom had been sold by their families to pay for rice so brothers and sisters might live. Beneath the foreign image of the silken glamour of Shanghai's glittering nightlife, there was desperation and degradation.

The Reds rounded up the whores – many of them forced into the life by gangsters – and shipped them off to re-education camp. They were treated for VD and taught a trade that could support them, and thus provided with a medical and economic foundation for a new life.

The pimps were lucky if they went to prison; most were shot. And a damn good thing, too.

'Silver bullets' was what the communists called prostitutes on the grounds that their temptations could be used as ammunition against the new regime.

## Good-time Girls

Prostitution has recently reappeared in China despite all the moral preachings of party and government. Working hard in a bustling factory brings a farm girl a good, solid wage, far more than her parents could ever have expected to earn.

But, as everywhere in the world, temptations lurk and, inevitably, there are always going to be women attracted by the fake glamour of big money and easy sex. While officially condemned, prostitution is condoned. In many cities, it is run almost openly by local police.

As far as I can gather, no force or coercion is used. Women take to prostitution in China for precisely the same reason they do in Los Angeles or Manchester – it's easy money.

It's also risky. AIDS is far less prevalent in China than many countries, but sexually transmitted diseases do exist. If you plan to indulge, take precautions.

There's another risk. Every so often, a Chinese city will go through a paroxysm of prudery. Prostitutes will be rounded up, some out-of-luck pimps arrested. The girls are jailed, the pimps – especially if there is any suggestion of rape or imprisonment – head off for a date with the rifleman at the nearest football stadium and the customer appears in court.

So, it's up to you. There's plenty of sex for sale in China, if you are sufficiently foolish to take the associated risks. And it's not just in the big cities, but also in holiday resorts frequented solely by Chinese. Don't blame it all on foreigners, my friends.

On a recent trip to Yunnan, I went by car down to the Stone Forest at Dali. If you like forests of petrified jagged pieces of rock, you will

*An attractive nightclub performer in Shenzhen.*

love this place, clambering up and down endless flights of sheer steps to get to remote pavilions where you can look at more jagged pieces of rock. After this torture, on the good highway back to Kunming, I spied a likely looking lakeside resort, a sprawl of restaurants and bars. "Stop!" I cried. The driver was reluctant, but I finally had my way.

Well, here was Sodom and Gomorrah, and doing brisk business. This was a wayside rest stop for travellers who couldn't wait to get to Kunming, 40 kilometres up the road, to meet some not-so-nice girls. Short leather skirts and flashing smiles signalled their occupation. I managed to have a beer and left. There were still dozens of girls on duty at 3 p.m.!

That night, I wandered through Kunming, which is a nice, friendly place. Very friendly, if you happen to be a foreign man on your own. In every hotel bar, I very quickly found a young lady beside me. Polite but firm is my motto: "No thank you, my dear, I'm too old and have no money." The "no money" part is usually persuasive. Back in my own hotel, I got in the lift. Two slim, attractive young ladies got in with me. I pressed the button for the 12th floor. They stood looking at me. I got off at my floor and walked down to my room. They followed. Not a word had been exchanged. I opened the door and went in; they casually started to stroll in with me. "No, no, no" I said. "No money. Poor old cripple." I finally managed to usher them out.

I'm no prude. But I'm careful. And if I was going to indulge, I'd like to make the selection.

The situation varies around the country, with prostitution being more blatant in some towns than in cities a few miles away. In all cases, commercial sex seems to be run with the cooperation, or, at least, benign connivance, of the local coppers. But there is no hint of coercion, the girls are on the game for precisely the same reasons that prostitution exists anywhere. They like the money, and the life.

## FALLING IN LOVE

It happens every day. And it often results in serious problems. The course of true love certainly does not run smooth, as Bill Shakespeare would have noted if he lived in Beijing.

Some Chinese who have had the misfortune to fall in love with a foreigner in recent years have been banished to some remote interior city. Others have been refused permission to leave the country when their spouse departed. This led in one case to a fiery Frenchwoman staging a lay-down protest outside the Chinese embassy in Paris, threatening to have her baby on the pavement if her husband was not allowed to join her. He was.

Things are easier now. Romance is much more common between foreigners and Chinese, although liberalisation has a long way to go. But ask yourself how you would feel if your daughter came home and announced she was living with or going to marry a foreigner from some country you had never heard of; what's this person like and will he look after my little girl? Of course, any parent is going to be alarmed.

The government puts itself in the place of vigilant Big Brother, not just for political reasons but because there is a widespread suspicion among many Chinese – and some sorry, sordid tales have borne these notions out – that devilishly randy Westerners are eternally scheming to ravish innocent Chinese damsels.

It is often difficult for Westerners to get to know locals of the opposite sex. There is ingrained prejudice and a large degree of ignorance about the outside world. While many young Chinese men and women would like nothing better than to date a foreigner, they have to overcome opposition from relatives and incessant joshing from friends.

Go to the Hard Rock Café in Beijing, single friends tell me. That's one place where you find girls – office workers and the like, decent ordinary women – who want to meet men. "You have to fight them off with a stick," one handsome young Australian told me. I wouldn't know, personally, but an attractive British businesswoman told me once that similar discos and nightclubs were not her cup of tea; all the foreigners had eyes only for the stunning Chinese girls and not busty blondes.

Getting to know each other can be tricky. Usually, the visitor to China will meet people in the travel industry or associated business such as shops. Businessmen may meet colleagues or people who work in similar industries but the opportunity for friendships to be formed are restricted. First of all, there is often the language barrier.

More imposing is the cultural hurdle. Despite the easing of bans on meeting foreigners and the general liberalisation of morals, China is still, by Western standards, a staid and proper society. There is very little casual sex. It happens, of course, but much more rarely than in American, European or Australian societies. For those who live in China, romance can and does bloom.

## *WATCH THOSE HANDS*

Respect Chinese women. Take care when you are dealing with waitresses and other service staff that you do not mistakenly insult them by taking perceived sexual advantage. When you are in a modern Western-managed hotel and a slinky, enormously sexy girl glides past in a high-cut cheongsam, do not make a mistake and think she is anything but a waitress. You'll be very sorry if you do.

A drunken, lonely and amorous Dutchman once patted a waitress on her shapely bottom in a Guangzhou hotel lounge. She didn't say anything but walked out of the room. Within 10 minutes, she was back, accompanied by two burly hotel security guards who in China are often unofficial representatives of the local Public Security Bureau. They were carrying his bags. Packed.

'You are leaving China on the next train,' the dumbfounded Hollander was told. He was marched out of the hotel, put in a taxi, given his train ticket, directed to the station and told not to return.

Serves him right.

## *COSTS*

China may still be a developing country. This does not mean it is a cheap one. Living in China can be as expensive as anywhere in the world. Decent apartments are virtually impossible to obtain for most foreigners so home is likely to be a permanent hotel room or a serviced flat in an apartment tower next to a foreign-run hotel.

Cheap they are not.

Living in a hotel service block is the most viable choice for anyone who does not have quarters provided by employer or the local Chinese organisation to which he is attached. Costs at the Garden Hotel in Guangzhou are US$55 a night for a long-term stay of three months or more. Apartments in the tower block adjoining the hotel range from US$2,000 a month for a 75-square-metre room to US$6,700 per month for a three-bedroom apartment measuring 185 square metres. In Beijing, add another 30% to these costs. Such accommodation comes with everything supplied.

But try to get one of these places; there's an enormous waiting list as brigades of international businessmen head for China.

Trying to get such services as water, garbage collection and staff privately can be a nightmare, even for Overseas Chinese who speak fluent Putonghua. For a foreigner, the maze of horrors through which one has to go to get a telephone connected is a bureaucratic atrocity. In a hotel service apartment, most of your problems of setting up house are solved.

Some people who know they are going to be based in China for a couple of years have the romantic notion of renting a wutung, living off a lane in one of the old traditional houses. This inevitably turns out to be more expensive than a hotel apartment and no matter how enthusiastically the idea is grasped at the start, the grim realities of getting anything done soon cause the experiment to be regretted.

On the other hand, in hotels where large numbers of students, foreign experts and long-term businessmen are quartered, there develops a warm, friendly community spirit. Such a place is the Friendship Hotel in Beijing where many overseas journalists who work in Radio Beijing are based, as are large contingents of Third

World graduate students. It's a merry place, despite the crumbling condition of the rambling old building, and the decrepit and tawdry bar has a happy club-like atmosphere. There is a feeling of camaraderie; I suppose inmates on Devil's Island were also matey with each other.

## COME OVER FOR DINNER

In Beijing, there are compounds where diplomats, journalists, permanent resident businessmen and others who live in the city for lengthy postings occupy large but not-too-comfortable apartments. Naturally, these have high walls around them. Nobody seems quite sure if they are designed to keep intruders out or to pen the foreigners in.

What used to cause rage and disgust to foreign residents was the discovery that their Chinese friends could not visit them. If they tried, officious guards demanded proof of identity and noted it down. The People's Armed Police are supposedly stationed at some Beijing compound gates to protect the inhabitants. From what, I've never learned.

That's changed. In every Chinese city in recent years there has been an immense building boom. Much of this was to provide well-designed and maintained housing for foreign expatriates. In Shanghai there are entire suburbs of such pleasant homes; don't think about the rents, which are as high as the Oriental Peal TV tower.

Many expatriates still choose to live full-time in hotels or in the serviced apartments, which are often found adjacent to large hotels and run as adjuncts. This makes for an easy life where everything is done for you.

These days, as suspicion continues to ebb, relations between Chinese and foreign residents are easier. But police still tend to keep an eye on visitors to diplomatic compounds and to blocks where journalists tend to live.

## *NIGHTLIFE*

Videos, satellite TV, movie theatres and concerts, added to an explosion in international-style bars and bistros, foreign guest artists in hotel lobbies and the galaxy of home-grown entertainment make China a lively place to be. Nightlife two decades ago was about as lively as being locked up in a Ming tomb. Dinner was at 6 p.m. and you were expected to go to your hotel room and stay there until breakfast; there was not much to tempt you to do anything else.

Now, nightlife sparkles. As in so much else in the country, Shanghai sets the pace. There are anything-goes local versions of the Spice Girls – indeed, one Beijing all-girl rock band preceded the British group in both sound and style. Rock-and-roll provides the beat to which young China swings away the evenings. Karaoke is all-pervasive; if you can croak out a tune, keep it to yourself or you'll end up being the exhausted, much-applauded star of the evening.

If you like Western classical music, you're in luck. Chinese musicians are excellent. Concert tickets are normally sold out months in advance. The Chinese love fine music and are very knowledgeable about Western composers. Every city has a school where Western music is taught. (But I can't go past the splendid Conservatory of Music in Shanghai without tears coming to my eyes. During the Cultural Revolution, the Red Guards destroyed many of the instruments – not only were they condemned as "old" but also sinned by being "bourgeois" – and locked the Director up in a cupboard beneath the stairs, where he remained in solitary confinement for seven years.)

In this more relaxed era, things are freer and a lot more easy. But still, most hotels have a staff member on every floor who keep an eagle eye open for non-guests. (This is another compelling reason not to indulge in casual sex; if you go to a room with a girl, it's probably noted.)

I had a furious row with Beijing hotel staff in 1994. I was in the capital on a job and needed 5,000 letters addressed and put in envelopes. I was certainly not going to pay the usurious rates demanded by the hotel business centre. So I asked one of my staff, a pretty Hongkong girl aged 23, to hire two students to sit in my room and process the work. They arrived after school, about 6 p.m. My staffer escorted the two girls up from the lobby to my room where I started to explain to them what to do. A few minutes later, the bell rang. Outside the door was an assistant manager. "Can I help you, Sir?" he asked. No, I didn't call. Must be a mistake. A few minutes later, there was another knock. This time it was the floor controller, a stern old biddy, and another manager. The layout was such that anyone standing in the corridor could only see the person at the door; the interior of the room was around the corner. The three girls were chatting and laughing. Suddenly, the penny dropped. They thought I was having an orgy. This was immensely flattering to me, although my wife of a quarter century would no doubt find it hilarious that three attractive young women would find me irresistible.

## INTO THE HOME

Most Chinese will skilfully avoid an invitation to your home. Even with a printed invitation to show the haughty guard, they will be questioned and have their names taken down. In times of political uncertainty, anyone going to see a foreigner (especially a newsman or diplomat) is likely to have to explain why. It's best for Chinese not to come to the attention of the authorities.

So if you want to meet a friend, it's best to go for dinner in a restaurant. This may seem outrageous to newcomers. To Chinese, it is, sadly, a fact of life.

## ON YOUR BIKE

One of the first purchases a foreigner who has gone to live in China is likely to make is a Seagull bicycle. This is the gift that China gave to President Bush when he visited Beijing and it was splendidly appropriate. The great bulk of people use bicycles for commuting and getting about their cities.

It's an enjoyable way of experiencing the cities. It's also eminently sensible and gives a foreigner a chance to see the sights through Chinese eyes. Bikes can be hired through most hotel concierge desks and pedalling about town is fun.

Incidentally, doctors stress to me that the reason China has such a low incidence of heart disease can largely be linked to the lifelong regular exercise people get pedalling to school and work and the marketplace. Add this to a healthy diet and the long life enjoyed by most people is explained despite the country's primitive medical infrastructure.

## KEEPING FIT

In many larger cities, foreign-run hotels now operate fitness and health centres. These come equipped with exercise machines, weights and saunas, and are staffed by keep-fit experts and aerobics instructors. With little else to do in the evenings, such centres are busy.

217

While jogging in China has not reached the craze levels of the Western world, it is still a common sight to see people pounding along pavements in the early light of dawn.

Much more common is to see people of all ages out under the willow trees and at lakesides carrying out the strict, patterned movements of tai chi exercises. For anyone living in China, it is easy to find an instructor. Simply join the local tai chi group which every morning gathers to do their exercises near where you live.

If you can't speak Chinese, ask a friend to go with you the first morning to explain who you are and that you want to take part in the exercises. You'll be shyly but warmly welcomed. Then just follow the leader as the group goes through the sedate movements of this ancient martial arts discipline.

You'll find tai chi relaxing as well as stimulating and although the pace is slow and easy, the various exercises stretch muscles and tone up all parts of the body.

## *QUALITY OF LIFE*

So what's it like to live in China? Opinions vary. There is, however, universal agreement that it is now a lot more pleasant, relaxed and comfortable than a decade ago or even three years ago. The turmoil and clampdown of 1989 has not affected to any extent the foreign community. Panicky Westerners fled Beijing in droves when the tanks rumbled into Tiananmen. There was no reason to leave.

Daily life can still be difficult. In Beijing, there is the International School. The standards of this institution are patchy. Many of the children, particularly those of Third World diplomats, are spoiled juvenile delinquents whose bottoms would do well to become acquainted with a rattan cane.

If you want lively entertainment, rock 'n' roll, wild parties, a wide variety of good, affordable restaurants, superb wines and opportunities to meet the opposite sex, don't go to live in China.

In most towns, pollution is a serious problem. This is largely caused by the habit of burning packed bricks of coal dust in the home. The air is gritty. Diesel fumes make the eyes weep. Most Chinese cities give little thought to urban beautification and even in the middle of showcase Beijing, outside splendid joint venture hotels that cost US$100 million, you are liable to find stretches of potholed pavements that look like Upper Volta on a bad day.

Changing times have brought immense improvement. High technology has played a part in this. Take the invention of the VCR. In most cities, foreign residents get films sent in from their head offices at home and enthusiastic bands of cassette swappers exchange movies. This gives something to do in the drabness of the long and featureless nights.

In most cities where there are foreign residents, permanent or temporary, one of the local hotels has been selected as the local bar where people gather. A friendly club-like atmosphere soon develops. German friends liken this to the *stammsicht* tradition in their homeland where one table in a bar is reserved for regulars.

A fresh face is always welcome and if you go into a bar in China and see a bunch of fellows drinking together, just ask if they live in the city. They will delight in welcoming you into their circle and there's no better way to get an idea of how a city works and what it is like than to sit down over a half-dozen beers with people who have been based there for a few years.

## *ENTERTAINMENT*

Cable TV and in-house movies have made a big difference to staying in China. Local TV is, naturally, in Chinese. You can go out to the movies, first checking that the show has English subtitles. But one visit to a Chinese cinema where people spit, eat and smoke throughout the show is probably enough to put you off a return trip.

Chinese-performed Western music, almost always classical, is excellent. The standard of musicians is among the best in the world. But getting concert tickets is normally very difficult.

*A balancing act by a unicyclist on the streets of Beijing. These street performances are making a strong comeback in China today.*

Ask your hotel or friends to let you know about performances of local acrobatic or magic troupes. They are astonishing, without doubt the best on earth.

Go once to a Chinese opera, for the experience. To the Western ear, Chinese opera is a dreadful cacophony. To the unskilled eye, the movements of the colourfully adorned performers are scenic but their roles are incomprehensible.

It is wonderful light entertainment, however, compared to Tibetan opera. A good friend took me along to one of these highland cultural performances one night, and in about a century, I will start to think of forgiving him. Tibetan culture consists of a performer with a voice that could cut marble singing at 100 decibels to one note hovering in the region of high C.

This lasts for three or four hours, when he departs, to be replaced by his identical twin who does likewise. Then a stream of other Tibetans, deities, goddesses, mountain herdsmen, feudal barons and people miraculously transformed into birds traipse across the stage, all of them bellowing at the top of their voices with amplification loud enough to wake up the monks in the Potala Palace, 3,700 kilometres away.

I'm told this is very cultural. Enjoy.

## *SERVANTS*

If your company is paying for a servant, or if you can afford to pay rapidly-increasing domestic helper salaries out of your own pocket, you can enjoy a holiday from the heavy housework while you live in China. In Beijing, the Personnel Service Corporation handles all applications and the person you get to work in your home is the one they assign to you. This could be marvellous or it could turn out to be less than fortuitous. It's all in the luck of the draw. There are similar arrangements in other cities.

It is difficult to come to some informal agreement to get someone to work for you. The language barrier is one obvious problem, shyness is another, but the major problem is finding some official to give a Chinese permission to work in close proximity to foreigners in a private arrangement.

In the capital and other big cities with large permanent foreign populations, there are few problems. You apply to the personnel department and in the fullness of time, a servant will turn up. Make sure in the initial interview that both of you know what duties are expected.

## *DRUGS*

The communists regard China as having been historically a victim of narcotics forced on the nation by outsiders. There is much justification for this view. It was a bunch of grasping Scots and English drug peddlers who insisted on breaking Qing laws by running drugs into China that sparked off the First Opium War. The result was the seizure of Hongkong Island by the British and the forcible opening of treaty ports up and down the coast. This humiliation of Chinese sovereignty (albeit the regime was Manchu) is still a prickly subject.

When the communists came to power, one of the first proclamations they made was that the use of narcotics had to stop. They gave fair warning. In six months, the party said, anyone found smoking, possessing, growing, trafficking or dealing in opium or any of its derivatives would be punished. The Chinese had heard many such threats before. For six months, nothing was done.

Then the communists proved themselves as good as their word. Six months to the day after the warning was given, police throughout the country swooped. Drug runners were lined up and shot.

They still are. With the opening of China, some greedy and foolish people have attempted to use Chinese airports as staging posts to smuggle drugs to the West. One favourite route is to pick up heroin in Bangkok and fly to China. There the tourist spends a couple of days and then flies on to the United States. Because customs officials know that drugs are virtually unknown in China, checks for narcotics on flights arriving from China tend to be casual. They are far less stringent than on flights arriving direct from Thailand, for example.

The profits of drug running in China are slim. If caught, traffickers are dealt with in a speedy fashion. It's arrest one day, up in court the next and that afternoon the drug runner has a date with the executioner in the local football stadium. There, with a placard around his neck detailing his crime, he gets a bullet in the brain in front of a crowd of spectators.

No Westerner has yet been executed simply because none has been caught smuggling drugs. The best anyone caught with drugs in China can expect is a lengthy prison sentence, at least 10 years in jail, to ponder the wisdom of his ways. You have been warned.

## *LAW AND ORDER*

China is a peaceable country. Even at the height of the pro-democracy struggle in the spring and summer of 1989, tourists were safe throughout the land.

There is little or no mugging. There is little theft. I feel no qualms about leaving camera gear worth thousands of dollars and wallets full of cash in hotel rooms anywhere in the country. I have never been threatened anywhere in China. Nobody I know has ever been robbed or had anything stolen.

This is not to say there is no crime in China. Read the local papers and you will see accounts of murder, rape, assault and personal crimes the same as anywhere in the world. Justice in China is swift and punishment certain. Robbers and rapists are shot. Murderers are almost invariably executed. The death penalty is also imposed for economic crimes against the state, for large-scale corruption and organised theft from state corporations.

Civil libertarians might protest these drastic measures but for tourists, at least, they result in a country which is safe to visit. Women can walk safely after dark in any Chinese city. If you get lost, any policeman will be glad to help you.

A few months ago, a tourist was found stabbed in his room at a five-star hotel in Shenzhen; it turned out he had met a girl in the bar, invited her upstairs where, saying she was going to the toilet, she opened the corridor door to a couple of robbers. The British guest fought. He died.

You can't protect people from themselves.

## NO SECOND CHANCE

The big campaign to crack down on civil crime is said to have started in 1983 after Deng Xiaoping and other party leaders witnessed a murder during their annual summer retreat to the northern beach resort of Beihaidei. Whatever the reason, after a period of relative leniency, the death penalty was swiftly reintroduced throughout the country for crimes of violence.

A few months after this began, I was down in rural Guangdong where one day I was sitting on a bus beside a local party cadre who was attached to the People's Armed Police. How was the law and order campaign going, I enquired. Did the death penalty, widely publicised and with executions being attended by many thousands of people, act as a deterrent?

He thought for a moment.

'Well,' he said finally. 'I suppose it is a deterrent. But I'll tell you one thing. We don't get any second offenders.'

Don't get the idea that the death penalty is some horrible communist custom; all Chinese societies take a tough view on crime and punishment and capital sentences are in the traditional mode.

# Chapter Nine

# CUISINE

*Hot oil or bitter cabbage –
every man to his own taste.*

*Viands have various flavours.
What pleases the palate is good.*

In the heart of the old French Concession in Shanghai is the old White Russian Garrison Church. It was built in 1933 by exiled czarists who had a hopeless dream of one day going home. After liberation, it was used as a store house but a few years ago, an enthusiastic Frenchman in Hong Kong with a vineyard in South Africa got a lease and turned it into a restaurant, with a German chef. Get the idea that China's food scene is cosmopolitan? You're dead right.

This place is called Ashanti (which happens to be in Northern Ghana) after the owner's vineyard, which is in South Africa. Do not drink his wine, which is appalling, but go to the place, buy a beer and wander about looking at the Red Guard-inspired art on the main floor and the wonderful naked Russian lady angels floating about in the church's dome on the upper floor. It's a fascinating building. Don't eat there, either – it's too expensive.

Instead, wander a few streets away to Park 97. This is a great place and as 2001 dawned was the hanging-out capital for swinging Shanghai. E-commerce yuan millionaires, models, movie stars, diplomats, journalists, businessmen...here's the cutting edge of the new China social clime. The food is good, too, with crunchy pizza and a great wine selection.

But for me, the best restaurant in China is down on the Huang He on top floor of one of the old European citadels of commerce. Here you find M on the Bund, an Australian chef-owner, a Dutch maître d'hôtel, English and Aussies in the kitchen, totally fabulous modern international food and reasonable prices. Wander outside with a glass of chardonnay from Shandong Province and the historical Shanghai waterfront is floodlit in front of your eyes. Down the Bund is the old Peace Hotel, now revamped to Victorian splendour, where the renowned geriatric jazz band plays 1920s Dixieland.

I mention these few places to give a hint of the flavour of modern China dining. There are similar restaurants, bars and nightclubs all over the country, but as in so many other ways, Shanghai is at the cutting edge.

This was not always the case. Foreign food in China used to be dreadful. By some twisted logic (the Red Guards were not too hot on common sense), people who liked Western food were identified as untrustworthy. So for a generation, foreign food languished. Of

226

course, there were no tourists, so that source of demand, too, was absent.

In recent years, there has been a reversal. Everything foreign was fashionable. That included food. And when the tourist armies came stamping into China, they wanted familiar dishes. First to cater for these culinary demands were the new hotels where tourists stayed, but in the past few years, restaurants with ethnic cuisines have been sprouting across the land with the startling rate of mushrooms in a Guangxi spring.

Please, I beg of visitors, always try the local dishes wherever you go. But after you have delighted in Chaozhou, Hunan, Taiwanese, Yunnan and Yangzhou specialities, and if you are in China for more than a few days, you should sample some of the foreign cuisine restaurants. Many are locally owned. Others are run by top international chefs. All the big hotels have very good international outlets. But my preference is for the small stand-alone family eatery.

There are many of them. Ethnic styles run the range. Portuguese is common, which is not all that surprising, given the long presence of Portuguese explorers, pirates and settlers on the China Coast. French, of course, is prevalent. American restaurants are always popular with Chinese, perhaps because of the massive size of the servings. Italian eateries are ubiquitous; there's scarcely a city in the land where you can't find a place called Angelo's or Pizza Palace.

For some reason, Mexican food is popular; I was told this was because people think it is a Western version of spicy Sichuan. And you will find places offering such exotic delights as Spanish and Swedish specialities. Given the huge German population in China – textiles, machinery, coal, steel, cars, aviation – and the preponderance of Swiss, Austrian and German chefs in the catering business, delicatessens offer pumpernickel and wursts of all descriptions.

Until a few years ago, unless you were in a major hotel in a key city, your dining choices were restricted. Now, the world's on your plate.

Most people eat to live. Chinese live to eat. This is not an exaggeration but a simple fact of life. All China adores food. Every man, woman and most children think they are gourmets. When Chinese from different regions meet, the second topic of conversation – after where they come from – focuses firmly on local regional delicacies.

Daily life revolves around food. A missed lunch is a minor tragedy. The delights of the table go back beyond Confucius. A gourmet himself, the great philosopher wrote glowingly of the importance of food. Through the ages, poets, emperors and warriors were expected to be connoisseurs of fine dining. The dinner table was one of the elegant highlights of a gentleman's or noble's existence and he was expected to be able to discourse knowledgeably on food, its history and preparation.

## A FEW EXAMPLES

One of the many hundreds of dishes attributed to a poet is that distinctive Hangzhou speciality, Dong Po Pork. The tale goes that the famed writer and calligrapher of the Northern Song, Su Dong Po, was in charge of dredging the jewel of the area, the willow-fringed West Lake. He had a work force of 200,000 men and, to encourage them to toil mightily, he ordered an army of chefs to prepare hearty dishes of fat pork casserole in the sweet rice wine of nearby Shaoxing. The city still delights in this 1,000-year-old dish.

To health-conscious Westerners, it glistens with soggy fat and clogged arteries spring to mind. To Chinese, it is a succulent, prized delight.

Military men were also expected to be familiar with kitchen techniques when they had done with military tactics on the battlefield. General T'so's Chicken recalls the campaigns of a fiery general who loved tender fowl fried in hot red chillies.

Mandarins bequeathed to China many delicacies because rulers of the state were expected also to be gourmets and scholars as well as administrators. But, naturally, most of the great dishes of China can be traced back to the grassroots, to the peasant villages where the bulk of the people always lived.

Among the best-known is Beggar's Chicken. There is fierce provincial and regional rivalry over where this aromatic dish originated with chefs in Jiangsu, Fujian, Anhui and Zhejiang all arguing heatedly that it was first accidentally baked in their home areas. While this is a lively way in which to spend an hour over a flask of Shaoxing wine, it doesn't really matter.

The legend is the same everywhere. A poor landless peasant was starving and as he roamed the countryside looking for edible roots or anything else to stave off hunger, he stumbled across a plump chicken. Within seconds, he had grasped the bird and wrung its neck. Eagerly, he lit a fire by the side of a stream and as the wood burned down to hot coals, he plucked the fowl.

Suddenly, the sound of horse hooves could be heard. Riding up came the local noble with an entourage of swordsmen. To be found with the stolen bird would mean death so the wily peasant swiftly plunged into the stream, scooped up mud and weeds growing on the bank and plastered them around the bird. He threw the ball of clay onto the fire.

The noble reined in his horse. What are you doing, he asked the peasant. Making bricks, sire, came the answer, pointing to the mud in the flames. On rode the horsemen.

As soon as they were safely out of sight, the beggar used sticks to pull the hardened clay out of the glowing coals. Using a stone, he broke the container and was enveloped in a magical cloud of heavenly steam. The weeds he had so hurriedly plucked were wild herbs and lotus leaves and they had cooked inside the sealed clay with the chicken. Today, that same feast can be enjoyed in many regions of coastal China. It is one of the true wonders of Chinese gastronomy. I love it. I adore ordering it, I cherish using the silver hammer to break the ball, I dote on plunging my head into the aromatic steam and I salivate as I plunge my chopsticks into the chicken and grab a huge chunk of meat and vegetable. This is truly good stuff.

Wherever you eat it, your local dinner companions will tell you it originated nearby. Nod in agreement and reach for some more of this succulent, juicy fowl and give thanks to that beggar of old.

## THE FOUR REGIONS

Just about every cookbook you read on China divides the nation into four culinary regions. There is justification for this. It's also incorrect. It ignores the huge variety of regional cuisines that are a matter of great local culinary patriotism in every corner of the land. We won't get into that argument here. There are more than 19,000 Chinese cookbooks in print that deal with the subject in depth.

The four basic gastronomic areas widely recognised by gourmets are the cuisines of Canton, Shanghai, Sichuan and Beijing.

### Canton

The culinary capital of the nation is without a doubt the great southern city of Guangzhou, a citadel of magnificent dining for more than 1,000 years and an area with a distinctive elegance in eating.

The secret in Cantonese cooking is freshness and lightness. Live prawns and vegetables picked from the market gardens that morning are steamed, simply and swiftly. The natural juices and taste of the ingredients stand by themselves without benefit of sauces, salt, sugar or any other additives. On a culinary map, what is known as 'Cantonese' food would cover the southeastern corner of the country. But within this area there is an enormous range of various local cuisines. Each hamlet has its own speciality and way of cooking and preparing food. And there are many strongly distinctive regional cuisines within the Cantonese food family.

The *dim sum* taken to the world by southern Chinese is a Cantonese custom. What you've had overseas is a pallid imitation. There is nothing else on earth that can compare with a crowded *dim sum* palace on a busy holiday morning. The extended family is there. All of them, three or four generations. People shout for different blends of tea. Serving trolleys roll through the crowded tables with aged crones to shapely young girls screeching out their wares. The sound crashes off the walls. In a good *dim sum* restaurant, it sounds as though World War III is being waged.

To Cantonese, the sound and the fury are almost as important as the food. Those heavenly prawns wrapped in translucent pastry, narrow baby pork ribs marinated in garlic, chicken feet steamed for hours in ginger and beef balls aromatic with coriander ... the dishes arrive in endless profusion.

For the treat of a lifetime, when in Guangzhou beg your hotel to make reservations for you to have breakfast at the Panxi teahouse. This is the premier Chinese teahouse on earth, set amid courtyards, ancient banyan trees and a placid lake in the Canton suburbs. Here presides the Queen of Dim Sum, Madame Lau, whose genius is recognised by gourmets worldwide. It is quiet and tranquil compared with other *dim sum* restaurants and a treat to be remembered.

## *Shanghai*

The cooking of Shanghai is a true melting pot. It would be much more accurate to label this gastronomic heritage Lower Yangtze Valley cooking. Shanghai was an insignificant hamlet before it was grabbed as a treaty port in 1841 so it has no traditional cuisine to call its own. Instead, it has borrowed widely from the surrounding rich delta areas, notably from the provincial kitchens of surrounding Jiangsu and Zhejiang provinces.

For a century, Shanghai was an international city and, despite 30 years of subjugation in the Maoist mould, there always remained a strong culinary influence from abroad. This was created by the once strong French presence in the city, by the huge influx of White Russians and Jews who flocked there between the world wars, and by the big foreign populations of British, German, Danish, American and

231

Japanese business communities. Stronger tasting, well oiled, cooked with more salt and copious quantities of sweet rice wine from the nearby city of Shaoxing, the food of the region is tasty and exciting.

## *Sichuan*

A couple of thousand miles upriver from Shanghai is the Red Basin of Sichuan. The land gets its name from the deep maroon soil rather than the politics of its turbulent native sons; Deng Xiaoping and many other revolutionaries sprang from this red earth. Here is the peppery kingdom; the spicy, tangy dishes of Sichuan and nearby provinces of Hunan and Guizhou are renowned. Full of zest and colour, Sichuan dishes such as dried shredded beef and red peppers look as attractive as they taste.

Geography has played a major part in creating the Sichuan palate.

Local gourmets tell you over a toast of *mao tai* (which originated in Guizhou) that the intense humidity of summer causes hot flushes and bad tempers. The way to get rid of this troublesome complaint is to eat lots of hot, highly spiced foods. The chillies and peppers cause the blood temperature to rise, which opens the pores in the skin, which in turn allows the internal organs to cool off. Is there any truth in this old wives' tale? Who knows.

Herbal doctors swear it's true and a lifetime addiction to hot red pepper didn't stop Mao Zedong (from Hunan) living to a ripe old age. So, enjoy that sliced cold duck smoked in tea and camphor, sip the fragrant tea from the Sichuan hillsides where the pandas prowl at night and tuck into the chicken sautéed with red pepper. It may burn the roof off your mouth and bring tears to your eyes, but it's going to open the pores.

One curious footnote to Sichuan cuisine is the presence on the menu of seaweed. Here you have a place thousands of kilometres from the East China Sea and there is often seaweed on the table. Why? Once again, the explanation comes from the herbalists. More than

1,000 years ago, the landlocked basin was noted for goitre. Many people suffered from the disease. Most of the local salt was obtained from bores where bamboo shafts were driven deep into the earth and a salt solution pumped laboriously to the surface.

Somehow, a herbal practitioner discovered the link between iodine salt in seaweed and goitre. Eat enough seaweed (they didn't know the specific chemical substance, of course) and goitre would gradually diminish. So up the Yangtze, struggling against the mighty flow of that phenomenal torrent, coolies have for centuries dragged big junkloads of seaweed to grace the tables of Sichuan's health-conscious gourmets.

## *Beijing*

The cuisine of Beijing, like that of Shanghai, is a misnamed hybrid. It should more correctly be described as the culinary tradition of the North China Plain. Most dishes that are commonly thought of as Beijing food (including the famed Peking Duck) originated from fertile, food-loving Shandong province where Confucius 25 centuries ago presided over a rich mixture of philosophy and gastronomy. Within this realm of northern provinces where 'Beijing' food is the norm – roughly speaking, Shandong, Hebei, Shanxi, Shaanxi and the Manchurian lands – there is incredible culinary diversity. Some rules, however, apply to most of the area. Wheat buns and pancakes are the staff of life here, not rice. The food is solid, substantial peasant fare, aimed at keeping a man hard at work in the fields during those frigid northern winters.

Until the end of the 18th century, the vast expanse of Manchuria, ancestral homeland of the Qing Dynasty which had ruled China since 1644, was largely empty. The forests and grasslands were deemed an enormous reserve for the pleasure of the ruling nationality and Han Chinese were rigorously excluded and confined to a slice of land close to the southern coast of present-day Liaoning province. Then, as Manchu rule collapsed, Chinese poured into these empty lands. It was at the same time as the Americans rolled across the Mississippi and conquered the Wild West. The Chinese settlers headed into the empty Manchurian plains with much the same exuberant enthusiasm as did the American settlers into the Great Plains. With them, they took their farming methods and culinary traditions. It explains why basic Shandong food serves as the strong foundations on which so much Northeast cooking skills are built today.

## THE FORGOTTEN FOUR

There are many culinary schools in China outside the basic four.

### Mongol

The Mongols, up on their harsh, windswept steppes, have their own traditions, adapted for the hard life of nomadic herders and roving invaders. Steak Tartar, that elegant dish served in Western restaurants, can trace its beginnings to the armies of the Great Khan. As Genghis and his extremely unfriendly horde galloped out of the steppes on their way to conquer the world, they rode fast and light. There was no large commissionary supply train rumbling in their wake. Instead, the rude, tough Mongols would cut a big chunk of meat off cattle, horse, sheep or goat and stick the raw, bleeding steak under their saddle. After a day of riding, the constant pounding of the meat broke down the gristle and sinews and made it tender. They would tear into the slab of raw meat at the end of the day, toss down a leather flask of fermented horse milk and be up before dawn the following day to ride off to sack, plunder and rape another city.

### Manchu

The Manchus were a little more civilised before they ascended the Dragon Throne. But not much. Their gastronomy was considerably elevated compared to that of the Mongols but nowhere near as civilised as the elegant Han they ruled. Lamb stews and beef barbecues were more their mark, along with heavy tubers and vegetables strong enough to last through the six-month-long icebox winters of their northern homeland.

## *Xinjiang*

Much more exotic is the food of the far western lands of Xinjiang. The name means 'New Dominion' and signifies the late date at which it was reincorporated into the Chinese empire after centuries of uncertainty over who held sway over this vast, arid land. Islam came early here, and with Xinjiang bordering Central Asia and the population a majority of Turkic Uygurs and other non-Han races, one expects the food to be different. So it is. The caravanserais of Kashgar and Urumqi smack of herbs and spices of Araby. Camels wander the streets amid stands of hot charcoal over which Uygur chefs bake kebabs of lamb, peppers and onion on wooden stakes. (To many Chinese, particularly southerners, lamb has a distasteful odour and the smell of cheese frequently makes them nauseous. Here, lamb and cheese made from goat, horse and camel milk are much loved staples.)

## *Tibetan*

The Tibetans, of course, have their own culinary culture which they seem to enjoy almost as fervently as their brand of Buddhism. The intricacies of both are likely to be lost on outsiders. Roasted barley flour, known as *tsampa*, is the basis of just about everything, mostly because little other grain has ever been successful grown in the harsh climate on the high ice plateau. Ground barley is added to everything, from tea to minced beef to vegetables. It is the basis of all Tibetan food. Tea carried up from the lowlands of Sichuan is mixed with smelly yak butter and heavy handfuls of barley to make a staple drink; it tastes as bad as it sounds. There may well be some tasty Tibetan native dishes; if you ever find one, please tell me.

Every racial group, region and county in China has individual culinary traits which locals regard with strong native pride. To a

*If it runs, crawls, leaps, flies, waddles, hops, swims, gildes or burrows, the Chinese will have a tried-and-tested recipe for it. This pangolin caught by tribesmen in Yunnan near the Vietnamese border made a prime dish. Serve it sautéed with a whisper of ginger and a hint of garlic, I was advised by a Yao chef. The recipe is simple: first, catch a pangolin...*

Chinese, food is absolutely central to life, and pride in the heritage of home village, county and province is supreme. Wherever you travel in China, always make sure to ask your guides, hotel staff and tour escorts what the local speciality is. Then try it.

## MANNERS MAKETH THEE HUNGRY

When I first came to Asia in the early 1960s, my initial touch of the Chinese way of life came with a jolly band of newspapermen in an open-air cooked food stall in Singapore. Platter after steaming, aromatic platter arrived on the table. Chopsticks flashed like swords in a *kung fu* movie as those ravenous scribes attacked the chilli crab, steamed prawns and fish cooked with spring onions and ginger. Unaccustomed to the simple intricacies of the chopsticks, my pickings of the meal were slim indeed. Then a burly Singaporean of Hakka descent leaned over, drained his Tiger beer and explained the first rule of Chinese culinary etiquette. 'Always make sure you don't go hungry,' he advised. This has stood me in fine stead ever since.

## THE RESTAURANT

About the worst fate that can befall a serious diner is to find himself alone at a Chinese table. How can he or she sample more than two or three dishes? What a tragedy. The optimum number of people to enjoy a decent repast is a dozen. That's why Chinese dining tables are generously sized round affairs, so 12 hungry gourmands can gather around the rim and lean over to get at the dishes on the lazy Susan in the middle that takes the dishes to within reach of all.

But if there are only two or three or four of you in a party, never mind. Just do your best and eat as much as you can. In many restaurants, the menu will list dishes in three sizes. If there are only a few of you, order the smallest size of every dish so you can call for as many different courses as possible.

The girth-conscious Westerner can eat till he bursts with an easy conscience because the Chinese diet is the healthiest on earth.

## The Table

Chinese eat as a family. That is why tables are so large. Based on the farming life, everyone could come in from the field and eat the steaming platters of vegetables and rice, along with the infrequent chicken, the festive piece of pork and the very rare bit of beef.

Chopsticks (*kuaizi*, or 'pick up small pieces') give longer reach. They are hygienic as well as efficient and well designed to allow deft diners to pluck tiny delicacies from stew pot or serving platter.

## Etiquette

Table manners are as complex as they are simple. On the most basic level, tuck in and eat your fill. On more formal levels, the etiquette can be as disciplined as the court of Louis XVI.

Formal banquets can be fun, once in a while. But if you are doing serious business in China and are going to a banquet a night, you can soon weary of the endless courses of rich dishes.

## Serving

The first platter at a banquet will be a spectacular selection of cold cuts and pickled vegetables. The host picks up a couple of choice items and places them on the plate of the guest of honour, then does the same for other guests within chopstick reach. Other members of the host party do the same. Then you have a toast – and tuck in.

Be careful. This is the first of a dozen dishes, so approach the meal like a marathon runner. This is no culinary hundred-metre dash. The waitress will display the courses so you can appreciate the appearance of the artistic creation (almost as important as taste) and then she will serve each diner. In less formal settings, the dishes will be put on the middle of the table and everyone helps themselves.

## *Timing*

They eat early in China. The morning meetings end at 11.30 a.m. so everyone can scurry off to the dining table. At night, it's up chopsticks at 6 p.m. Until the tourist influx caused a change in habits, at least in the bigger hotels, meals were served from 6 p.m. and service stopped at 6.30 p.m. If you had not dined by then, well, tough. You had to wait till breakfast or munch a packet of dry biscuits in your hotel room. As in so many other areas, there have been changes. Hotels now serve until 10 p.m. or so. But don't leave things too late or you might still go to bed hungry.

At a banquet, when the last course is served, usually fresh fruit, it is time to drink up and go. You don't sit around the dinner table for small talk. You've been at table for a couple of hours mixing conversation with the courses. Now you eat your orange or melon, raise your glass in a final toast, shake hands all round and repeat your sincere thanks for a marvellous meal – then depart. Chinese good manners call for a speedy end to conclusions once the final course is consumed.

## *EVERYTHING UNDER THE SUN*

There's a saying: Chinese will eat any creature whose backbone points to the sun. In other words, any animal, fish or fowl is good for the pot. The hidden message here is that the only animal whose backbone does not point to the sun – man – is not eligible for the pot. This stricture has been relaxed among the Chinese communities of South America where upside-down sloths are sometimes a delicacy adapted to the Chinese kitchen.

In China, just about anything goes into the wok.

## *No Puss or Poodle*

There is a story about eating in China that simply refuses to go away. Dozens of people will tell you they've heard of it second-hand.

Nobody can ever give a time, date, place or name.

The story goes like this ...

An elegant foreign couple, normally identified as French, go into a restaurant. Sometimes, the tale has them in Hongkong, other times in a city in China. With them, the pair have a well-trimmed poodle on a leather lead. They cannot speak Chinese. A helpful waiter brings a menu. The couple cannot decipher a single character. The waiter points to what other diners are having. The couple look, nod. The waiter kindly offers to take the dog outside while the couple dine.

In come the courses. Each, washed down by cold Qingtao beer, is tastier, more succulent, than the last. The couple dine excellently. The bill is called for. So reasonable for such a feast! The couple pay, leaving a big tip. Thank you, they say. Now, where is our pet? The waiter looks astonished. There is a communication gap. Finally, the message gets through. The dog? The waiter points proudly at one of the dishes in which the poodle has been tastily presented with garlic and ginger. The lady faints.

I've heard this story a score of times. Nobody has yet to persuade me it ever happened.

## *Munching on Monkey*

Another great gastronomical horror story sworn to be true by hundreds of people who have never seen it is the old saga of eating the brains of a live monkey. This is usually said to take place in Borneo or Indonesia, but I've also heard tell of it being a practice in Guangxi or Yunnan provinces. It is a lot of nonsense but never let it be said I would ruin a good story just because it is not true.

The recipe for this imaginary feast is to take a live monkey. The circular table has a round hole about five inches in diameter cut in the middle. You (somehow) sit the monkey on a stool and strap it in place so the skull protrudes through the hole. Then, using a sharp knife, you cut off the top of the head and pick at the live brain.

This is total garbage, of course, but thousands of people who have never seen it swear it is true. The old European ethnocentric fears about dining on dog or enjoying a well-sautéed cat steak in a Chinese restaurant is sheer nonsense. Old China Hands love to repeat such ridiculous yarns to turn the tender stomachs of the delicate newcomers.

Fear not. There is no way in the world anyone will be served dog instead of beef in a Chinese restaurant anywhere on earth. One reason this is unlikely is simple economics.

Chinese, especially in the south, do eat dogs in winter. But they are normally the plump Zhou puppies with black tongues, specially bred for the stew pot. Restaurants are not going to feed this delicacy to ignorant foreigners, if only because Zhou flesh costs about 15 times more than prime beef. It is eaten for medicinal purposes (it is supposed to make the blood thick and protect the elderly against winter chills) and is very difficult to find.

Nobody is going to waste this on a foreign devil who wouldn't appreciate such a fine dish.

## *Delicacies*

That's not to say the Chinese don't have some peculiar tastes. If you should have a hankering after stir-fried scorpions, hasten up to the western region of Shandong province and all your wishes will be answered. The poisonous creatures up there are a much adored speciality.

Truth to tell, they don't taste too bad. Every peasant farm seemingly has its own backyard scorpion plot; do not ask me how one breeds them. Whenever honoured guests appear on the horizon, Mrs Tsang goes outside and scoops up a couple of hundred 5-cm-long scorpions. As any Shandong housewife will happily tell you, they have to be cleansed thoroughly twice in dry salt, then washed in salty water, to remove the venom in the tail. Then stir-fried, they end up a crunchy delicacy tasting not unlike English whitebait. They are, I must admit, an acquired taste.

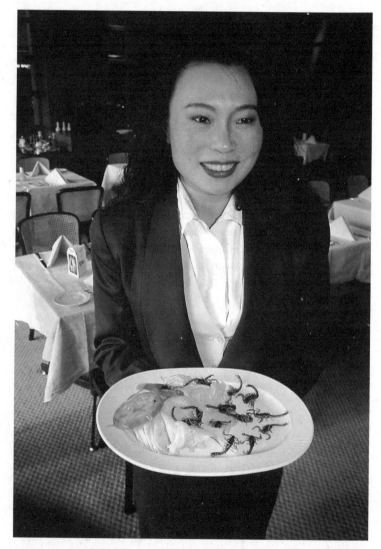

*Nice, crunchy scorpions, anyone?*

Rice birds? In the great southern ricelands, young sparrows 3 cm or so long are trapped as they flutter around the ripening crop. Marinated and then baked, they are eaten bones and all.

Snakes? You name it, Chinese eat it. Cobras are big favourites in Guangdong while pythons are the choice delight in Fujian. The true delicacy is the gall bladder. To the table, the waiter (brave fellow) brings a writhing 3-metre black king cobra. On his finger, the waiter wears a ring with a sharp hooked blade. He loops the hissing snake over the table, flashes his wrist and the gall bladder pops out of the snake and, twisting and oozing greenish bile, it sinks to the bottom of the glass of snake vodka in front of you. Being the only foreigner and therefore the guest of honour, you have won the great distinction of getting the gall bladder. There is no way you can get out of this. Lift your glass in a polite toast to the host and swirl down the contents with a satisfied smile. The first dozen times are the worst.

Bear's paws? These taste rather like rich oxtail stew. Pretty good. Now the central government has declared bears a protected species so this is a rare dish.

Camel hooves? Because it is now largely impossible for chefs to get bear's feet, they make do with camels. The awkward beasts plod by the millions over the steppes of Mongolia and the sands of Xinjiang so they are in no way an endangered species. Bad luck. This means there are an endless supply of camel's hooves to go around. A well-simmered, marinated camel's foot, boiled for hours with herbs and vegetables by a master chef and served with great flair and style, tastes just like what it is – the well-worn hoof of a critter that has walked through every sewer between Ulan Bator and Kashgar. Humps, another northern delicacy, are a delight compared to the hooves.

Pandas? No way. Anyone killing a panda for the pot in China faces life imprisonment if they are lucky and execution if the judge feels virtuous.

Sea slugs. The only dish I flatly refuse to touch is this vile creature that oozes itself over shallow seas off the China coast. They are a prized delicacy. Imagine a truck tyre that had been on a vehicle used for 40 years or so to run about a farmyard. Cut off a chunk of tyre, throw it on a plate and you get some idea of what a good piece of sea slug tastes like.

Beancurd. Marvellous. Wonderful. The stuff of life. The pressed whey of beans, usually soy, is one of the most healthy and joyous inventions of the Chinese kitchen. Alas, many Westerners do not like the texture of *tofu* although doctors will tell you this protein-rich vegetable cuts cholesterol, replaces meat and has vast dietary advantages. Bland in itself, *tofu* can be mixed with a vast variety of other ingredients to give it a huge array of tastes. Thankfully, this marvellous dietary invention is now becoming popular among sophisticated Western foodies.

Years ago, in the Hunan capital of Changsha, I was dining with a bunch of top party officials in a restaurant which Mao Zedong was said to have frequented when he was a young teacher in the town. How about a dish of the *tofu* which was the late Chairman's favoured dish, I suggested. This is a preparation called, with extremely good reason, Bad Smell Beancurd. There was some hesitation but the waiter was called and the dish eventually appeared. Never has a culinary invention been so aptly named.

It lay on the plate looking like something that had been deposited in a paddy field by a very sick water buffalo. It smelled bad, it looked bad and it tasted a lot worse. I took a hesitant mouthful with my chopsticks. Eyes turned in my direction. I swallowed, reached for a glass of the local fire-water. The party secretary, mayor, propaganda chief and assorted officials looked anxiously on. My verdict? Well, I said, if this is the sort of stuff that Chairman Mao used to have to eat, then I was not surprised that he set off on the Long March.

Silence while this was translated. Then roars of laughter all round and calls for more rice wine and beer as the Bad Smell Beancurd was, thankfully, carried away to oblivion.

## *Exotica*

Softshell turtles steamed in their shells with herbs, peppers and spices are a speciality of Guangxi. Zhuang tribesmen swear by the dish as a protection against the chills of winter. They hint also of the vast potential aid in the sexual department which a steady diet of stewed turtle provides.

A few years ago, the famed Cajun chef, John Folse of Louisiana, was in Hongkong cooking at the Hilton Hotel. One of his specialities from the Louisiana bayou was turtle. Astonishing. The dish tasted precisely as it was prepared in Guangxi. In some excitement, I talked to the chef after lunch. The recipe he gave me was exactly the same – the ingredients and the preparation – as that used in the hill valleys of southwest China. Come to think about it, we agreed after a lengthy discussion, why not? Both Louisiana and Guangxi are inhabited by people who are a minority (Cajun and Zhuang) and live in hot, humid areas, richly watered, and thickly forested where game and wildlife abounds. So it really shouldn't be too much of a surprise that the dishes were based on the same animals and vegetation and cooked in the same manner. The moral of this story is that no matter how strange a dish may sound, it's well worth trying. It could be something just like mother cooked back home.

There are exceptions. I doubt if anyone's mother ever cooked fat frog soup, unless she was a Liaoning herbalist's mum. The winters in Manchuria are ferociously cold. Many animals, including the humble frogs, hibernate. In the autumn, a special breed of frog eats furiously, then burrows down into the fields and streambanks to create a warm environment for the coming deep freeze. The creatures are protected not only by their burrows but by rich, deep layers of fatty tissue built up during their summer-long feast. When the snows fall and the earth freezes solid, Manchurian gourmets set off in search of the buried frogs. They know how to find the animals in their deep hollows; don't ask me how. Once caught, the sleepy frogs are skinned and the layer of fat scraped off their hides. The fat is boiled and made into a soup which supposedly does for the human diner what the fat was originally supposed to do for the frog. It keeps him warm in the plunging temperatures.

Worry not. No Chinese restaurant or hotel is going to press such delicacies on a squeamish Westerner. But such potions, part food, part medicine, are common on the kitchen tables of China. They are the extreme equivalent of the Jewish mum's chicken soup. Most Chinese grandmothers, however, use duck as the raw ingredient.

## A Diet of Desperation

Ever seen a shark's fin? They are ragged pieces of gristle and skin. There is not much taste to them and not a great deal of nutrition. So why are they now so vastly expensive and how come shark's fin soup is a renowned delicacy?

The questions hark back to the days of famine along the coast. Why eat a fin if large chunks of succulent shark flesh were available? Simply because there was not enough food to go around and if the fin was all that was left to boil up to keep alive, people would eat it. Probably by accident, someone discovered that the fin, boiled sufficiently long, produced a strong gelatinous substance. In time, this was added to chicken broth to produce the tasty, rich dish known today as shark's fin soup. Originally, however, it was eaten because there was nothing else. It was part of the diet of desperation that led Chinese over the centuries to place many items of exotica on the table.

## BUYING FOOD

The shops of China are bursting. Unlike the pitiable display of foodstuffs available in the Soviet bloc, China luxuriates in plentiful supplies of the basic necessities of life. Cooking oil and grain sold under controlled prices are sometimes rationed but there is always plenty available at slightly higher prices in the free enterprise markets.

Shops and outside markets are normally bustling. This is partly because of the traditional insistence on the freshest possible ingredients (fish are scooped live from holding tanks, chickens beheaded and plucked in front of you) which sees housewives going to market every morning. This desire for fresh food is compounded by necessity; not every home in China has a refrigerator and daily buying is vital.

The shopping visit is partly recreational. It's an opportunity to talk to the neighbours, see friends, stop for a chat and find out what's going on in the neighbourhood. You don't only load up on spinach and carp, you also collect the daily ration of gossip.

For foreigners, Western-style delicatessens now offer well stocked premises, usually in joint venture hotels. But people who live in China will probably buy most of the basic vegetables, poultry, fish and canned foods from local markets. For one thing, it's a lot cheaper. For another, it's more fun.

## DON'T JUST EAT FOOD, TALK ABOUT IT

Just about every Chinese considers himself an expert on food. It is a national fascination. Sophisticated cosmopolitans and simple peasants alike are happy to discuss food, knowledgeably and with great enthusiasm, with just about anyone. If the novice businessman in China wants to swiftly gain friends and influence people, he would be well advised to bone up on Chinese cuisine so he can make intelligent table talk. (Chinese consider it polite to talk about food and to ignore more controversial matters like religion, politics and money.)

I was once at a high-level political seminar at the Great Hall of the People in Beijing. There were senior cadres there from every province and a collection of top party and government officials. Up to me came a member of the State Council who quietly took me aside for a chat. The other foreign newspapermen were, understandably, anxious to know what we had discussed so earnestly in the 15 minutes we were chatting animatedly in a corner.

'Matters of mutual interest,' I announced, copying a line much loved by diplomats. This, of course, infuriated my colleagues. They thought I'd got a scoop. Alas, no. What the Great Man wanted was to talk to me about a recipe in one of my recently published Chinese cookbooks. The ingredients were a bit different in my directions from the way the dish was prepared in his home province. We spent a lively time swapping anecdotes about smoked duck (every region has a distinctive method of preparing this delicious dish) and sundry other dishes. I didn't get a story that night but it did me absolutely no harm at all to have been seen cornered with one of the most powerful men in the land at a public function. In months to come, down in the provinces, when I saw local leaders who had been at this reception, I got an overwhelming welcome. It took some time for my Western colleagues to get over their ire. When I eventually told them later that night we had discussed cookbooks and recipes, they flatly refused to believe me.

But it is the mark of a scholar, gentleman and sophisticate (and conniving journalists) to be able to knowingly talk about haute cuisine. The kitchen door opens many other doors in China.

## *WELCOME TO FAT CITY*

The eating scene is changing as rapidly in China as every other aspect of life. And it's not always for the better. The golden arches of McDonald's beckon a young generation towards obesity and the risk of heart attacks, doctors warn.

The basic Chinese cuisine, north and south, was heavy on rice and wheat, with many tasty vegetables and perhaps, minor portions of meat. Add bean curd and as many fish as you could afford, and this became not just a tasty cuisine, but a recipe for a long and healthy life. In the era before vehicles became common, almost all China rode to work on bicycles. Exercise and a good diet equal the longevity so prized by ancient philosophers.

Then came rising income, one-children families and the Western culinary invasion of fast food outlets. Dripping with fat and heavy with meat, the dishes were consumed with passion. Not only did Chinese like the finger-lickin' taste of those outrageously expensive snacks, it was thought fashionable to eat them. The main Beijing McDonald's soon had more people queuing at the door than there were at the nearby entrance to the Forbidden City.

# Chapter Ten

# THE FAMILY

*With perfect harmony in the family*
*No evil influences can injure*

*Everything prospers in a united family*
*Though events do not happen according to men's calculations*

Chinese society is built on the solid foundations of the family. It's the basis of life and society today as much as it was when the first Han stuck their wooden ploughs into the soft soil along the Yellow River. It is an institution that has prevailed throughout the ages. It remains inviolate today, the base of Chinese culture and community. Many of the strengths, and not a few of the weaknesses, of modern China can be traced to the reverence for family ties. Confucius lauded them and the princelings of party bosses today cash in on the reverence in which family values are prized.

The family was the obvious first organisation to exist when cave-age men started scratching the fertile earth in the Great Bend of the Yellow River to grow their meagre crops. The legendary first ruler of the early Chinese state, Fu Hsi, is reputed to have formulated the extended family clan system and to have laid down rules for the use of family names sometime in the late 29th century B.C. Through all the agonies and triumphs of Chinese history since then, the family has remained the strongest strand running through civilisation.

## *THE WONG FAMILY*

The family today is Mr Wong, Mrs Wong and one little Wong. There is a generation growing up which largely will never know the dubious joy of having a brother or sister. The stringent restriction on children may be for the good of the nation but it cuts across the ingrained attitudes of thousands of years.

## *GOING HOME*

The casual tourist to China today is unlikely to visit a Chinese family in their home. This is especially so in the cities where accommodation is in very short supply. Many people live in such crowded conditions that to the Westerner would be intolerable.

So don't expect to be invited home by some casual acquaintance. Through television and movies, most Chinese you meet, especially if they speak a foreign language, are fully aware of the chasm between their homes and what foreigners enjoy. They are hesitant to ask foreigners home, even if they feel like it, because of mutual embarrassment when a visitor is ushered into a flat the size of a modest bedroom in a Western home.

If an opportunity should arise, grab it. They don't happen often.

The average home in a city is likely to be in a concrete block no more than five storeys high. These are the new uniform buildings thrown up the length of China to accommodate the mushrooming urban population. Housing the 250 million people now crammed into ever-swelling cities is a vast headache for central planners who have called on international urban experts for advice on how to house people in liveable conditions.

You are much more likely to be asked to enter a home when you are strolling through some village a bit off the beaten track. If this should happen, nod your thanks and go inside.

Generally homes in the southern hamlets are larger than in the north. There are two reasons for this, both basic. The south is richer, therefore they can build more spacious homes. In the north, homes have to be heated for six frigid months of the year so the snugger the better.

When you are ushered into a Chinese home, city or country, it will appear to you to be spartan beyond belief. Pride of place will probably be given to a television set and radio. There will be pictures of relatives and ancestors mounted on the main wall. Take one of the chairs offered, sip your tea and say '*Xie xie ni*'. Your politeness will be appreciated.

When exchanging, through your interpreter, details of where you come from and what you do, glance around. To your eyes, the situation may appear grim. But the householder is obviously proud to show off her home. Why? Because for her, a decade ago such luxuries as you see would have been unthinkable. It is the economic revolution of Deng Xiaoping that has made it possible. So admire what you see, ask for details about the family pictures and think only to yourself how far the Chinese people have yet to go to achieve a better standard of living.

## FAMILY PLANNING

Since the 1970s, China has been desperately trying to bring down soaring population growth. There's a very good reason for this – survival. Projections on unchecked growth are terrifying. If nothing had been done to check the rising human tide, China would by 1989 have had 1.3 billion people. As it was, members of the Family Planning Commission in Beijing could report there were 1,127,000,000 Chinese in April of that year. With an extra 200 million mouths to feed – 'avoided births' as officials put it – much of the economic progress made in recent years would have been nullified.

When Mao Zedong proclaimed the People's Republic in 1949, there were 540 million people in China. By the trends that became apparent in the early 1970s, the population by the turn of the century would have reached 1.5 billion, a staggering burden to support. Even with the stringent family planning programmes introduced by worried officials in 1972, China will still have 1.2 billion citizens when the nation enters the 21st century.

Why? One direct reason is better health care. By Western standards, the hospitals in rural China may be primitive. But the Barefoot Doctors scheme introduced in the 1950s had hardy volunteer paramedics tramping through every village in the land preaching simple lessons of hygiene, basic first aid, ground rules in caring for newborn babies. China didn't have much money, drugs or modern facilities and in that hostile era there was no foreign aid but the message got through. It helped keep alive millions of babies who otherwise would have died. So did vaccinations that saved millions more from diseases like polio, measles and smallpox. With fewer people dying and more being born, the population soared.

## ONE-CHILD FAMILIES

In 1979, officials ruled that married couples should not be permitted to have more than one child. 'One is enough,' proclaimed posters that went up all over the land. With 150,000 doctors, counsellors and advisers on the staff and with another 300,000 auxiliary staff stationed throughout the country, the Family Planning Commission spread the message enthusiastically.

Those who obeyed were rewarded with housing, job promotion, choice perks and public acclaim. Those who determinedly kept breeding lost out on financial bonuses, were publicly scorned, had job opportunities blocked and in extreme cases were sacked; if they were members, they were expelled from the Communist Party.

The twin carrot and stick approach worked. The birthrate dropped, but not sufficiently. Still, the economic impact was considerable. The education campaign, abortions, the supply of free birth control pills, condoms and other scientific aids and financial inducements – plus the patriotic urging to help the nation by making the sacrifice of having only one child – meant there were 200 million fewer people born than would otherwise have been the case.

Traditionally, much of the wealth of the peasants had been measured in the number of children they had. There were many reasons for this. The major two were the necessity for a son to carry on the sacred family name and to provide children to worship the ancestors. The other was to ensure that in old age, an infirm peasant would have an ample supply of filial sons to support him.

Attempting to change the inherited habits and inbuilt mores of thousands of years was no easy matter. Particularly in rural areas, there was great opposition. Horrifying stories emerged from rural areas, backed by official statistics, about girl babies being killed or simply left to die so parents could try again for the prized boy baby needed to carry on the family line.

To counter this, the policy was relaxed. If a couple had a girl, they could try again, after a waiting period of a few years, to produce a boy.

## *The Super Brats*

Some cynics say the one-child household has produced a breed of brats. They contend that with only one baby on which to expend their

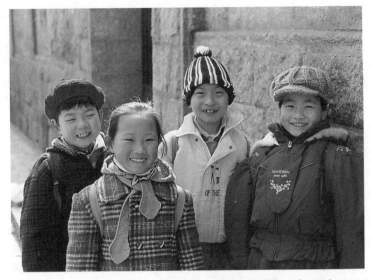

*Many among the new generation will grow up without siblings, but with over a billion Chinese in the country, there'll always be lots of friends.*

love, parents spoil solo children, and that doting grandparents add even more to the problem.

Others argue that children cannot have too much love. Certainly, the new generation of China could be called with some justification The Prized Generation. They are bigger, heavier and brighter than children born 40 years ago. A special institute at Hangzhou University has been established to track the physical growth and mental development of the nation's youngsters. Statistics show children today are healthier, livelier and have a higher IQ than in their grandparents' time.

Any visitor to China can see the beneficial results of one-child families. The children are well dressed, well loved, well clothed, well fed, well educated. Because parents know they can only have one of them, they strive to give their children the best.

The spoilt generation? I think not. The lucky generation is more like it. Anyone who has travelled in other Asian lands and seen the child beggars starving in the streets and then observed the happy, adored children of modern China has no doubt of the success of the one-child, one-family policy. Go to the Philippines, for instance. Starving, sick children beg in the streets. Pitiful eight-year-old girls totter in high-heel shoes in clubs for perverts and paedophiles, a short drive from the home of the Catholic prelate. If you are a parent, there's no doubt which system you would prefer.

## FAMILY STRUCTURE

The structure of the Chinese family was well in place before Confucius set down the guidelines that have endured for some 2,500 years. Traditional social values emphasising respect for the elders and reverence for the ancestors are still a living part of Chinese daily life. In every humble peasant cottage to which I have been invited over the years, the main room is dominated by a montage of photographs and portraits and a shrine which contains incense.

The family is not just dad, mum and the kids as in the Western world. The extended family (*jia ting*) probably all live under one roof. This is how the first peasant families grouped before the dawn of history. A man and his wife and their children and grandchildren would live in one building. The man was the patriarch whose whim was law.

In modern China today and in the great Overseas Chinese communities abroad, parents are respected and deferred to in a degree that foreigners find incomprehensible. A successful middle-aged businessman or bureaucrat will still pay formal respect to his humble peasant parents and unabashedly follow their wishes.

## RELATIONSHIPS

Confucius laid down precepts for how people should relate to each other. The basic ones are:

1. Between husband and wife
2. Between parents and children
3. Between brothers and sisters
4. Between sovereign and subjects
5. Between friends

There is also a special relationship between students and teachers, one that does not end with graduation but which extends throughout a lifetime. This is similar to the bonds between parents and children; what the father does in the home, the teacher continues in the classroom.

## *OLD AGE*

The venerable old man is a familiar and much loved part of Chinese literature and painting. 'A man of 70 is a rarity from the ancient times,' proclaims a proverb from the Tang Dynasty. True; life expectancy in those days was such that few reached their three score years and ten.

The elderly were – and are still – granted reverence not because they are rarities today in an era when Chinese longevity produces many millions of septuagenarians, but largely due to the deep experience in life and wisdom they are felt to have garnered over a lifetime.

When a man or woman completes the cycle of the 60-year calendar (time for the party of a lifetime and a banquet at which every family member will make enormous sacrifices to be present) he or she reaches a social plateau. With every year that passes, they acquire more dignity and status.

In the old days, a man of 60 could carry a staff within his village. By the age of 70 he could walk with the aid of the staff – a symbol of longevity – in the country, and by the age of 80, he could carry it before the Dragon Throne and did not have to kneel before the emperor. Anyone who reached the age of 90 was regarded as being sufficiently venerable for the emperor to heed his advice.

Instead of being sent away to institutions and old folks' homes to spend their last days, a concept that profoundly shocks most Chinese, the elderly are treasured. Sons and daughters feel it is an honour and a privilege to have their parents living with them, even in the confines of a crowded city apartment or a small village house.

## KINFOLK

Unlike the normal Western family of a couple and their children, the Chinese bonds extend much further. Unmarried daughters live with their parents. When they are married, they traditionally sever links with their own family and their names are added to the ancestral family tablets of the husband's clan. The newlywed bride then owes allegiance and obedience to her mother-in-law with whom she will probably live. (The tyrannical attitude of the imposing matriarch over the pretty wife of First Son is a common, popular and enduring theme in Chinese literature that can be traced back at least 3,000 years.)

Sons were encouraged to live with their parents until the elders died. This may have been possible when families clustered together in a clan village as tillers of the soil. Obviously, this is quite unrealistic in a modern urban industrial community. The custom for the eldest son to stay with the parents, however, is still common. After all, he is responsible for paying homage to the ancestors and when his parents do go to join the generations that went before, First Born will take his prideful place as head of the family.

The extended family will make great efforts to gather for special occasions, notably the great annual celebration of Lunar New Year. This remains constant under the communist regime; at New Year holidays are given so millions can travel from one end of the country to the other.

## FAMILY TREES

Chinese genealogists can trace back the history of notable families for many generations. Wealthy and scholarly families proudly display the well-thumbed, hand-bound books of characters that form their family trees. For peasant families, there is no such need for paper proof of their forebears; they have tilled the land around the village for centuries and the names are recorded in the hamlet temple.

The system is highly structured. Not only does it extend upwards and backwards, but also sideways. Second Aunty's Third Daughter is a close relative. Fourth Uncle's First Born is a close cousin, much more so than in the West. The relation of an individual to the rest of the clan extends outwards in a pattern similar to a boulder thrown into a goldfish pond. The most distant ripple may be far away, but it is still connected to the original splash of impact; so is a fourth cousin on the mother's side of the family still a relative and a person to be considered before any outsider.

The complex pattern of kinship is like a spider's web. Everyone is connected. In some charts that lay out an extended family, the person who is paying a genealogist to have his family mapped out will appear in the centre. Above him are his ancestors, below his descendants, children and grandchildren. To the right are his male relatives, to the left his father's female ancestors.

## *THE FAMILY NAME*

Taking precedence over all other consideration is the sacred family name and the filial duty of preserving it and passing it on to another generation. Hence the intense pressure to produce sons. If the eldest son has no son himself, tradition rules he must adopt the eldest son of his next youngest brother. If this cannot be done, the search goes on, spreading through the kinship network of male cousins.

If no acceptable candidates can be found within the clan, the search for an adoptive son can go outside, preferably to a sister's child. The sister, of course, is technically now a member of another family. The last alternative to keep alive the family name is for the husband of a daughter to be invited to join the father-in-law's family; their sons will bear the ancestral clan name and through this stratagem the honoured surname will live on and the ancestors will be worshipped for further generations.

## *CLOSE BONDS*

Relationships of all kinds are far more important to Chinese than to Westerners. The intense bonds of the nuclear family can be grasped more easily by foreigners. But there are links of surprising closeness and strength between more distant relatives and friends.

These bonds extend to classmates in middle school, the Western equivalent to high school. Decades after they have graduated, businessmen who went to an obscure high school will gather at old boys' nights. College alumni have similar feelings of affection and gratitude to their alma mater to a much more intense degree than Europeans or Americans.

Close associations are also found within professional and trade groups where affiliations are strong. This Chinese feeling of togetherness, of close association with people of the same background and similar interests, extends to all walks of life.

## *BIRTH*

Some traditions surrounding pregnancy and birth date back to prehistory. Praying for a son is one of them. Modern Chinese will sometimes say they don't care if their sole baby is a boy or girl; one suspects the yearning for a male heir to carry on the family name is as ardent in the heart of a sophisticated city cadre as it is in a peasant in a rural hamlet.

Despite great advances in medicine which were aimed specifically at lowering the appalling death rate among babies in pre-revolutionary times, old superstitions die hard. Old wives' tales often linger on in the field of midwifery. Babies were traditionally not bathed for three days. Relatives were invited on the third day to view the newest family member.

If the baby survives a month, the official celebration is held when friends and acquaintances join in the fun. At First Moon parties, drinks and food are served. The male child's hair was once shaved off on the 29th day of life and wrapped in red cloth which was sewn into the baby's bedclothes. One hundred days later, the hair was thrown into a lake or river. This was meant to ensure the boy grew up brave and strong. This and other old superstitions are not practised these days – or are not admitted to.

## MARRIAGE

The institution of marriage was ordained by the first of China's mythical rulers, the great Fu Hsi. Miraculously born as a divine being with a serpent's body in the 29th century B.C., he is credited with the discovery of the famous Chinese trigrams used in divination and thus contributing to the development of writing. He is said to have instituted marriage and the offered the first open-air sacrifice to heaven. Rites for wedlock were laid down in recognisable forms by the Duke of Zhou 3,000 years ago and were carried out in that style until the end of the Qing Dynasty in 1911. Some elements of these old customs are still used today.

In the age of matchmakers, an 'old crone' representing the man's family would approach the woman's clan. Token presents (a symbolic plump goose was favoured) were given, horoscopes exchanged. If the offer was not wholly unacceptable, the girl's details would be written on red paper and given to the matchmaker who would return to the man's family.

After a professional seer had scanned the horoscopes and all parties were satisfied, red cards with the family background of the pair were exchanged. This signified a betrothal. The potential bride and groom at this stage were not consulted.

Then presents were exchanged between the families and yet another professional was paid to find an auspicious date. Finally, the groom, relatives and friends went to the girl's home and accompanied her to his home, where she would then become part of his family. In olden times, this was often the first occasion the two most concerned with the procedure had met.

The young Republic of China passed laws simplifying these ancient procedures. In the first year of its rule, the communist regime passed the new marriage law that made free choice of partners the basis for wedlock, gave women equal rights and legal protection.

## *WEDDING PARTIES*

The customary puritanism of the new regime banned traditional expensive frills like wedding parties. In the past decade, there has been a reversion to lavish nuptial celebrations. These have been roundly criticised in the official press although some of the most expensive banquets of recent times have been held to mark the weddings of the offspring of senior cadres.

The newly prosperous business elite are returning to the old days with a vengeance. The bridegroom's family foots the bill for huge banquets in the best restaurant in the city and traditional robes are worn.

## *DIVORCE*

Before reform laws this century, divorce was relatively easy. If you were a man. Should you have been a woman, divorce was impossible.

Customary laws under dynasties stretching for thousands of years allowed men to unload their spouses for trivial failings. These included:

1. Inability to bear a male child
2. Wanton conduct
3. Being disrespectful to her parents-in-law
4. Being talkative
5. Theft
6. Jealousy
7. Having an incurable disease

Jealousy could include a wife's reluctance to accept her husband taking in concubines. This was a common custom before the communist takeover. In theory, Confucian preachings held that a man could take a concubine if his wife was infertile or bore only daughters. In practice, a man could pack his home with as many women as he could support. The wife was supposed to be a devoted and dutiful spouse and to grin and bear it. The positive side of the argument was that if any of the concubines had children, they officially became the offspring of the Number One wife.

In theory and practice today, divorce is comparatively easy for Chinese, both men and women. In reality, the rate of marriage collapses is rare.

## DYING

If you see people shrouded in white with their heads bound in similar material, you are watching a family grieve for a loved one. White is the colour of mourning in China.

Just as modern China has tried to eliminate or reduce the extravagances of marriage ceremonies, so have efforts been made to cut down the costs of funerals. In legend and literature, stories of families going into debt to pay for a fitting farewell to a patriarch are familiar. The genteel poor once saved half their lifetimes to pay for a decent funeral. The poor joined funeral societies in which they pooled their money to ensure that all members were sent off to the uncertainties of the next life in a fitting fashion.

This meant to be well clothed, buried in a coffin carved from good wood (if possible, wood from the Nan tree that grows in Sichuan) and laid to rest in a plot of ground guaranteed not to disturb the many deities of the Chinese heavens.

With the deep belief in ancestor worship and the twice yearly pilgrimage to family graves, this has in effect meant a great deal of land throughout the nation was being used as graveyards. Flying over China, you can see how hillsides around villages are pitted with gray spots. These are tombs of former generations.

### Funerals

Once grandiose, the final ceremonies are now more spartan and confined to the family. But, as in so many other spheres, there has been considerable relaxation in recent years and ancient ceremonial trappings are making a reappearance.

These include the use of fiery offerings to the dead. If a man in life liked good food and drink, then cardboard and paper imitations of a feast may be burned at his funeral, reminders to the gods to cater for his needs in the afterlife. There are also wardrobes of paper clothes, paper boats, motorcars and, of course, huge wads of paper money printed by the Bank of Hades with minimum denominations of a million yuan to provide ample spending money in the next world.

## *FRIENDS*

Many Westerners, even in such modern and open societies as Hongkong and Singapore, complain it is hard to make Chinese friends. I've never found this a problem.

# Chapter Eleven

# DOWN IN THE COUNTRY

*When you drink water,*
*Think of the source.*

The great cities are booming. Skylines change dramatically almost by the day. But deep down in the countryside, in tens of thousands of tiny hamlets, the heart of China still beats in the village. The rural communities with their surrounding fields of rice, wheat and vegetables remain the heart, soul and belly of the land. Roughly speaking, five-sixths of the Chinese people, about a billion of them, live in villages or small towns where the pure 'Chineseness' of the people can be seen.

*Rice paddies, neat plots of vegetables and stone houses, the common conception of how the countryside should look often turns out to be reality as scenes like this appear out of the Hubei mist like a scene from a willow pattern plate.*

In many ways, the prodigious output of the Chinese farmer more resembles gardening than farming. Plots are very small by Western standards; a family in the fertile south where classical rice paddy farming is practised probably has less than two acres. Every inch of ground is used.

North of the Yangtze in the wheat and millet growing areas, agriculture is equally intense. The land is nurtured with nightsoil and commercial fertiliser. The ceaseless pattern of preparing the fields, fertilising the soil, planting seeds, weeding, raking, hoeing, reaping, harvesting is as set in the mores of Chinese rural life as the rising and setting of the sun. In the south, with three crops a year, thanks to the warm, humid climate, the pattern is a bit different from the arid, cooler north where the frigid winters reduce crops to one a year. Everywhere, there is a pattern, a rhythm to life, that has been established down the ages. Around the confluence of the Wei River with the Huang He, man has planted the same fields for at least 6,000 years.

That good earth of China still supports the nation. The village is the foundation of Chinese culture. Old Hundred Names, the peasant, is the sturdy, patient, ancient stalwart who ultimately is the basis of the state, the nation and the race.

## A FRENZY OF CONSTRUCTION

Drive from the port city of Qingdao along the spectacular coast of southern Shandong towards the sacred mountain of Laoshan. Who lives in these imposing, spacious new homes made of locally-hewn stone? Fishermen and peasants, says the woman guide. Nonsense, I think. A couple of miles on, I ask the driver to stop. I get out and go to the nearest house and knock on the door.

A housewife answers and after getting over the shock of talking to an unanticipated foreigner, we chat about housing, then stroll about the neighbourhood. Sure enough, my new friend and her neighbours are all local farm folk who have invested profits from crops in expansive mansions. These houses are much more substantial and impressive than anything a Hongkong newspaperman can afford, I reflect.

It's the same all over China. As money from cash crops pours into the peasants' pockets, new housing is built. The danger is this wave of new construction can eat into valuable farmland, something district officials are anxiously trying to avoid.

This process has been going on for years. Back in 1983, Madame Guo Xiao-lin, the Governor of Jiangsu, one of China's richest provinces, was trying to tell me that in the previous five years, more than half the 60 million peasants in Jiangsu had moved into new homes. Pure propaganda, I thought. Couldn't be done. Fifty per cent of the population in new houses in five years? No way. Over the next couple of weeks, I travelled hundreds of kilometres through the province. Looking out the train windows, directing my hire car drivers down lonely side roads to remote villages, peering from the decks of ships sliding down the Yangtze, I kept count. Sure enough, China's top woman politician had been telling the truth. Staggering as it seemed, the claims were correct.

The building boom in rural China continues in a frenzy of construction. The sturdy houses being constructed in every province are comfortable, superior in every way to the lamentable hovels which traditionally provided humble roofs over the head of the Chinese peasant. I am no propagandist for the communist system. But the visitor to China cannot escape the plain fact that the man-in-the-paddy-field is on the whole better housed today than at any time in the past 5,000 years.

Housing differs in accordance with the climate. Everywhere, however, the new homes tend to be bigger, constructed of higher grade materials and offer superior accommodation. This frantic building boom has not been without its drawbacks. The demand for materials, notably cement, roofing tiles and timber, has caused shortages and has led to inflation. Much more seriously, the new-found peasant wealth, created by the economic policies that let them plant what they want and sell their produce, has created many problems.

The most obvious of these can be seen by anyone flying at low level over any part of densely populated, heavily tilled East China. For centuries, the villages have clustered amid the fields. The richest land was closest to the village. As new houses have gone up, they ringed the existing settlement, eating into the fields. The old homes in the centre of towns have often been turned into halls or commercial areas and as new larger homes have been built on the fringe, they have devoured some of the most productive agricultural land in China.

This situation is worrying economists and agronomists in Beijing. The statistics they produce show why; in the past decade, China has lost a staggering amount of prime cropland because of housing expansion – fields equal to the entire arable area of France have fallen out of agricultural use. When you consider that China's cultivable land is a mere 10% or less of the total area, little wonder that central government planners become frantic about this effect of prosperity on future production.

## THE GREATEST ACHIEVEMENT

Beijing can boast with considerable justification of the success of its agricultural policies. They manage what many considered impossible; they feed 1,210,000,000 people. There is no famine in China. Although there is some worry about lack of grain – largely because farmers prefer to grow more profitable crops of vegetable, cotton or even flowers – there is ample food to feed the enormous population. To many people, this victory is the greatest achievement of the Beijing government and goes a very long way towards balancing deficiencies in other areas.

Is it better to have democracy or a full belly? Western idealists may have one answer. A starving Indian peasant in Bihar who has rights at the ballot box and a dying baby may well have an opposite opinion.

## THE GOOD EARTH

Credit for the well-stocked markets of China does not belong merely to the central government. When the communists came to power, they had already 20 years experience in governing rural areas, first in the Soviet area of Jiangxi province, then in large areas of the north which they governed after the Long March. They had learned from earlier mistakes and realised that Soviet-style policies would not work in agriculture.

Still, the ardent revolutionaries attempted to tamper with Old Hundred Names and the way in which he tilled the good earth of China. They also tried to force a major change in lifestyle. First,

269

*Harvesting sugar in Guangxi: women are a vital part of the rural workforce.*

peasants were encouraged to work in collectives. By 1958, the commune system was widely introduced; it merged large-scale agriculture with local government, public works and industry. This was the so-called Great Leap Forward which resulted in a Huge Plunge Backwards.

At the very least, three million people starved to death as a direct result of the Great Leap, one of the most disastrous economic policies ever attempted. In Guangdong and other areas, people in what had once been prosperous counties awash with rice were resorting to cannibalism to stay alive.

At the same time, experiments in communal living were suggested with children being taken away to special schools and adults sleeping in dormitories. This madness took two or three years to dissipate until even Mao Zedong was forced to admit the lunacies of his idealistic Brave New World policies.

For the peasants, these years were a living nightmare. The very foundations of rural life, the eternal Chinese family structure, was threatened. In the countryside, the Cultural Revolution of the next decade went largely unnoticed. It was the Great Leap debacle that devastated rural China.

The political policies that shackled China's farmers were lifted in 1978 when the central government announced new rules. Put simply, these meant the people-on-the-land could by and large grow what they wished and sell it to whom they wanted for the best price they could obtain. Simple enough, you might think. But in the Chinese context they were revolutionary moves. They let the peasant get on with what he knew best, growing crops and raising livestock, and removed the nonsensical political burdens. The result was swift – farm income rose dramatically.

## PROSPERITY STRIDES THE LAND

The results of this soaring income are obvious. First, there are those new homes. Wander into any Chinese village, find the centre of town and sit down at a stall or restaurant. At first, if you are in a small place away from normal tourist haunts, the people may be reserved. Chances are, they are shy. Smile, and you'll reap a rich harvest of beams. Try out your patchy Putonghua. You'll soon be the centre of a crowd of curious folk. Give out cards (make sure you've printed a couple of thousand) that give not only your name, but your home town and country. Almost certainly, you'll soon be invited into a nearby home. In the cities, such an invitation is rare. Down in the countryside, the doors are flung open. All over the land, I've noticed the same warm greeting.

The inquisitive visitor who wants to see how national policies are affecting the normal people can stroll away by himself down some back lane, wandering through the narrow lanes just wide enough for a water buffalo or a donkey cart. Peer into the courtyards where much of family life is concentrated. The sight of a foreign face will soon have the kids coming out, then the grandparents. '*Ni hao*' and waved invitations beckon you into the courtyard. Hands are shaken. You are gestured and bowed inside.

By the standards of the Western world, the room may seem a poor enough place. Viewed through Chinese eyes, it is a treasury of prized possessions. The main room is probably about 5 by 3 metres. It is dominated by the inevitable TV set which, if China Central Television is on the air, is turned on although nobody is watching.

On the wall, above a small shrine, are family photographs. In many homes, the patriarch will be pictured as a young man in military uniform, particularly if he was in the Peasants and Workers Red Army before Liberation. In a surprising number of homes, a portrait of Chairman Mao will be clustered with the family pictures. (I have never seen a portrait of Comrade Deng in a family collection.) On your unexpected impromptu visit, you will notice many signs of prosperity. Out in the yard, there are likely to be a couple of bicycles. Costing about three months' pay for the average factory worker, these are sizeable investments. Inside, the main room will have a bed because it is probably here that the main husband and wife in the household live. Other beds, usually foldable, are stacked in small rooms alongside. Cooking is usually done over coal stoves in a separate annex across the courtyard.

Under the family portraits, there will be a radio or, in recent years, a colour TV. A sewing machine may stand in a corner. If you are polite, you will express curiosity about the home. Chinese are unabashed askers of personal and financial questions. How long have you lived here? Where did you live before? How much did the television cost? Do you get the coal issued free (as happens in some of the coal-rich northern provinces) and if not how much do you pay every year? How much does rice cost a kilo? What about cooking oil? What do you grow? How much do you get for your crop? Who do you sell it to? How much does fertiliser cost? Where does the rest of your family work?

In turn, the peasants will want to ask you similar questions about your life back home in the Midwest or Midlands. I usually take a few dozen small coins with me when I go to China. It would be insulting to offer money to your sudden hosts who will press hot tea on you and offer you food. But if you offer a Hongkong $1 coin (worth about US15 cents) to a child, pointing out the head of Queen Elizabeth II, the family will be delighted with such an exotic talking point. (This, however, can lead you into deep political discussions; what had the English monarch got to do with a Chinese city like Hongkong?)

Voluble, humorous, lively, inquisitive, shy and hesitant at first, but then open and friendly, the Chinese peasant at home is a relaxed and cheerful host.

## *LIFE DOWN ON THE FARM*

Just as the lure of bright city lights dragged generations of European and American youths from the farms into the towns, so did similar urges work in China. The new prosperity in the countryside seems to have at least partially stopped this trend.

The best wage a young factory worker can expect is about 150 yuan a month. Then he has to pay for food and lodging. If he stays down on the farm, he is likely these days to do a lot better. Farm income is soaring. Families that live close to major cities can easily earn up to RMB10,000 a year. The main source of income is fresh vegetables and fruit which are taken to city or suburban free markets for daily sale. The profits, incredible for China, have fuelled a buying spree in the countryside.

The age-old sight of a water buffalo plodding through a muddy field in front of a farmer is now rare. These days, the peasant is more likely to be driving a small tractor which is made in factories in almost every province. (Interestingly, the tractors differ from place to place, with designs adapted to various climatic and typographical conditions. Most can also be swiftly converted from ploughing machines to small trucks to carry the harvest to market.)

## CRAFTS

Traditionally, the Chinese peasant made just about everything he needed. Or, to be a lot more accurate, she did. Wives and daughters spent much time around the home weaving, making rattan furniture and creating household goods like wooden buckets. These days, the old folk crafts are largely disappearing, another victim of prosperity. Why spend many long hours laboriously making a watertight bucket out of wood when a plastic bucket that will last for eternity can be bought for a couple of yuan at the nearby market town?

The more basic crafts and arts have long been a feature of village life. Although the elegant arts were confined to the cities and the courts, the daily crafts were always practised in the villages and towns. They are still flowering today.

In many small villages, there are traditions of pottery and weaving rattan. In some tribal areas, vivid local arts, drawings, sophisticated carvings and beautiful pottery can be found for sale at very cheap prices. You've got to be lucky.

My tip is for you to wander about any marketplace you spot. Chances are the only thing you get will be photographs of squirming tanks of snakes or a wandering herbalist making his potions from stomach-queasy ingredients. On the other hand, you may find some local artist who is selling his pots or local crafts that intrigue or attract you. I like buying some of the exotically shaped steamers and pots used by peasants for winter hot-pot cooking. Not only are they very functional, they are also things of simple beauty. Teapots are another fascination for me and I snap up pots of all shapes and sizes to add to my collection. You never know what you are going to spot in country markets. It's always worth the effort to wander around and have a look.

## FUN

Just as Western culture has its harvest festivals, so do the peasants of China celebrate bringing in the crops. Travelling through the country in the autumn (the weather is better then, too), the visitor is likely to see crowds gathering in the streets. Sometimes, large temporary sheds will be thrown up or outdoor stages erected. Contortionists, acrobats, singers, opera shows and all sorts of open-air entertainment take place.

Wander in. If there is a charge, someone will show you how much to pay. It will be very cheap. This is how the people of China entertained themselves for centuries when troupes of minstrels, thespians and singers wandered the country, bringing lively artistic shows to the most remote areas. Television has killed much of this tradition (just as the music hall died in the Western world) but some traces remain.

In rural areas, always ask your guides or at hotels what local festivals are being held. There's not going to be a great deal else to do, so wander down to the town square or marketplace and see how the rural folk of China enjoy themselves. In remote areas, you'll probably find yourself the star attraction.

*— Chapter Twelve —*

# TIPS FOR SURVIVAL

*Seeing once is better than hearing a hundred times.*

## *HOME AWAY FROM HOME*

On the outskirts of Beijing, Shanghai, Nanjing and scores of other cities across China, rows of modern town houses stand behind tall fences, flanked by neat lawns. They are imposing residences. They would grace any residential neighbourhood in Sydney or Cincinnati. Equipped with modern kitchens, satellites to bring global TV and computers whizzing in the worldwide web, they have every modern convenience.

You could be in a suburb anywhere in the Western world, except that there is a servant in the kitchen to allow madam to avoid the drudgery of housework.

These modern additions to the suburban skylines are typical of homes being built to house the floor of foreigners pouring into China. When the long-delayed World Trade Organisation becomes reality, that flood can only increase.

These stretches of glamorous homes are meant to bolster the confidence of inmates – sorry, residents – and reassure them that although they are geographically in the People's Republic of China, it is in fact home sweet home. It may as well be, too, for all the contact the occupants have with normal Chinese. They have created a cocoon that keeps them segregated from the rest of the country.

Well, if that's what they want, who can argue? But it's a terrible pity that a family can live in China for three years while the breadwinner is posted there and never have a proper close Chinese friend, breath the atmosphere of the backstreets or ride hard-class in a train. It's their loss.

## A SOCIETY INCOMPREHENSIBLE

Most foreigners who go to China do so as tourists. Their stays are going to be for less than a month. No matter how strange a new society is, it can be borne for a few weeks even if the food is weird, the language totally incomprehensible and the daily habits and customs of the inhabitants are sufficiently bizarre as to be matters of constant wonder.

It's different for those whose job or academic path takes them to a new society for a much longer period. They have to learn to make adjustments to fit in with their new environment. China is not going to change to suit them. If they want to survive, they have to adapt to their temporary homeland. This is now a lot easier, especially in the big cities, than several years ago. But there are still considerable difficulties.

## *YOUR FAMILY*

You think it's tough being a businessman in China? You've got it easy, pal. Every day, your mind is occupied with problems, you have the stimulation of meeting new people, seeing fresh faces, gaining extra insights into the society with which you must now cope. Things are much tougher for the wives left to spend the day in an apartment or, even worse, in the confines of a hotel room.

These days, there are women's associations and organised social groups, often attached to the growing number of international schools. Many women find the aerobics and exercise sessions in hotel fitness centres a place to meet people and make friends. With quality housing now becoming more affordable and findable in most cities, middle-class Western families have home lives not all that different from the rest of the world.

### *Teenagers*

Life can still be stifling for children accustomed to the more relaxed lifestyle of the West. Imagine yourself a Western teenager in China. Back home, life would be an endless round of school, parties, picnics, sports events, fashions, dating, overnight stays with friends, trips to the countryside, movie-going, hobbies and all the other joys of growing up and exploring life. In China, life is much more restricted. There are far fewer opportunities for enjoying the best years of your life.

Western children in China are well aware of how they are being deprived of what they see as the fun and glamour of life back in Los Angeles, Munich or Nottingham. And frequently they are not grateful to their parents for dragging them off to live in a country where teenage jollity is frowned upon. They feel deeply that while their counterparts back home are dancing, loving, dating and enjoying themselves, they are confined in a society where there is nothing to do. This leads to intense family pressure which in many cases can lead to divorce and complete fracturing of the family.

Once again, there have been dramatic changes, with bars, discos, karaokes and other places of entertainment booming in every town. Despite this, jaded young people are likely still to complain that China is:"boooorrring".

These are problems that must be faced before you accept a posting to China. Don't just ask how the job will affect your career but try to sum up what it will do to your family.

If your wife is reserved and does not easily make friends or mix with strangers, a Chinese posting for you can be a personal disaster for her. If she relies heavily on daily visits from her mother or friends, living in Beijing will be like being a castaway on a desert island.

And remember that Beijing or Shanghai are lively cosmopolitan places compared to most other Chinese cities. A German wife whose husband ran a factory in Qingdao described her life there a few years ago as 'death before burial'. And that is in one of the most pleasant cities in the country.

## *Alternatives*

So if your boss calls you into the boardroom and announces that you've got that big promotion and it means a two-year spell running the joint venture factory in China, don't automatically leap at the opportunity. Weigh things up. What will it mean to your family?

At different stages of your life, the scenario changes significantly.

If you are young and single, it can be that great chance to leapfrog a few rungs up the corporate ladder. Life for a single man or woman in China can be thrilling, exhilarating and exciting. True, many foreigners tend to stick together and are unadventurous. The language barrier cuts many off from the bulk of the population and despite all the advances of recent years in both buildings and freedom, there are still significant differences between lifestyles of China and, for instance, Britain.

The different perception of sex and relations between men and women means sex can be tricky. There are of course other foreigners you meet in tourist hotel bars where visitors gather. These days, especially for men, there are huge temptations as young girls make it clear they would adore to be married to a wealthy foreigner. Be cautious. Love and lust may be universal, but China has strict and sometimes hard to comprehend laws. These are seldom if ever enforced, but if you live in China, make sure if you intend to stray off the straight and narrow that you discuss the risk with people who have lived in the community for some time.

There are compensations. A spell in China will broaden your horizons. After all, if you can succeed in running a trade office or a factory in China, you can soar anywhere. It's a chance to prove yourself.

The picture changes drastically a few years on if you are married and have young children. How will your wife cope? First, there is the accommodation hurdle. There remains in China a vast shortage of urban housing suitable for foreigners. In the past, it meant enforced living in a service apartment next to a tourist hotel. New housing complexes for foreigners have gone up many cities; decent apartments are still in short supply. And houses can be as expensive as New York. Most available decent housing has long been snapped up by companies with permanent offices in China. There is a staggering waiting list. Many hotels in places like Guangzhou are converting entire floors from overnight rooms into apartments for permanent guests.

Your wife and children will be confined largely to where you live. There is likely to be a pool and health centre attached. But there will probably be little else in the way of entertainment for small children. There will be a maid to do the housework but many expatriate wives complain the presence of a person in the flat who doesn't speak a word of English and with whom communication is impossible only makes things worse. It also means she doesn't even have the chores to do to fill in those yawning empty hours when you are at the office or attending the inescapable and endless round of business banquets.

What to do? Some couples choose to separate for the period of the posting with the wife staying at home base with the children. This can be hard on a marriage. Living together in China, however, can impose even tougher burdens. Many firms give a foreign resident in China four rest and recreation trips annually to Hongkong and one of these is normally a fully-paid fare to the home city in America or Europe.

Individuals and families have to discuss things carefully and make a choice. Can their marriage survive such lengthy separations? Can it survive the stresses of living together in China?

One solution is to speak to the executive who held the job earlier. What option did he choose? How did it work out? Are there any other members of local chambers of commerce who have lived in China? If so, contact them and you will probably discover they are only too eager to recount the horror stories of their stay. As a last resort, if your boss insists you are the man for the job, say you want to go to settle in, taking your wife with you on an exploratory trip. If she likes it and, after speaking to as many foreigners as possible and discussing shopping, schools, entertainment and other aspects of life in your temporary home city, if she thinks she can bear it, she can then return with the family. She may, however, opt to stay home with the kids and impatiently await your return.

At another stage of life, when the children are grown up and a couple is mature and liberated from parenthood, a posting to China can be invigorating personally as well as professionally.

Back home, they would have been Mr and Mrs Average, senior middle management with the mortgage mostly paid off and the children working and starting families of their own, plodding along in contented middle age. But a posting to China has liberated them from the bonds of surburbia, set them free to explore a whole new life. They hurl themselves enthusiastically into China and the Chinese way of life. The wife goes busily to class to study art and language as the husband heads off to tackle production problems in a computer assembly plant or to teach at a university. For them, housing is no problem because a hotel suite is all they need. Schooling difficulties do not exist. Money is ample. And after two or three decades of being tied to the responsibility of raising children and buying a home, they have suddenly been given a new lease on an exciting fresh life. You won't hear any complaints from this group about expatriate life in China.

All the above applies in spades to retirees. For people who have ended their careers and who don't feel ready for the retirement village or the cemetery, China offers enormous opportunities for an extension to a useful lifetime. This is particularly so for management and technical experts in industry, education and agriculture who wish to serve in China in various voluntary roles. If you are interested, ask your country's foreign office for details of aid programmes in China that require volunteer staff.

## *Support Groups*

In every city in China where there are sizeable foreign communities, local expatriate wives regularly get together for coffee and complaints. These are forums where problems rise swiftly to the surface and solutions are found. Remember, you are not Marco Polo. You are not an intrepid explorer to unknown lands breaking fresh ground. Every hurdle a newcomer faces in China has been met and overcome by people already living there. They have been in your boat – confused, perplexed, bewildered, irritated by the unexplainable – and are pleased to soothe your fears and explain the form. If in doubt, ask.

Most communities in Beijing have clubs or associations formed around their embassies. These groups are in existence precisely to aid people like you, newcomers to China who need help. Most have published their own guides to survival in China. Don't hesitate to call your embassy to ask for help. Why else have you been paying taxes all these years?

There are other sources: the huge and helpful American Women's Association in Hongkong can provide names of people who have lived in China and who are back in Hometown, USA. The excellent Australian Business Association of Hongkong likewise knows how to prepare people for leaping into the unknown.

## *Spouses*

If you are a spouse accompanying a husband or wife on a China posting, realise from the start that life was not meant to be easy. Your husband or wife has the job to fill in at least eight hours of their day. You have to find something else to do with your time.

Without wishing to appear to be a sexist pig, life in China is easier for a jobless wife than a supported husband. Regulations make it officially impossible for a foreign spouse to take a job (although these are being relaxed) and it is a fact of life that a lone man with nothing to do to occupy his day is far more cut off from social contact than a woman. There are probably going to be a comparatively large number of wives – but few workless husbands – without jobs. The lone male will find it awkward to go to the coffee mornings with the other spouses, all of whom may be women.

For both sexes, studies provide one obvious outlet. Tutors are available to teach Chinese language, culture and cuisine. The two- or three-year posting in China can be the opportunity to open windows of learning that would otherwise never exist.

But many people keep the shutters closed tightly. They sit at home and brood, discontented malcontents. When they return home, they are full of stories of the dullness and blankness of expatriate life in China. Does fault lie with the country or with the individual who retreats snail-like into a shell?

Incidentally, some wives of Chinese diplomats who have served in New York have complained to me of the drab dullness of life in the Big Apple. It all depends on what you want from life.

## THE THREE BURDENS

The Chinese tourist industry used to be likened to a gnarled old peasant climbing a steep mountain. On the back of this stooped, tortured figure there were three huge boulders. One was marked CAAC, another was labelled Bank of China and the third had written on it, China International Travel Service.

This is no longer true. The state-owned airline monopoly was years ago broken up. Three huge modern companies now run China's aviation. The planes are new, the service good and the safety record – thank you, Buddha! – vastly improved.

I used to be able to dine out for weeks on tales of some of my trips on domestic services inside China. Now, there's no fun. You get onto a new Boeing or Airbus and are greeted by a smiling, smartly-tailored hostess. There is a safety belt. The plane takes off on time and flies to the correct destination. Is this miraculous? Yes, indeed, if you are accustomed to the old days when you bounced uncertainly around the skies of China in a prop-powered Soviet-built flying wreck that could once have taken Joe Stalin to Yalta.

## CAAC

There was once universal agreement that CAAC was the worst airline in the world. I used to argue about this judgement; it was not that good. The initials stand for Civil Aviation Administration of China. Many contend they also could be read as China Aircraft Always Crash. You had to be brave, foolish, adventurous or have had a couple of good shots of *mao tai* to fly in the old days, circa 1983.

Passenger services were utterly lamentable with staff arrogant, high-handed, contemptuous of passengers and haughty in the extreme.

Today, the many smaller component airlines are comparatively slick and efficient. Having said that, there is still a tendency for Chinese airline staff to refuse to give anything but the most basic information to passengers. And maintenance and safety remain a worry, although both have improved markedly.

## CITS

China International Travel Service has vastly changed. It now helps travellers; if you find this statement strange, that's because you never had to deal with them in the past when it ran almost everything, and none of it well. This huge bureaucratic agency has had to compete with free enterprise organisations in places like Hongkong; as a result, the official travel service has had to sharpen up its act.

You still sometimes get treated like a pauper begging for a handout instead of a valued customer. But staff are now trained and sometimes go out of their way to be friendly. So what, you ask? Isn't that their job? Well, yes, but in formative years when CITS was struggling to cope with the swelling torrent of foreign visitors, angry staff made no secret of their contempt for customers and their anger that they were expected to do some work and not laze about reading newspapers all day.

Unless you are a poverty-stricken student with endless time and nothing to do, always get CITS to buy your tickets. (Or get your hotel to do it for you. Or American Express, in go-ahead places like Shanghai.) Otherwise, you will be subjected to pushing, shoving masses of people at train stations or CAAC booking offices. If you can't speak Chinese or do not have exactly what you want to know written out in Chinese, once you battle your way to the front of the queue, you will then have to try to explain to a rude, impatient and unsympathetic clerk where you want to go. Meanwhile, a couple of thousand restless and short-tempered commuters will be elbowing you in the ribs in their urgency to get at the sole service window.

Having done this once, the traveller returns to the surly and arrogant CITS staff with warm feelings of brotherhood.

During one trip in about 1984, while I was down in the magnificent province of Guangxi in the southwest, I had to catch an early morning train for the 34-hour journey from the local capital of Nanning to Guangzhou. The ticket had supposedly been bought and paid for by the local foreign affairs office. It had to be picked up from CITS. So on a Sunday afternoon, I found their office.

Naturally, it was locked. There was noise from inside, but nobody answered my hammerings on the stout front door. After prowling around the building, I found a rear open door. Stumbling through the unlit corridors, I eventually found the CITS office. Inside was the local tourist boss with a clutch of his cronies, watching a football match on colour television, smoking and drinking beer. Where was my ticket? Go away, he said, come back tomorrow at 9 a.m. But, I protested, the train left at midnight. Ticket, please. Go away, he waved. We're busy. I ripped the plug of the television set out of the wall, to irate disapproval. Ticket, please. Enraged, he pulled open his desk, got my ticket which was inside and hurled it at me. Then he and his pals returned to the football game.

This was typical, for the era. Now CITS staffers sometimes act like normal human beings.

## *THE BANK*

In China, when you refer to The Bank, it means the Bank of China. As well as being the reserve bank of the nation, it is also a huge domestic and retail banking arm. When you want to change money, you get the best rate by going to the nearest branch of The Bank rather than at your hotel.

Like all other service sectors in China, standards have improved immensely in recent years, although to Westerners accustomed to smiling, friendly service, the attitude of staff sometimes seems to be haughty and resentful.

## *THE ASSIGNMENT SYSTEM*

Many people in offices, shops and departments in China are not there because they want to be. They were ordered to do a certain job and had totally no say in the matter. This is why so many people obviously have no interest at all in what they are doing for a living. Blame the old system.

One of the most hated aspects of life for urban students was the way in which people were assigned to education and jobs. The former system often took no account of where people wanted to spend their lives or what they wished to do. Some angry university students have complained to me about the way they were directed to study subjects in which they had no interest and, even worse, were prevented from following the disciplines they wanted. The system was both inefficient and corrupt, a legacy of the desperate early years of the 1950s when China was striving to survive and to produce badly-needed engineers, doctors and technicians. But it has resulted in two generations of young people being forced into careers in which they have no interest.

Hopefully the new economic system will do away with this awkward and unpopular practice, as it has eliminated so many other formidable curses of the gigantic, unfeeling bureaucracy. It was a system that put many square pegs into unsuitable round holes and which has ruined many lives. People were condemned on a whim to spend their lives in jobs in which they had no interest. Now, people can largely decide themselves on what work they will do – providing they can get the right job, as anywhere else on earth – and employers are no longer obliged to keep lazy and incompetent staff on the payroll. It's been a change of huge significance.

And now, by and large, the young people of China can choose for themselves what fields they want to follow in their careers. It's made for an amazing improvement.

In "famous and listed" state-run restaurants you still find the bad-tempered staff who think the world owes them a living and who resent customers. Do not go to them. There are many friendly, efficient free enterprise restaurants. Let the official places keep their bad attitudes and they will inevitably go bust one day soon.

## MUTUAL BENEFIT

Traditional Chinese business philosophy holds that every party to a commercial agreement should make a profit. In the best of all possible worlds, this is self evident. But emerging from a commercial cocoon that has enshrouded them all their lives, young Chinese (for example, any businessman aged under 70) have never had experience about making business decisions except under the incompetent guidance of the communist system.

The new generation that has risen through management ranks in the past 15 years are canny and skilled in Western ways. China has had to manage the transition from "pure" socialism to a market economy with deftness and determination. The changes have been pressed ahead, but at sweeping social cost. An entire generation that was promised jobs for life has seen that vow of certainty – and equal poverty – removed. An element of stability has been taken from them in exchange for the opportunity to make vastly more money. Most people support this. Understandably, those who had a tiny apartment, a dull but secure job for life and no ambition for anything greater may resent the changes.

For bosses, it has meant they can hire and fire. In the past, they had to accept whatever staffers were assigned to them, no matter how unsuitable or unwilling. Now they can pick themselves, and get rid of unwanted staff.

Gone in the economic revolution are thousands of state-owned companies which employed millions of people. Obviously, these could not be shut down overnight nor scrapped at once. It would have caused a social upheaval. Slowly, but very surely, the nation's planners have been getting rid of this gigantically inefficient industrial dinosaur of state-owned enterprises. There are still many thousands of them in existence, but even here people now have to work for a living instead of leaning on a broom or reading *People's Daily*.

## *IT WAS NOT ALWAYS THUS ...*

Often, Chinese state entrepreneurs are anxious to sign deals. They sincerely want to be helpful. But there is also often a feeling that they have to squeeze out the last possible profitable dollar from a deal just to show they are as smart, as tough and as shrewd as any capitalist. The result, all too often, is that they price themselves out of the market and the foreigner who was eager to do business in China throws up his hands and relocates his factory, instead, in Thailand or the Philippines.

Instead of lamenting the lost deal, the unskilled, inept cadre is likely to give himself a pat on the back for refusing to allow himself to be fooled by the foreign plutocrat. The fact that he has lost China a badly-needed new factory will not occur to him. Such short-sighted bloody-mindedness is now not so common. But this brand of self-defeating commercial blindness can still be encountered far too frequently.

## *CLOTHING*

Try to walk through Kunming, the capital city of gorgeous Yunnan Province. If you have a Western female by your side, progress will be slow. The shops are crammed with inexpensive silks, cheap but well-made fashionable shoes, skirts and blouses of modern cut and attractive hue. It's the same in any city in China, where tailors, department stores and fashion shops offer great quality and range at affordable prices. Most of the customers are local Chinese, spending the (comparatively) large wages they now receive.

In the mid-80s, the streets of China were drab and bleak. The pedestrians and cyclists – there were few vehicles, then – dressed uniformly in dark blue or gray high-buttoned Mao suits. If there seemed a lot of uniforms on the pavement, that was because soldiers, police and other officials had nothing else to wear when off-duty.

Today, clothes worn by both men and women on the streets of Chengdu or Dalian or any other big city are colourful and stylish. In Beijing, lanky models stride the catwalk showing Chinese designs. The garment shops in every city are filled with identical modern clothes that factories throughout the nation are making for export abroad.

Progress in economic terms has meant Chinese officials now tend to be more dress conscious. They wear suits and largely expect visitors to do the same at interviews and official meetings. To me, this is a step backwards – I loathe ties.

## *DRESS CODES*

There are few formalities in China's dress code. The very most you will ever need is a suit. In summer, shirtsleeves are the norm. For women, a simple dress or slacks and a jacket are adequate for anything short of an official state banquet in the Great Hall of the People.

Women should not wear clothes that are excessively revealing: tank tops, for example, are embarrassing to Chinese. So are short shorts. Use your commonsense.

You seldom see a senior official or top executive wearing a Mao jacket. (In reality, this garb is merely a rather formalised version of standard Chinese clothing.) I have a couple which I like; they are simple cotton, unlined, loose, comfortable and have plenty of pockets for notebooks, pens, business cards, camera, film and all the other paraphernalia of the roving scribbler. At business meetings, dress for the climate. If it's a cold day, bundle up and keep warm. If it's stifling hot, nobody will expect you to wear a jacket and tie.

When it comes to dress, the Chinese are pragmatic. Be comfortable. But not too relaxed. It's not done, for example, for men to wear shorts to official business meetings although it's perfectly acceptable to wear shorts when you are going on an inspection tour of a farm.

## THE OTHER SIDE OF THE COIN

You know what you think of the Chinese you have met. What do they think of you? Probably, they are more baffled than you are. Some people say the Chinese have a love-hate relationship with the outside world. I don't think that is strictly correct. It's more a fascination-repulsion complex.

Many Chinese, even these days, have never met and spoken to a Westerner. In the cities where tourists go, foreigners are no longer an item of overwhelming curiosity. They are now often taken for granted. But they are still, up close, creatures of bizarre habits, weird requests, outlandish behaviour and peculiar beliefs.

Television has given Chinese a perverted sense of the rest of the world. On the one hand, Westerners are all rich beyond the dreams of any Chinese, live in splendid mansions, drive magnificent cars with gross abandon, own yachts and private aircraft and enjoy a life of perpetual excitement and glamour. With their own eyes, Chinese in Beijing and other cities witness huge Americans eat gigantic meals with disgusting amounts of meat and hardly any vegetables. Little wonder these White-skinned Ghosts are all overweight and bloated.

As any reader of *China Daily* or other newspaper can tell you, Americans are likely to have AIDS and other diseases because of their truly odious, hardly believable, sexual promiscuity and the universal habit of taking drugs. They live in cities choked with marauding gangs of criminals and oppressed minorities which are ripe for revolution. Their irresponsible government makes millions of Americans homeless and prices basic medical care well out of the reach of the sick. Many millions are unemployed, the nation is crippled by racial hatred, children defy their parents, the school system is on the point of collapse and the streets are lawless canyons roamed by armed criminals. Are you not fortunate to be a Chinese in a socialist state? Despite this, there remains an enormous fascination with all things American and many Chinese believe the official line to hide the fact that everything in the US of A is marvellous.

These are the contradictory viewpoints which many Chinese still have about America. And you can't really blame them. After all, with cable and satellite TV and Western films in every city, Chinese watch movies from all over the world. How are they supposed to tell fact from fiction? They probably think Eddie Murphy is a typical American detective and that Meryl Streep is Mrs America.

There are similar glaring errors about most other nations, the result of both ignorance and propaganda. Just as you go to China with twisted notions of how they have developed, so the Chinese tend to have some astonishing ideas about the state of the rest of the world. While you will have plenty of questions to ask during your time in China, you should also expect to answer a lot. There are possibly more misconceptions about you and your way of life among the Chinese than you have about how they live.

## COMMON NOTIONS
Chinese tend mentally to lump all foreigners together as non-Chinese.

There are exceptions. Below are some common Chinese view-points of different groups. These racial stereotypes are how Chinese friends in different provinces describe various nationalities to me.

I wish to stress that they are not universal Chinese viewpoints of other people. They are, however, widely held concepts and prejudices. Chinese are more ambivalent about America than about any other country. They think there is much to admire about the sheer richness and freedom of the United States while, at the same time, the greedy consumerism and unpalatable sexual and drug appetites of many Americans make most Chinese feel uncomfortable and disgusted.

**Americans:** All crazy, but also generous, friendly people led by treacherous warmongering politicians. If they are female, probably have sexual designs on innocent Chinese boys. If male, likewise, except these are on Chinese girls as well as boys.

**Arabs:** Constant tormentors of Western countries who keep Western barbarians occupied outside China. Therefore good. Often encourage Islamic extremism which causes ripples among the many millions of Muslims in China's north and west. Therefore most dangerous and untrustworthy.

**Australians:** Acceptable as business partners. Generally a rowdy, hard-drinking people. A likeable bunch of lunatics who speak an incomprehensible dialect.

**Blacks:** Sex-crazed, drug-addicted womanisers who want to attack Chinese females. Suspected of having AIDS, black marketeering, and smuggling. Also, totally beyond the pale because they are black. Also, assumed to be great dancers.

**British:** Devious, tough, ruthless and brutal. Not to be trusted in any deal unless there is an obvious advantage for them that will make them keep their word. After having Chris Patten as the Last Viceroy of Hongkong, China's official leadership now loathes everything about him and the British democracy he preaches. On the other hand, Chinese leaders adore Mrs Thatcher; why not, she gave them back Hongkong with virtually no strings attached. For reasons no Britons can understand, Chinese think them stylish.

**Canadians:** Nice, honest, open and generous farmers who can be trusted. Easy to do business with because they are a bit simple.

**Filipinos:** Brown Yankees who yodel and pluck guitars. Not serious people. But they are no threat to the sacred Motherland, so are tolerated.

**French:** Flamboyant and foppish, not serious but very artistic. Verging on constant anarchy.

**Germans:** Clever, technically brilliant people, generally hard-working, but overweight and often drunk.

**Hongkongers:** Cunning Chinese in three-piece suits and haughty manners, in China to make millions by providing sophisticated industrial infrastructure. Great that they have been back in the fold since 1997.

**Indians:** Toadies of Western liberalism whose addiction to democracy makes them totally untrustworthy. Also to be regarded with deep suspicion because of recent emergence of Indian industry as a challenge to China's export-led economy. Also, many Indians are brown and Chinese are bluntly and sometimes obviously intolerant of coloured people.

**Italians:** Cultural robbers who stole the idea of the noodle from China and called it spaghetti. Smooth and handsome romancers who drive fast cars. Watch out for them.

**Japanese:** Suspected of ulterior motives in offers of help to develop China. Probably awaiting opportunities to rob China's riches and to control the country. They did it before; how can we trust them again?

**Latin Americans:** Victims of grasping American bankers (which makes them good guys) and conspirators who flood the world with drugs (which makes them bad guys).

**New Zealanders:** Poor cousins to Australians except they get drunk faster. Always complaining about everything and saying how much better it is back home. Why don't they go back?

**Non-Chinese:** Pitiful barbarians who, if they become troublesome to China, can be speedily kicked out of the country.

**Russians:** Brutal thugs itching to steal more northern territory from China. Not to be trusted. But they serve as an excellent lesson to 1.2 billion Chinese of what happens when a totalitarian state collapses, therefore most useful to the leadership.

**Singaporean Chinese:** Almost as bad as Hongkong Chinese except there are not as many of them. Too much money, too slick and smart.

## *TOURISM*

In 1978, China welcomed a grand total of 10,000 tourists. In 1988, 4,340,000 arrived. Nowadays, more than 70 million foreigners arrive a year plus millions more Overseas Chinese, who tend to blend easily into the general population. China's tourist industry brought in

US$48.4 billion in 1999. Add to this a gigantic surge in internal tourism, domestic tourists numbering 719 million in 1999 (check out www.china1st.com), and there is little wonder this vital industry has suffered growing pains.

In a decade, China has had to build 1,495 new hotels and train about a million to run them. So if you have complaints (which is almost certain) there are plenty of excuses.

Standards are rising very fast. Prices have kept remarkably steady, with a very good hotel room in a major city costing about US$75. Beware, however, of travel at peak times when rooms are commonly sold out.

And check when travelling about special events; at the twice-yearly Canton Trade Fair, all hotel rooms in Greater Guangzhou are totally sold out and the price goes up fourfold.

## *The Turbine*

In many ways, the tourism-travel-hotel industry has fuelled China's growth. It has also played a vital role in education. As money from Overseas Chinese built new hotels and famed international chains were hired to run them, the country had to suddenly find hundreds of thousands of multilingual accountants, drivers, waiters, reception-ists, bartenders, chefs and executives to staff the new hotels, tourist agencies, restaurants, tour guide companies and all the other plethora of interests that grow from mass tourism.

By and large, much of this training – everything from personal hygiene and appearance to computer programming – was done by the hotels. They promptly lost these skilled staff; in many hotels, turnover was more than 150% a year.

This was not because staff didn't like the work. The problem all too frequently was the guests liked the staff too much. I know of hundreds of examples. A foreigner goes to a Chinese city to set up an office. The only clean, intelligent, English-speaking, efficient and presentable person he meets is a hotel receptionist at check-in. So he offers her a secretarial job at four times the pay.

The hotel, which may have 3,000 staff (like the huge China Hotel complex in Guangzhou used to have) and cannot meet such enormous pay bills. So the worker leaves, the hotel recruits and starts training anew – and a few months later the wheel moves again and the new staffer is lost for the same reason.

## *Tourism Booms*

The number of visitors was rising steadily until the spring of 1989. When the tanks rolled into Tiananmen, the boom came to an abrupt halt. Politics aside, the crackdown didn't stop canny tourists who found prices were rock bottom as foreigners cancelled trips. You could get a splendid room at a hotel like The Palace in Beijing for US$20 – then you would ask for an upgrade to a suite!

It was too good to last and within a couple of years, the tourists were back in even greater number, pouring vast sums into Chinese government coffers, providing a million jobs directly and opening a showcase in every city that showed average Chinese people how the rest of the world expected higher standards. The Chinese learn quickly.

# CULTURAL QUIZ

## SITUATION ONE

At the hotel tour desk, you are endeavouring to find out about local excursions. The service staff is busy chatting or reading books. You say "Excuse me" several times but they ignore you completely.

Finally you …

A   Walk off in disgust.

B   Slam your fist on the counter, scream "You stupid idle fools" and demand action.

C   Wait patiently then ask quietly to see the supervisor.

D   Complain to the hotel management.

E   Find the head office of the city tourist bureau and complain.

## *Comments*

This seldom happens any more. But if you come across a similar situation, none of these courses of action will do you much good. I've tried all these tactics and all have ended up with a similar response, a smirk and a sneer. The temptation to lean over the counter and deliver a sharp slap around the ears is almost overwhelming but this would be the most disastrous course which would end up in a stand-up confrontation which you would be certain, one way or the other, to lose. *C* and *D* are probably the courses of action that are most likely to get you what you want, which is knowledge about city tours. *E* will probably get you lost looking for the tourism office. But complain, certainly. Write a letter on hotel notepaper and post it to the local newspaper – or, better still, *China Daily* in Beijing – describing what happened. All Chinese cities are pressing for tourism and are touchy about criticism. It might not help you but could result in making things a bit better for the next visitor.

## *SITUATION TWO*

You are at a formal dinner party. The local wine is flowing smoothly, the beer is frothing in the glass and the *mao tai* (or provincial equivalent of the fearsome fire-water) is poured evilly into tiny toasting glasses. Your host, sitting on your left, lifts a glass, raises it into the air with his right hand and touches the bottom of the glass with the fingers of his left. He is welcoming you with a respected gesture, giving you much face.

Do you:

A  Say "I don't drink" and ask for orange juice.
B  Lift the identical glass that he has in his hand and return the gesture, merely touching your lips to the glass but not drinking.
C  Quaff the lot with one snap of the head, say "Terrific!" smacking your lips, and signal the waitress for more.
D  Ask suspiciously "What's this stuff?" and refuse to touch it.

## *Comments*

*A*, *B* and *C* are all acceptable. If you don't touch hard liquor, that's perfectly okay. Merely explain politely to your host (the Chinese respect for the liver is similar to that of the French). Chances are, he will probably heave a hearty sigh of relief and join you with the orange soda. Most Chinese do not drink as heavily as many Westerners; he may well have had to entertain a string of foreign boozers over recent days and welcomes the chance of giving his constitution a break.

On the other hand, Chinese have an almost reverent regard for the rollicking Western tippler. Being obviously drunk and out of control is odious and disgraceful (as it would be in polite salon society in Europe) but enjoying a good bellyful of beer, wine and *mao tai* with a meal is a sign of distinction. Remember to return the toasting gesture, first to your host, then to other members of the party. Keep rank in mind and go down the list in order of importance as you rise to offer toasts between courses. Don't mind if you get precedence a bit blurred; you're only a poor benighted foreign devil, after all, and you are obviously doing your best.

## *SITUATION THREE*

You are a Western housewife whose husband has just been sent to China. For the first time in your life, you have a maid. Unaccustomed as you are to dealing with a domestic helper, you are a bit flustered about how to treat her. She can speak only a few words of English and your lack of Chinese is total. What does she *do*? Where do her duties begin and end? How do you go about getting your relationship on a sensible working basis?

Do you …

A   Go to your husband's office and ask his secretary or Chinese assistant to help out.

B   Take the kids for a walk and leave the servant to it.

C   Follow her around the house seeing what she does and then showing her how you want it done.

D   Contact other expatriate housewives who have lived in the city for some time, talk to them about how they solved the problem, then follow their advice.

E   Get rid of the maid and do the housework yourself.

## Comments

Option *D* is probably the best course. Others have been there, done that, so profit from their experience. You'll find the maid will want to help make you happy if only because having a contented employer will make life easier for her. The problem is getting the message to her about what you want done. To start with, you've got to work out where her responsibilities start and end. Does she merely clean the house or does her employment contract include washing clothes, making beds, ironing, cooking and looking after a couple of small kids. Find out – right at the start. It's no use beginning a relationship on a basis of ignorance and later complaining that you didn't know the ground rules. Get things sorted out to your mutual agreement before she starts work. That way, there can be no confusion and no room on either side for later recriminations. *A* is not really satisfactory; it's hardly office staff job to run the home. *B* is a cop-out, *C* is plain stupid (neither side will understand) and the final option will rob you of an opportunity of exploring your new environment. You're probably never going to be able to employ a maid back home in Perth or Portland, so enjoy it while you can.

## SITUATION FOUR

The family is living in Beijing. There is not a great deal for teenagers to do and your son has made friends with a group of kids from the embassy compound. They seem a raucous group made up of many nationalities. You are worried about your child because he seems to be mixing with a rough crowd. This feeling of concern becomes outright fear when cocktail party gossip turns to talk of Third World diplomatic children being involved in brawls with Chinese youngsters, of shoplifting and vandalism. You talk things over with your spouse and come up with the following options.

A   Send the child back home to boarding school or to live with relatives.

B   Warn the lad his newfound friends are not very nice people and have a dreadful reputation with the Chinese authorities. Ask him to stay away from them.

C   Shrug the situation off with the comment "Boys will be boys."

D   Speak to officials of your country's embassy and ask for advice.

## *Comments*

You definitely have a problem here. Some foreign youngsters in China are very spoiled. Now the country has satellite TV and internet, there are opportunities for young people to act and live more like they used to back home. But life can still be drab for a foreign teenager. Parents may find the place exciting and professionally beneficial. Young people are unlikely to think the cultural privilege of visiting the Forbidden City ranks with dancing in a disco back home. That's changing as China's entertainment offerings become as jumping and exciting as the rest of the world; many foreigners are cut off from this by language barriers.

Many people with teenagers who are sent to Beijing go the boarding school route. Most companies pay for at least one passage a year for the offspring to visit China during long school holidays. *B* is about as likely to work in China as it is back home; best of luck.

Option *C* is asking for trouble. The police in Beijing have been restrained to a remarkable extent in dealing with provocations and outright insults by foreign children. One day, they are likely to snap, and when they do, it will be children who are not covered by diplomatic immunity who will bear the brunt. Option *D* is a viable alternative if you have no choice but to keep the children in China.

## *SITUATION FIVE*

You're starving! So are the Western friends and relatives from your home country who have descended on you. They are your first house guests and you wish to impress them with the progress you've made and on how well you are settling down in China. So out you go for a meal. Of course, you've taken precautions and prepared in advance. What you have done is:

A  Nothing at all. You'll just head out and hope for the best.
B  Studied your Chinese cookbooks and phrase books so you can order dishes in your newly acquired Putonghua.
C  Spoken to Chinese friends and staff where you work and with whom you have dined before. They have telephoned the restaurant, reserved the seats and ordered the meal.
D  Booked a table at a restaurant where you know there are English-speaking staff and menus.

## *Comments*

If you chose *C*, you're smart, cautious and not prone to taking risks. All should be well. If you opted for *D*, this is probably equally safe but a lot more fun; at least you and your guests can look at the menu, make your decisions after discussing Chinese food and customs. Quite a civilised choice. Those who selected *B* are likely to have a good time but the chances are the waiters will not be able to understand your Chinese. Good luck. Those who picked *A* are brave folk. Best wishes to you. Chances are, all tables will be filled, nobody will understand a word you say, restaurants you remember will be closed and you'll end up back at your apartment with a bowl of soup. It's all part of the learning experience. Remember, smile and people will fall over themselves trying to help. Point to dishes that look good. Bon appetit!

## SITUATION SIX

Your office has moved into a new building. You go and inspect the premises and are delighted. You have a view looking out over a wooded hillside and from your desk on the 14th floor you see directly out onto the crest of the hill.

Later, you bring your staff to the new offices and they seem less than pleased. In fact, they appear downright unhappy. Nobody will tell you what is wrong but eventually one of the staff approaches you and says the new office is in a very unlucky spot.

The 14th floor is badly selected because in Chinese the word four is pronounced *shih* which is also the way to say 'death'. And the view you so admired stares defiantly into the very eye of the dragon spirit that inhabits the hill.

How do you solve this dilemma?

A  By asking the advice of the staff, and when senior members tell you seriously to consult a geomancer to examine the situation and to suggest remedies, you follow their advice.

B  By telling the staff they are acting like a bunch of superstitious old women and to grow up.

C  By ignoring the situation.

## Comments

Please, follow the first course. It may cost a couple of hundred yuan, but it is a small price to pay for peace and happiness in the office. You don't have to believe in *feng shui* yourself to take the advice of a geomancer. After the ceremony and the careful siting of chairs and desks, you can then offer roast pig and beer to the assorted spirits which have been placated before drinking and eating the offerings which have already (in a spiritual sense) been consumed by the demons and deities. After all, how does this differ all that much from the ritual Western office Christmas parties?

## SITUATION SEVEN

You are a lucky executive. Since you have been in China running your company's joint venture plant manufacturing specialised textiles, you have heard a dozen horror stories about other expatriates whose Chinese counterparts are stiff, awkward and who insist on running their factories and offices on the old, inefficient Iron Ricebowl system. But Mr Wong, your workmate, is young, breezy, informal, a hard worker and a delight with whom to work. What's more, the factory is doing well and production schedules are well ahead of expectations.

So when Mr Wong informs you, shyly, that his wife cannot come to a reception because they are having a baby, you want to show your friendship and appreciation. What's more, you realise how important is the advent of a baby in the Chinese one-child family.

What do you choose as an instant gift for Mrs Wong?

A  A huge bowl of fruit bought from the local joint venture hotel which includes unseasonal tropical delights unobtainable in wintry China.

B  A bunch of expensive white roses flown in from the Southern Hemisphere.

C  A slinky piece of lingerie.

D  A large box of chocolates.

## *Comments*

Buy the fruit. It will be considered a very thoughtful and welcome gesture, signifying that not only are you an appreciative boss and partner, but that you are a true friend. The flowers would be accepted with a smile by Mr Wong but never taken home to his wife. Flowers are generally offered only to the sick and having a baby is a sign of extreme good fortune. To make this gaffe worse, white is the colour of death and mourning. Chocolates would be nice but fruit is a much better choice. To give something as personal as lingerie to a Chinese woman would be disastrous. Not only would it be offensive in the extreme but would be regarded as a degrading insult.

When giving gifts to anyone on any occasion, you can't go wrong if you stick to fruit. Chinese also worship education so books are also an excellent gift. If you know a friend has a child studying a second language, a simple book in that language on some inoffensive topic such as geography or culture will be greatly appreciated.

When Chinese accept a gift, incidentally, they seldom make a great public fuss. They will often put the gift aside after a cursory glance. Don't think this means they do not like it. That's just good manners on their part.

## *SITUATION EIGHT*

The business trip has been a great success. You've been wined, dined, shown the plant and you've signed the contract. It's your last evening in China and you're trying to get away from the Chinese officials with whom you've been negotiating for the past few days so as to relax and have a few drinks. But they don't seem to take the hint and go.

What's going on?

A   Are they hanging about for some obscure reason. If so, what?

B   Do they expect some sort of gift?

C   Is there something else to do in regard to the contract?

## *Comments*

You are being outrageously rude. When you arrived, they greeted you, welcomed you, met you at the airport and, that very first night, took you out to a welcoming banquet hosted by the most senior person in their organisation. Since then, they've taken you around, shown you the plant and sat in on negotiations and discussions.

Now it's your turn. You have to host the farewell banquet. If you fail to do so, it will brand you forever a low-born, ignorant churl and the chance of your venture succeeding will be blighted.

You should already have made arrangements for a full-scale dinner party with at least a dozen courses. You should have sought the advice of the hotel management to reserve a private dining room, on what choice local delicacies to serve, what wines to drink, what small gifts to distribute. Well before this, you should have invited them to attend a humble dinner so you could express your thanks. They are probably standing about thinking you are going to surprise them with some special function. They can't imagine you intend to merely shake hands and walk off by yourself. It's just not done.

If you had sophistication, you would have brought with you to China some wine from your homeland (well, French wine, if you are British) and hard liquor like Scotch whisky or Bourbon. I went to an Australian banquet once where the host had the foresight to bring Australian chardonnay and rum; it was a raging victory not so much because his guests liked the drinks but because they deeply appreciated his thoughtfulness to introduce them to some delicacy from his homeland. This canny Aussie also had a couple of dozen tiny koala bears which he gave to the guests for them to give to children and grandchildren. Plus a large illustrated book on Australia for the company's reception room. He was voted an extremely civilised person.

## *SITUATION NINE*

For months, you have been meeting regularly with a fluent English speaker, a middle-aged man who has nothing to do with your business but whom you met in a park one day and began discussing Chinese art. It is not an intense relationship but you can relax in each other's company and you regard him as a genuine friend, one of the few you have managed to make in China.

One day, he brings along a teenager whom he introduces as his nephew. He seems a nice enough lad. The next time you meet, your friend asks you, at first hesitantly, then bluntly, then insistently, what you can do to help the boy go to your native land to study at university. You attempt to shrug off the approach but it becomes obvious at future meetings you are seriously expected to act. You feel embarrassed and upset. Your friend has used your relationship in an attempt to manipulate you into a situation you wish to avoid. He is trying to cash in on your goodwill.

What to do?

A  Agree that the boy should go abroad to study and do your best to help obtain a scholarship, university place and a student visa for your homeland.

B  Tell your friend, bluntly, that you are upset because he is using your friendship to try to obtain favours which, anyway, you are in no position to obtain.

C  Shout your outrage and say the friendship is ended and you never want to see anyone in the family ever again.

D  Advise the boy to apply through normal channels at your consulate, offering to pick up the application papers for him and to ask

311

for printed information about universities back home.

## *Comments*

Welcome to the land of *guanxi*. Your artful friend sees nothing wrong at all in his behaviour. After all, you are friends and friends are meant to help each other whenever possible. And his nephew is family. So helping his nephew is the same as helping him. Why are you upset? Don't you understand?

Under no circumstances agree to the first choice. This is like leaping into quicksand. As soon as the youth is on the plane overseas, approaches will be made to you to aid his sister or some other relative or a friend to join him. It's the start of a slippery slope, indeed. Much as you may want to help, once you start you will be inundated by requests. Virtual strangers will approach you; if you've got a reputation of being a soft touch who can get things done, half of China will besiege you seeking educational placement abroad.

I strongly advise taking the last course. There's little chance, unless you've got personal pull with your country's Minister of

Education, of helping someone jump the queue. It's a lengthy bureaucratic process and the forms have to be filled out, considered back in your homeland, the I's dotted and the T's crossed. It can't hurt to get a couple of dozen forms from your embassy and give them to friends, but stress absolutely you have no *guanxi* back home with the authorities and there is nothing more you can do to help. You will then probably be asked to sponsor or guarantee a student financially. This, of course, is up to you. I have had people I hardly know approach me asking that I pay several thousand dollars to sponsor someone to study abroad and sign guarantees that I will pay their medical expenses, plane fares back to China and other commitments. No way. Sorry about that, but no, no, no.

Chinese will then look at you mournfully and say: "But I thought you were my friend." This may hurt your feelings. It will hurt you a lot more if you wade into this mire. I did help, once, to get the son of a close friend to apply for a visa. What I did was nothing more than pick up application forms and help fill them out. I was then virtually surrounded by supplicants for weeks asking that I help their relatives, and their relatives' friends, and their relatives' friends' friends. And so it went on.

Choices *B* and *C* may seem rough. You may be tempted to resort to them. Don't. Why should you, on the basis of a casual acquaintanceship, be held responsible for making a serious economic and financial commitment? No reason at all. Don't let yourself be suckered by guilt and sympathy into doing so. You'll only be making trouble for yourself in the future. Firmly stick to Choice D and advise them to go through the normal procedure.

# DO'S AND DON'TS APPENDIX

## *DO:*

• Remember that 'face' is very important to the Chinese. Don't make them lose face by making them appear dumb, or because you are confrontational and make someone back down in public. Even when fiercely bargaining in a market, you should take care not to make people lose their pride in front of others. A laughing, joking attitude when driving to clinch a hard deal works a lot better than banging and shouting: "Hey," I protest to an old lady trying to charge me 10 times the going rate for a painting. "I'm a poor, old, starving, crippled, unemployed, poverty-stricken ignorant foreign devil." She cackles, and cuts her outrageous price.

• Be polite. It costs you nothing but pays a fortune. Never force someone into a corner where they are going to have to publicly shame themselves. You may win a point, but you've made a lifelong enemy and shown yourself to be an arrogant bully. This doesn't apply to official Chinese diplomacy, naturally. When Beijing wants something, it can be highly objectionable and rude. (Former Hong Kong governor Chris Patten was branded a shameless political harlot when he failed to promptly kow tow to China's demands).

• Use both hands to receive and give things, e.g. a glass at a table, returning a borrowed pen, accepting your bill in a restaurant. It shows respect and indicates that you are a civilised human being.

• Remember that life is China depends on *guanxi* (connections). It's who you know which gets things done. In Chinese society, it is totally acceptable to use friends, relations, odd acquaintances, school chums or anyone at all to ask for favours or special treatment. This is far more extensive than the British Old School Tie network and applies to anything from a business license and train ticket to a place in school for a neighbour's kid or a job.

## DON'T:

• Expect to get the truth all the time in China. That's because people tell you what they think you want to hear. You can sit about at a bus station or airport and nobody will tell you that the service has been cancelled or delayed. They simply do not want to be bearers of bad news.

• Be surprised to get giggles as a response. When something disastrous happens – a waitress spills your snake soup all over your lap, for instance – instead of weeping, she will probably burst into a giggle. She's highly embarrassed and concerned and this is her cover-up.

• Scream in rage or lose your self-control, if you can help it. This makes you look shameful in front of the Chinese.

# GLOSSARY

The first question a tourist is asked in China is "Where are you from?" If you are American, you come from Mei guo (in Putonghua) which, literally translated, means 'Beautiful Country'. From England? That's Ying guo. Here are some other words to help you along...

**Countries**

| | |
|---|---|
| America | Mei guo |
| Argentina | A gen ting |
| Australia | Ao da li ya |
| Brazil | Ba xi |
| Canada | Jia na da |
| Denmark | Dan mai |
| England | Ying guo |
| France | Fa guo |
| Germany | De guo |
| Holland | He lan |
| India | Yin du |
| Ireland | Ai er lan |
| Japan | Ri ben |
| Malaysia | Ma lai xi ya |
| New Zealand | Xin xi lan |
| Norway | Nor wei |
| Pakistan | Ba ji si tan |
| Scotland | Su ge lan |
| Singapore | Xin jia po |
| Wales | Wei er si |

**Eating**

| | |
|---|---|
| Eating | *Chi dong xi* |
| I'm hungry | *Wo e le* |
| Go to a restaurant | *Qu fan guan* |
| Food | *Shipin* or *Shiwu* |
| Food (Chinese) | *Zhong can* or *Zhong cai* |
| Food (Western) | *Xi can* or *Xi cai* |
| Menu | *Cai dan* |
| Boiled | *Zhu (de)* |
| Stirfried | *Jian (de)* or *Chao (de)* |
| Deepfried | *Zha (de)* |
| Roast | *Kao (de)* |
| Steamed | *Zheng (de)* |
| Hot and spicy | *La* |
| Sweet | *Tian* |
| Sour | *Suan* |
| Salty | *Xian* |
| Breakfast | *Zao can* or *Zao fan* |
| Lunch | *Wu can* or *Wu fan* |

| | | | |
|---|---|---|---|
| Dinner | *Wan can* or *Wan fan* | Beer | *Pi jiu* |
| Snack or dessert | *Dian xin* *Tian pin* | Ice water | *Bing shui* |
| | | White wine | *Bai jiu* |
| Chopsticks | *Kuai zi* | Red wine | *Hong jiu* |
| Knife | *Dao zi* | Bottoms up | *Gan bei* |
| Fork | *Cha zi* | Tea | *Cha* |
| Spoon | *Tang chi* | Coffee | *Ka fei* |
| A bowl | *Yi wan* | Milk | *Niu nai* |
| Rice | *Fan* | Mineral water | *Kuangquanshui* |
| Bun | *Man tou* | Fruit juice | *Guo zhi* |
| Meat | *Rou* | Orange juice | *Ju zhi* |
| Beef | *Niu rou* | Spirits | *Lie jiu* |
| Pork | *Zhu rou* | Vodka | *Fu te jia* |
| Lamb | *Yang rou* | Whisky | *Wei shi ji* |
| Chicken | *Ji* | Brandy | *Bai lan di* |
| Duck | *Ya zi* | | |

**Dinner** group continues:

| | |
|---|---|
| Fish | *Yu* |
| Shrimp | *Xia* |
| Crab | *Pang xie* |
| Squid | *You yu* |
| Soup | *Tang* |
| Vegetables | *Qing cai* |
| Fruit | *Shui guo* |
| The food is delicious | *Hen hao chi* |

**Buying**

| | |
|---|---|
| Buying | *Mai dong xi* |
| I would like that ... | *Wo yao neige ...* |
| How much? | *Duo sho qian?* |
| Expensive | *Gui* |
| Cheap | *Pian yi* |
| Change | *Ling qian* |
| Where can I buy ...? | *Zai na li ke yi mai ...?* |

**Drinking**

| | |
|---|---|
| Drinking | *He dong xi* |
| I'm thirsty | *Wo ke le* |
| Let's go to the bar | *Qu jiu ba* |
| I want to order ... | *Wo xiang dian...* |

**Walking**

| | |
|---|---|
| Left | *Zuo* |
| Right | *You* |
| Forward | *Wang qian* |
| Stop | *Ting* |

317

# CALENDAR OF FESTIVALS AND HOLIDAYS

China has nine national holidays. There are hundreds of local celebrations which are not recognised by the Central Government, ranging from dragon boat festivals and other folk celebrations to religious holidays marked only by adherants. In recent times, Beijing has warmly extended May and October holidays to almost a week, which sends millions of domestic tourists flocking across the country.

| *Public Holiday* | *Date* |
|---|---|
| New Year's Day | January 1 |
| Spring Festival (Chinese New Year) | First day of the first month in the Lunar calendar |
| International Women's Day | March 8 |
| International Labour Day | May 1 |
| Youth Day | May 4 |
| International Children's Day | June 1 |
| Birthday of the Chinese Communist Party | July 1 |
| Anniversary of the founding of the PLA | August 1 |
| National Day | October 1 |

## Lunar New Year (January to February)

This is the biggest blast of all. In every corner of the Chinese world, families make extreme efforts to be together. It's the start of a new year, signalling a fresh beginning. The Chinese world largely grinds to a halt for three days.

## *Lantern Festival (February)*

This is fun. Held on the 15th day of the 1st month of the lunar new year, it's a colourful time, with hordes wandering about with paper lanterns lit inside with candles. As this is the dry season in most of the nation, there are plenty of fires sparked by this ancient celebration.

## *Guanyin's Birthday (March/April)*

Happy birthday to the Budhhist Goddess of Mercy (19th day of the 2nd moon). Guan Yin's birthday is also celebrated in Bendigo and throughout Asia, particularly in countries such as Malaysia, Thailand, Hong Kong and Taiwan.

## *Ching Ming Festival (April)*

Grave sweeping is the big thing to do in the first week of April, what is called in Cantonese the Ching Ming festival. You go to the tomb, place offerings of pork and oranges, light incense sticks and in the dry season in southern China, set half the countryside ablaze while worshipping your ancestors. Descendants clean the grave sites and pay homage.

## *Water Splashing Festival (April)*

This local riot in Xishuangbanna in Yunnan is in mid-April. It celebrates the Dai Calendar New Year and is held by the Dai people in the sixth month of the Dai calendar. This festival has its origins in the Buddhist legend of a dragon sprinkling fragrant showers on Lord Buddha at his birth. It's huge with tourists who like tribesmen throwing dirty water over them.

The festivities include bathing Lord Buddha, sprinkling water onto each other for good fortune, dragon boat racing, launching rockets and fairs. Young girls dance the Peacock Dance, and boys and girls throw finely embroidered purses to the object of their affections.

## *Mazu's Birthday (May/June)*

Along 2,000 miles of coast, this gives millions of fishermen a good reason to put ashore and get happily boozed as they eat enormous meals. No wonder Mazu, Goddess of the Sea, gets such plaudits from her followers. In Guangdong, she's called Tin Hau and she's venerated all the way down the coast to Vietnam.

## *Dragon Boat Festival (June)*

Have a ball! This is my favourite festival. Falling on the fifth day of the fifth lunar month, I usually lounge about on a beach drinking beer all day and eating prawns and laughing and joking as a bunch of drunks splash about in long skinny boats, most of the crews ending up in the water.

More seriously, this marks the death of Qu Yuan, a legendary poet-statesman served as minister to the Zhou Emperor. A wise and articulate man who fought against the widespread corruption at court, he was loved by the common people. Court officials pressured the Emperor to have him removed from service. In exile, he travelled, taught and wrote for several years. Hearing that the Zhou had been defeated by the Qin, he fell into despair and threw himself into the Milou River. To prevent the fish from eating Qu Yuan's body, the fishermen rushed out in long boats, beating drums to scare the fish away, and throwing steamed glutinous rice balls into the water. Called *zong zi*, these rice balls are usually wrapped in bamboo leaves and have a filling of egg, beans, dates, fruits, sweet potato, walnuts, mushrooms, meat, or a combination of these. Dragon Boat races are an most exciting part of the festival, drawing crowds of spectators.

## *Hungry Ghosts' Festival (August)*

The superstitious light fires in the streets and on staircases, terrifying normal people and giving firemen nightmares. The reason for these conflagrations in steel cans and on pavements is that it is believed that demons, ghosts and evil spirits escape from hell and roam the earth during this time. Families will prepare sumptuous dinners to serve to the dead souls wandering about. Of course, the family eats the food; the ghosts eat the spirit of the food, token offerings being placed on the ancestral altar for that purpose. The Chinese will also burn joss sticks, hell money in large denominations, and paper mache models of clothes, shoes, TV, radio, cars and more for their relatives to use in hell. It's a bad time to get married or travel.

## *Birthday of Confucius (September)*
Birthday of Confucius. The sage preached his patriarchal message in modern day Shandong province, and local tourism officials never let you forget it. His hometown of Qufu goes mad as believers in his teachings flock to the area.

## *Mid-Autumn Festival (October)*
Also known as the Full Moon Festival, the Mid-Autumn festival falls on the fifteen day of the eighth lunar month. At this time, the moon's orbit is at its lowest angle to the horizon, making the moon appear brighter and larger than any other time of the year.

This festival is a celebration of a bountiful harvest. There is also an enchanting legend behind it. There was a fairy on the moon living in a spacious but cold crystal palace with her sole companion, a jade rabbit. A heavenly general and friend would occasionally pay her a visit, bringing along his fragrant wine. She would then dance a beautiful dance. Tt is traditionally celebrated outdoors with moon-gazing and the eating of mooncakes. Mooncakes are a flaked pastry stuffed with a wide variety of fillings, such as egg yolk, lotus seed paste, red bean paste, coconut, walnuts, and dates.

# RESOURCE GUIDE

## *EMERGENCIES AND HEALTH*

Be careful where you eat. That's about all you need to remember. Pay a bit of attention and China is no more hazardous than anywhere else. It's a damn sight safer – in terms of crime – than USA or most of Europe.

Large cities like Beijing and Shanghai have good, modern medical facilities. Isolated and backward regions like Mongolia, Tibet or Xinjiang have poor medical support; well, it's the same comparing New York with Alaska or London with Albania. Many hotels have resident doctors or are in touch with local doctors of proven ability. Big cities have hospitals offering services for foreigners.

Medical services are generally cheap. But they may be basic. If you are not well, tell your hotel. They'll get a good reliable doctor quickly. If it's anything critical or complicated, grab the next plane to Hong Kong or Tokyo. Your biggest danger is probably road accidents.

Buy health insurance. If you go to a Western-style clinic – mostly run by Europeans or Americans for profit – you either pay by cash or credit card, and this can be as costly as a private clinic in Los Angeles.

## *Emergency numbers*

Throughout the nation, emergency numbers are the same. Good luck if you don't speak Chinese.

| | |
|---|---|
| Alarm Report | 110 |
| Ambulance | 120 |
| Local telephone enquiries | 114 |

## *Hospitals*

Shanghai and Beijing have the best, naturally. Here are some:

**Shanghai Huashan Hospital**. 12 Wulumuqi Zhonglu, Shanghai. Tel 86 21 6248 9999.

**Shanghai First People's Hospital**. 585 Jiulong Lu, Hongkou, Shanghai. Tel 86 21 6324 3852 ext 1921.

**Guangzhou No. 1 People's Hospital**. 602 Renmin Beilu, Guangzhou. Tel 86 20 8108 3090 ext 681.

**Beijing Union Medical Hospital**. 53 Dongdan Beidajie, Beijing. 86 10 6529 6114.

## *Medical services*

**Asia Emergency Assistance**. 1 Xingfu Sancun Bei Jie, Beijing, behind German embassy. Tel 86 10 6468 9100. Fax 86 10 6462 9111.

**The International Medical Centre**. Lufthansa Centre, 50 Liangmaqiao Lu, Beijing. Tel 86 10 6465 1561. Fax 86 10 6465 1560.

**International SOS Assistance (SOS)**. Tel 86 10 65003419. Fax 86 10 65016048.

**China International Travel Assistance(CITA)**. Tel 86 10 66031185 Fax 86 10 66012040.

**Pioneer International Clinic**. 3003, Peace World Plaza, 352 Huanshi Donglu, Guangzhou. Tel 86 20 8384 8911.

## *Lost and found*

If you are robbed, go to the nearest police station and ask for the Foreign Affairs Branch of the Public Security Bureau. You will have a lot of paperwork to do. (I've had exactly the same experience in Spain; you get robbed and next thing you know you are a clerk). Get a copy of the report for your insurance company. It can be a wearying process. Better to report any major loss to your hotel or consulate and ask them for advice and help.

## *Handicapped facilities*

This is getting much better, my wife reports. She teaches rehabilitation science in Hong Kong and takes her courses to a half-dozen universities and hospitals on the Mainland, so she should know. But compared to other countries, China makes few adjustments for the disabled. Foreign-run hotels are the exception.

Some hotels have rooms designed rooms for handicapped. Some travel agencies deal specially for handicapped folk; ask them for advice before leaving home.

## *HOME & FAMILY*

## *Accommodation information*

Real estate and renting are developing in China along Western patterns. Once it was all handled by the state. Apartments in Beijing can cost from $2,000 to $10,000 a month. Check out: www.asiagateway.com/China/Property/Property_Agents/. Some of my recommendations are: P&L Real Estate, Beijing Ying An Real Estate Co Ltd and Vigers Shanghai.

## *Child-care and schools*
**SIS Yew Chung Shanghai International School**. Tel 86 21 6242 3243. www.sis.ycef.com.

**Concordia Family Centre**. Tel 86 21 5899 0380.

**Shanghai American School Parent Teacher Association**. 86 21 62211445.

## *Budget hotels*
You can check out the following websites: www.sinohotel.com and www.cnhomestay.com. Here are some recommendations:

*Beijing:*
**Jinghua Fandian**. Nansanhuan Zhonglu, Yongdingmenwai. Tel 86 10 6722 2211

**Lihua Fandian**. 71 Yangqiao, Yongdingmenwai. Tel 86 10 6721 1144.

**The Yuanding Fandian (Far East Hotel)**. 90 Tieshuxie Jie, Qianmenwai. Tel 86 10 6301 8811. Fax 6301 8233.

*Guangzhou:*
**Guangdong Luyou Dasha (Guangdong Luyou Dasha)**. 179 Huanshi Xilu. Tel 86 20 8666 6889. Fax 86 20 8667 9787.

**Guangzhou Youth Hostel**. 2 Shamian Sijie. Tel 86 20 8188 4298 Fax 86 20 8188 4979.

**Qiabao Huodong Zhongxin**. 31-33 Shamian Dajie. Tel 86 20 8188 5913. Fax 86 20 8186 8690.

*Shanghai:*
**Changyang Hotel**. 1800 Changyang Lu. Tel 6543 4890

**Lao Zhengxing Hotel**. 556 Fuzhou Lu, Huangpu District. Tel 6351 5496/6322 224.Rates: 200RMB for a standard double.

**Linglong Hotel**. 939 Yanan Xi Lu. Tel 6225 0360/6252 2714.

**Pujiang Hotel**. 15 Huangpu Lu, Hongkou District. Tel 6324 6388.

## *ENTERTAINMENT & LEISURE*

### *Restaurants and cafés*
*Shanghai:*

| | |
|---|---|
| **1221** | Tel 86 21 6213 6585 |
| **Dragon and Phoenix Room** | Tel 86 21 6321 6888 |
| **Ashanti Dome** | Tel 86 21 5306 1230 |
| **M on the Bund** | Tel 86 21 6350 9988 |

*Beijing:*

| | |
|---|---|
| **Beijing Tuanjiehu Roast Duck** | Tel 86 10 6590 3388 ext 5247 |
| **Quanjude Restaurant** | Tel 86 10 6511 2418 |
| **Sihexuan Fandian** | Tel 86 10 6500 2266 |

*Guangzhou:*

| | |
|---|---|
| **Hard Rock Café** | Tel 86 20 8388 0688 |
| **Hollywood East** | Tel 86 20 8766 0303 |

### *Shopping districts*
*Shanghai:*
A fantastic range of new shopping streets have been opened by the go-ahead city government. The famed Nanjing Lu and Huaihai Lu are

packed with shops, but for specialities go to places like Old Shanghai Street. Bargain furiously.

**The Hualian department store**, 635 Nanjing Donglu.

**No. 1 department store**, 830 Nanjing Donglu.

*Beijing:*

Major shopping areas are along Wangfujing, Dachilan, Liulichang and Jianguomenwai.

*Guangzhou:*

Beijing Lu and Zhongshan Lu is still the in-place to shop. Near Qingping Lu antiques are hot and the jade market at Wenchang Lu is pretty good.

## *Theatres*

*Shanghai:*

| | |
|---|---|
| **Shanghai Grand Theatre** | Tel 86 21 6372 8702 |
| **Shanghai Concert Hall** | Tel 86 21 6386 9153 |
| **Madmen & Fools** | Tel 86 21 6247 2621 |

## *Cultural and social organisations*

**Shanghai Historic House Association**. Fax 86 21 5403 0811. Shanghai_House@hotmail.com.

## *Clubs*

**American Women's Club** (Shanghai). Tel 86 21 5984 0362.

**Australian Women Social Group**. Tel 86 21 6255 9030.

## *Museums*

**Shanghai Museum**. Tel 86 21 6372 3500.

**National Museum of Chinese History**. Tiannmen Square.

**Miltary Musuem**. Fuxing Lu.

## *MEDIA*

### *Newspapers and magazines*

There's virtually no censorship. Global newspapers and magazines are available. China has a number of local English language papers and new ones open all the time. The excellent *South China Morning Post* of Hong Kong is available on the same day in most large hotels in big cities.

### *Television and radio*

All hotels have CNN and many other global channels. Shortwave radio can pick up the world; take one with you. Radio Beijing has 40 foreign language services but you can't pick it up in China. (You can't pick up the BBC foreign service in England, for that matter).

### *Language institutes and classes*

A helpful website is for those wishing to learn Chinese is: www.chinapage.com/learnchinese.html. And China Education and Research Network (CERNET) at www.edu.cn/english/index.php is a good place to start for information on educational institutes in China.

## *RELIGION AND SOCIAL WORK*

### *Religious institutions*

*Catholic Mass:*

English Services at **Christ the King Catholic Church**. 361 Julu Lu. Tel 86 21 6217 4608.

*Protestant Mass:*

Shanghai Expatriate Protestant Worship at **Hengshan Community Church**. 53 Hengshan Lu. Tel 86 21 6406 5394.

## *Volunteer organisations*
**Guangdong International Volunteer Expatriate Service (GIVES)**.
Tel 86 20 8778 0089. GIVES-GD@hotmail.com.

# *GENERAL COUNTRY INFORMATION*

## *Weight and measures*
Metric is used. But Chinese measures are sometimes used by old people.

| metric | Chinese |
|--------|---------|
| 1m | 3 chi |
| 1km | 2 li |
| 1L | 1 gongsheng |
| 1kg | 2 jin |

## *Appliances and utilities*
Electricity is 220V, 50 cycles AC.

## *Pre-entry vaccinations*
Some fanatics get jabs for tetanus, polio, typhoid, Hepatitis A, Hepatitis B, tuberculosis. Others also are protected against meningitis and encephalitis. China's as healthy as most places and a lot healthier than many.

## *Embassies*
**Australia**. 21 Dongzhimenwai Dajie. Tel 86 10 6532 2331. Fax 86 10 6532 6957.
**Cambodia**. 9 Dongzhimenwai Dajie. Tel 86 10 6532 1889. Fax 86 10 6532 3507.
**Canada**. 19 Dongzhimenwai Dajie. Tel 86 10 6532 3536. Fax 86 10 6532 4072.

**France**. Unit 1015, Tower A, 21 Gong Ti Beilu, chaoyangqu. Tel 86 10 6539 1300. Fax 86 10 6539 1301.

**Germany**. 17 Dongzhimenwai Dajie. Tel 86 10 6532 2161. Fax 86 10 6532 5336.

**India**. 1 Ritan Donglu, Jianguomenwai. Tel 86 10 6532 1908. Fax 86 10 6532 4684.

**Ireland**. 3 Ritan Donglu, Jianguomenwai. Tel 86 10 6532 2691. Fax 86 10 6532 2168.

**Israel**. Room 405, West Wing, China World Trade Centre, 1 Jianguomenwai Dajie. Tel 86 10 6505 2970. Fax 86 10 6505 0328.

**Italy**. Qi Hua Tower – Apt 11/A-B, 1375 Huai Hai Zhong Lu, 200031, Shanghai. Tel 86 21 6471 6980. Fax 86 21 6471 6977.

**Japan**. 7 Ritan Lu. Tel 86 10 6532 2361. Fax 86 10 6532 4625.

**Kazakstan**. 9 Sanlitun Dong Liujie. Tel 86 10 6532 6182. Fax 86 10 6532 6183.

**Malaysia**. 13 Dongzhimenwai Dajie. Tel 86 10 6532 2531. Fax 86 10 6532 5032.

**Mongolia**. 2 Xiushui Beijie, Jianguomenwai. Tel 86 10 6532 1203 / 86 10 6532 5045

**Netherlands**. 4 Liangmahe Nanlu. Tel 86 10 6532 1131. Fax 86 10 6532 4689.

**New Zealand**. 1 Ritan Dong Erjie, Jianguomenwai. Tel 86 10 6532 2731. Fax 86 10 6532 4317.

**North Korea**. Ritan Beilu, Jianguomenwai. Tel 86 10 6532 1186/86 10 6532 6056

**Philippines**. 23 Xiushui Beijie, Jianguomenwai. Tel 86 10 6532 1872. Fax 86 10 6532 3761.

**Russia**. 4 Dongzhimen Beizhongjie, west of the Sanlitun Compound in separate compound. Tel 86 10 6532 1267. Fax 86 10 6532 4853.

**Singapore**. 1 Xiushui Beijie, Jianguomenwai. Tel 86 10 6532 3926. Fax 86 10 6532 2215.

**South Africa**. 5 Dongzhimenwai Dajie. Tel 86 10 6532 0171. Fax 86 10 6532 0177.

**South Korea**. 9 Sanlitun Dong Silu. Tel 86 10 6532 0290. Fax 86 10 6532 6778.
**Spain**. Sanlitun Lu, 9.- 100600. Tel 86 10 6532 3629/6532 3728. Fax 86 10 6532 3401.
**Sweden**. 3 Dongzhimenwai Dajie. Tel 86 10 6532 3331. Fax 86 10 6532 2909.
**Thailand**. 40 Guanghua Lu, Jianguomenwai. Tel 86 10 6532 1903. Fax 86 10 6532 1748.
**United Kingdom**. 11 Guanghua Lu, Jianguomenwai. Tel 86 10 6532 1961. Fax 86 10 6532 1937.
**United States of America**. 3 Xiushui Beijie, Jianguomenwai. Tel 86 10 6532 3831. Fax 86 10 6532 6057.
**Vietnam**. 32 Guanghua Lu, Jianguomenwai. Tel 86 10 6532 5414. Fax 86 10 6532 5720.

## *General and tourist advice bureaus and websites*

For travel tips including tourist visa application form by email – www.cbw.com/tourism. Also visit:
**Chinese Embassy in Canada** – www.chinaembassycanada.org/eng/index.html
**China National Tourism Administration** – www.cnta.com
**Beijing Tourism Administration** – www.bjta.gov.cn
**China Now** (guide to city life in China) – www.chinanow.com
**Pearl River Delta** – www.pearlriverdelta.org

## *Immigration, residency and nationality issues*

You can take 400 cigarettes, two bottles of booze, and 50g of gold or silver. Fresh fruit is banned, as are chilies. There is still an official ban on importing printed materials, film and tapes which are "detrimental to China's politics, economy, culture and ethics." I've never known this to be applied, however. Residents can get a "green card" if they are English teachers, foreign experts or long-term students.

## COUNTRY STATISTICS

**Country name:** People's Republic of China
**Government type:** Communist state
**Capital:** Beijing
**Population**: 1,261,832,482 (July 2000 estimate)
**Area**: 9.5 million square km
**Provinces**: 23 provinces: Anhui, Fujian, Gansu, Guangdong, Guizhou, Hainan, Hebei, Heilongjiang, Henan, Hubei, Hunan, Jiangsu, Jiangxi, Jilin, Liaoning, Qinghai, Shaanxi, Shandong, Shanxi, Sichuan, Yunnan, Zhejiang. China considers Taiwan its 23rd province. 5 autonomous regions: Guangxi, Nei Mongol, Ningxia, Xinjiang, Xizang (Tibet). 4 municipalities: Beijing, Chongqing, Shanghai, Tianjin.

**Ethnic groups:** Han Chinese 91.9%, Zhuang, Uygur, Hui, Yi, Tibetan, Miao, Manchu, Mongol, Buyi, Korean, and other nationalities 8.1%.

**Religions:** Officially atheist. Taoism, Buddhism, Islam, Christianity.

**Languages:** Standard Chinese or Mandarin (Putonghua, based on the Beijing dialect), Yue (Cantonese), Wu (Shanghaiese), Minbei (Fuzhou), Minnan (Hokkien-Taiwanese), Xiang, Gan, Hakka dialects, minority languages.

**Currency:** 1 yuan = 10 jiao. 100 CNY (China Yuan Renminbi) = US$12.09. US$1 = 8.27 CNY.

**GDP (purchasing power parity):** US$4.8 trillion (1999 estimate)

**Industries:** iron and steel, coal, machine building, armaments, textiles and apparel, petroleum, cement, chemical fertilizers, footwear, toys, food processing, automobiles, consumer electronics, telecommunications.

**Agricultural products:** rice, wheat, potatoes, sorghum, peanuts, tea, millet, barley, cotton, oilseed.

**Exports:** machinery and equipment, textiles and clothing, footwear, toys and sporting goods, mineral fuels, chemicals.

**Imports:** machinery and equipment, plastics, chemicals, iron and steel, mineral fuels.

## *BUSINESS INFORMATION*

### *Business organisations*
**American Chamber of Commerce**. Tel 86 21 6279 7119.
**Belgian Business Association Shanghai**. Tel 86 21 5879 6522. Fax 5879 6534.
**British Chamber of Commerce**. Fax 86 21 62185066. www.britaininchina.com. britcham-sh@online.sh.cn.
**Canadian Business Forum in Shanghai**. Tel 86 21 6279 8400.
**China Australia Chamber of Commerce**. Tel 6248 8301. Fax 6248 5580. caccsha@uninet.com.cn.
**Chinese American Professionals in Shanghai (CAPS)**. Tel 86 21 6217 5626.
**Danish Business Association of Shanghai (DBAS)**. Fax 86 21 6219 2711. DBAS@uninet.com.cn.
**Dutch Business Association Shanghai**. Tel 86 21 6437 6598.
**Expatriate Professional Women's Society (EPWS)**. Tel 86 21 6415 2369. ahabdf@public2.sta.net.cn/epws@hotmail.com.

### *Legal aid agencies*
**Lehman, Lee & Xu**, Beijing. Tel 86 10 6532 3861. Fax 86 10 6532 3877. www.chinalaw.cc. mail@chinalaw.cc.

## *USEFUL TELEPHONE NUMBERS*
*Beijing:*
Taxicab Administration: 6601 2620
Airport Information: 6655 2515
Beijing Railway Station: 6512 8931
European Assistance: 6505 319 395

*Guangzhou:*
Baiyun Airport: 8666 6123

International Passenger Service: 8666 1803
Ticket Service, China Southern Air Company: 8331 2332
Guangzhou Railway Station: 8666 1789
Guangzhou taxicab Company: 8666 2014
Zhoutouzui Passenger Service(Hong Kong and Macao Lines),
Guangzhou Harbour: 8444 9495

*Shanghai:*
Ticket Service, China Eastern Air Company: 6247 5953(international)/6247 5953(international)/6247 2255(domestic)
Ticket Service, Shanghai Air Company: 6268 1551
Hongqiao International Airport: 6268 8918
Shanghai Railway Station: 6317 9090
Passenger Service, Shanghai Harbour: 6326 1261

# BIBLIOGRAPHY

It is impossible to publish a full bibliography of works on China. Such a list would itself fill a sizeable volume. In recent years, hundreds of books have been written about many aspects of life in modern China.

Here is a list of suggested books that give readers a grasp of China today. For a start, I suggest that anyone who wants to understand the nation today reads the classic *Red Star Over China* written in 1937 by American newspaperman Edgar Snow. He risked his life (with my old friend, George Hatem, better known as Dr Ma Haide) to penetrate the Kuomintang cordon around the communist area of Yanan in Shaanxi to meet the shadowy Mao Zedong and the Red Army shortly after they finished the epic journey which has gone down in history as the Long March. It was Snow's explosive book that first told the world about the communists, who they were and what they meant to do. The aspirations expressed by Mao and other leaders like Chu Deh, Chen Yi, Liu Shaoqi, He Long and Zhou Enlai laid the framework for the modern state.

## *A Guide to the Guidebooks*
Since China opened its doors to tourists in 1978, a number of guide books have been regularly published. Most are comprehensive volumes which divide China by provinces and give tips on what to see, where to stay, what to eat and general outlines of the country and some of its customs. Almost all are intended for the casual visitor rather than those who plan to spend a lot of time in China.

My favourite is *China; A Travel Survival Tip* which injects a bit of badly needed humour in its wry observations. Prices have not been included because these change from country to country.

BIBLIOGRAPHY

## Guide Books

*China; A Travel Survival Kit*. Alan Samagalski and Michael Buckley, Lonely Planet, California, USA, 1984.

*The China Guidebook*, 1984 edition. Fredric M. Kaplan/Arne J. de Keijzer, Eurasia Press, New York, USA, 1984.

*The China Guidebook*, 1989 edition. Fredric M. Kaplan, Julian M. Sobin/Arne J. de Keijzer, Eurasia Press, New York, USA, 1988.

*The Rough Guide to China*. Researched and written by Catherine Sanders, Chris Stewart and Rhonda Evans, Routledge & Kegan Paul Ltd, London, UK, 1987.

*Through the Moon Gate, A guide to China's Historic Monuments*. Edited by the China People's Publishing House of Fine Arts, Oxford University Press, Hongkong, 1986.

*60 Scenic Wonders in China*. Edited by The Editorial Department of New World Press and The English Language Service of Radio Beijing, New World Press, Beijing, China, 1980.

*Fielding's People's Republic of China 1989*. Ruth Lor Malloy, Fielding Travel Books, New York, USA, 1975.

*The China Business Handbook*. Arne J. de Keijzer, Asia Business Communications Ltd, Weston, CT and China Books & Periodicals, Inc., California, USA, 1986.

*China, the Encyclopedia-Guide*. Nagel Publishers, 1978.

*Fodor's Guide to Beijing, Guangzhou and Shanghai*. John Summerfield, 1984.

*Economy*, China Handbook Series. Compiled by the China Handbook Editorial Committee, Foreign Languages Press, Beijing, China, 1984.

*Geography*, China Handbook Series. Compiled by the China Handbook Editorial Committee, Foreign Languages Press, Beijing, China, 1983.

*Handbook for China*. Carl Cow, Oxford University Press, 1933.

## General Reading

*Travels in Tartary, Tibet and China, 1844–1846.* Evariste-Regis Huc and Joseph Gabet, Dover Publications, Inc. New York, USA, 1987.

*Red Star Over China.* Edgar Snow.

*Forgotten Tribes of China.* Kevin Sinclair, Intercontinental Publishing Corporation Ltd, Hongkong, 1987.

*The Yellow River.* Kevin Sinclair, Intercontinental Publishing Corporation Ltd, Hongkong, 1987.

*Over China.* Kevin Sinclair, Intercontinental Publishing Corporation Ltd, Hong Kong, 1988.

*Chronological Handbook of the History of China.* Dr E. Faber, Shanghai, 1902.

*Imperial Life in the Qing Dynasty.* Edited by Grace Wong and Goh Eck Kheng, Historical and Cultural Exhibitions Pte Ltd, Singapore.

*Spectrum of Chinese Culture.* Lee Siow Mong, Pelanduk Publications (M) Sdn Bhd, Malaysia, 1987.

*China, Land of Discovery and Invention.* Robert K.G. Temple, Patrick Stephens Limited, UK, 1986.

*Outlines of Chinese Symbolism & Art Motives.* C.A.S. Williams, Dover Publications, Inc., New York, USA, 1976.

*Chinese Mythology.* Anthony Christie, The Hamlyn Publishing Group Limited, Middlesex, UK, 1968.

*Confucius.* Editor-in-Chief, Miao Fenglin, Shandong Provincial General Publishing House, Shandong Pictorial, Shandong Province, China, 1989.

*The Essence of Chinese Civilization.* Dun J. Li, D. Van Nostrand Company, New York, USA, 1967.

*Your Chinese Roots, the Overseas Chinese Story.* Thomas Tsu-wee Tan, Times Books International, Singapore, 1986.

*China Modernisation and its Economic Laws.* Peter P.F. Chan, The Hong Kong Economist Newspaper Limited, Hongkong, 1982.

*This is China, Analyses of Mainland Trends and Events.* Edited by Francis Harper, Dragonfly Books, Hongkong, 1965.

*A Land of Fascination, The Definitive Guide for Travel to Hangzhou and Zhejiang Province.* Edited by He Qi, People's Publishing House, Zhejiang Province, China, 1987.

*The Handbook of Chinese Horoscopes.* Theodora Lau, Arrow Books, London, UK, 1979.

*The Fontana Collection of Modern Chinese Writing.* Edited by Christine Liao, Fontana/Collins Books Australia, in association with The Chinese Literature Publishing House of Beijing, Beijing, China, 1983.

*China, Old and New.* John Logan, Publications Division, South China Morning Post, Hongkong, 1982.

*Best Chinese Idioms, Volume 1.* Compiled by Situ Tan, Hai Feng Publishing Company, Hongkong, 1986.

*Best Chinese Idioms, Volume 2.* Compiled by Situ Tan, Hai Feng Publishing Company, Hongkong, 1988.

*The Chinese People's Liberation Army, From the Long March to the Hydrogen Bomb.* Samuel B. Griffith II, Weidenfeld and Nicolson, London, UK, 1967.

*Chinese Temples and Deities.* Evelyn Lip, Times Books International, 1986.

*Proverbs and Common Sayings from the Chinese.* Arthur Smith, Paragon Book Reprint Corp. and Dover Publications, Inc., New York, USA, 1965.

*A Collection of Chinese Proverbs.* Rev. W. Scarborough and Rev. C. Wilfrid Allan, Paragon Book Reprint Corp., New York, USA, 1964.

*The Great Chinese Revolution 1800–1985.* John King Fairbank, Harper and Row, New York, USA, 1986.

*Chinese Cavalcade.* Kwan Kim-Gaul, Herbert Jenkins Limited, London, UK, 1963.

*Recent Discoveries in Chinese Archaeology.* Edited by Foster Stockwell and Tang Bowen, The Foreign Languages Press, Beijing, China, 1984.

*China – A Short Cultural History.* C.P. Fitzgerald, Praeger (1935) 1961.

*Mao Tse Tung.* S. Schram.

*Red China Today: The Other Side of the River.* Edgar Snow, Penguin, 1970.

*The Arts of China.* Michael Sullivan, Cardinal, 1973.

*Dragon by the Trail.* John Paton Davies, Robson.

*Morrison of Peking.* Cyril Pearl, Angus and Robertson.

*The Chinese.* David Bonavia.

*Deng.* David Bonavia, Longman Group (Far East) Limited, Hongkong, 1989.

*Coming Alive – China After Mao.* Roger Garside, Deutch.

*China After Mao: China's Second Revolution.* Harry Harding, Washington, Brookings Institute, 1987.

*China the Beautiful Cookbook.* Kevin Sinclair, IPC.

*Scrutable Chinese Cooking.* Kevin Sinclair and Lily Levin, Lily's Way Inc., 1984.

# THE AUTHORS

**KEVIN SINCLAIR** has spent most of his life as a newspaperman in Asia. For three decades, his byline has been familiar in Hongkong, where he is now a columnist on the *South China Morning Post*. Author of a dozen books on Hongkong and China, covering every subject from cuisine to anthropology, geography to sport, history to salvage operations, Sinclair admits to being obsessed by China. The former Chief Correspondent of *China Review*, he was made a Member of the Order of the British Empire in 1983 for his services to journalism.

**IRIS WONG PO-YEE** has risen swiftly through the editorial ranks since she and Sinclair trekked to remote areas of China. The communications graduate from Baptist College is now Deputy General Manager of *The Hongkong Standard*. Fluent in English, Cantonese and Putonghua, Wong's byline appeared in many publications when she was a freelance journalist. She has worked as a researcher on major books on China, as a hotel executive and now in senior management of a leading newspaper company.

*Iris Wong and Kevin Sinclair*

# INDEX